# *Great White*
# SHARK

# Great White
# SHARK

## Richard Ellis and
## John E. McCosker

With Photographs by Al Giddings and
Others, and Paintings by Richard Ellis

HarperCollins*Publishers*

*in collaboration with*

Stanford University Press

1991

The publication of this book has been a collaborative effort.
Stanford University Press saw the book through manuscript development, illustration selection, copyediting,
design, layout, and typesetting. HarperCollins arranged
for the book's printing and binding and is handling the
marketing, warehousing, and order fulfillment.

Illustration credits appear on page 261.

FIRST EDITION

*Library of Congress Cataloging-in-Publication Data*

Ellis, Richard, 1938–
    Great white shark / text by Richard Ellis & John
McCosker ; original paintings & drawings by Richard Ellis ;
photographs by Al Giddings and others. — 1st ed.
      p.   cm.
Includes bibliographical references and index.
ISBN 0-06-016451-4 (cloth)
1. White shark.   I. McCosker, John E.   II. Title.
QL638.95.L3E45   1991
597'.31—dc20       89-46528

Printed on acid-free paper

91 92 93 94 95 NK/HC 10 9 8 7 6 5 4 3 2 1

# Preface

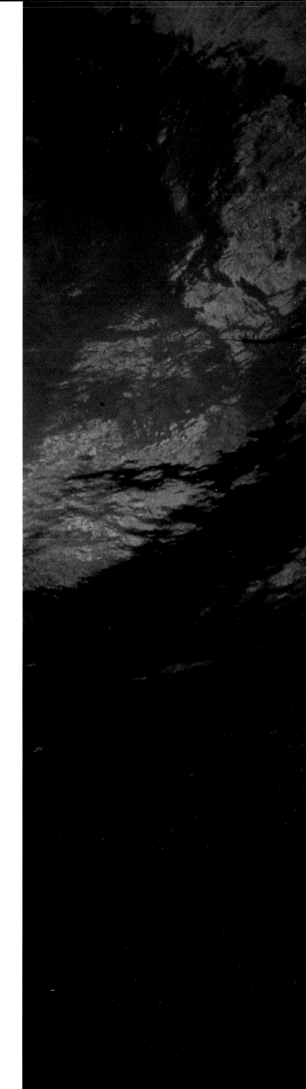

The development of this book was both very simple and very complicated. It was simple in the sense that we had both long been fascinated by sharks, we both knew a good bit about them, and we both felt a particular reverence for the great white. One of us exercised that reverence by painting the shark's portrait and writing about it, while the other took a completely different route, via graduate school in ichthyology and, later, the job of directing the Steinhart Aquarium in San Francisco, sharks and all. The project became complicated when we tried to translate our separate and communal reverence into a manuscript that would be both accurate and interesting, one that would speak with one voice and simultaneously serve science, the public, and the white shark. Simple or complicated, for us the idea seemed reasonable, but Al Giddings, the principal photographer for this work, had especially ambivalent feelings about the subject: he had saved a friend from the jaws of an attacking white shark, as you will read in this volume.

It was not alone through aquarium, laboratory, and library science that we came to know about great white sharks: we have both had the singular experience of diving with them off South Australia. Together we have visited Año Nuevo Island, off the California coast, to examine sea lions and elephant seals for white shark attack scars. Separately, we have looked for white sharks in the waters of the Farallones (outside San Francisco Bay), the Azores, New England, South Australia, and South Africa, and in the voluminous literature of sharks and the sea. We wrote one article together before we embarked on this many-sided project, and after "Speaking of Sharks" was published in 1985, we believed that we had had enough experience working together to co-author a book.

Beyond that article, neither of us had done much co-authoring, and we spent many hours trying to work out a way to work together from opposite sides of the country. We investigated modems, faxes, and other such hookups, but in the end—and in the interest of sanity—we resorted to an old-fashioned, more or less foolproof, system: according to a schedule we had worked out in advance, each of us wrote the sections or chapters that we felt qualified to write, and when, for example, McCosker had completed a draft on morphology, or California attacks, he sent it to Ellis, who transcribed it and rewrote it as seemed to him necessary.

Although there were other conflicts, this approach at least eliminated the problem of one person's text appearing on the other's computer screen, with the recipient deciding to change it where the sender wanted it to remain as written. When a copy of the manuscript had been assembled, the transcriber sent it to the ichthyologist for further revisions and corrections, generally with arguments about how much more material we needed on, say, the structure of the brain stem. After what seemed like years of mailing changes back and forth (and countless hours on the telephone discussing them), we ended up with a "clean" manuscript, and submitted it to the editors. That was only the beginning. A book with two editors, one on each coast, could have produced such a profusion of changes, corrections, additions, queries, and opinions that the two-author problem would have paled by comparison. In the end, however, the editors worked well together and, more importantly, worked well with the two authors. Of course, there were moments when the authors despaired of ever seeing the book in print, but as you can see, all the problems were smoothly ironed out, and we believe we have produced a seamless, accurate, interesting, and useful study.

The white shark is not a simple animal, neither in the sense of "primitive" nor in the sense of "uncomplicated." Its history and its life story are complex, and surprisingly rich in excitement, drama, and mystery. There are, as well, very few animals whose stories are so fraught with controversy. There are those who believe that *Carcharodon carcharias* is a menace to be eliminated as expeditiously as possible, and there are those who believe that the species is one of the most fascinating animals on earth, and should, on that count alone, be preserved. The white shark—not unlike nearly all the large land predators—is a species in danger of endangerment, at least in the parts of its range where we know it best.

This is a scientific book. It is filled with Latin and Greek names, charts, tables, footnotes, and a bibliography that will make your eyes glaze over if you are not familiar with this sort of thing. But we have tried to keep everything readable, and we have avoided the use of parenthetical source citations, which in most scientific works enable the reader to refer immediately to the source of a quotation or figure, but tend also to muddy things up. You will seldom encounter such formulations as "(Carey et al. 1982)" in this book, but wherever possible (and as unobtrusively as possible), the source of a particular bit of information has been identified in the text, and the source has been included in the Bibliography.

The nature of the subject profoundly affected the nature of the book. The white shark does not confine itself to charts and tables; it does not always keep its distance. It tends to intrude itself into our lives—and into our literature and movies—in a manner shared by no other undomesticated animal. Of all the animals on earth, the white shark is perhaps the most feared by the most people.

We are concerned about scientific accuracy, and we have tried to make this an accurate and dependable book, but we have also thought to convey our fascination for the subject. We are concerned, as well, about the fate and future of the white shark, and if this book has a purpose beyond exposition, explanation, and entertainment, it is to make very clear the plight of this great fish, so reviled, feared, and assaulted that it may be in danger of disappearing forever. The world would not be a better place without the white shark. It would be sorely and criminally diminished if, through fear and ignorance, we allowed one of the most interesting creatures ever to have lived to be eradicated. We do not apologize for the shark; it needs no defense from us. We intend rather to encourage an awareness of its place in what Henry Beston called "the net of life and time . . . the splendour and travail of the earth."

Richard Ellis  John E. McCosker
*New York*  *San Francisco*

# *Acknowledgments*

I n the creation of a book of this sort, the authors and the photographer incur debts for assistance, wisdom, and cooperation to so many people that only a brief acknowledgment of each can be committed to print. And of course the mere listing of them does not begin to recognize the impact of their contributions. During the years that we have studied and photographed the white shark, we have found ourselves talking and working with people from all walks of life, around the world, people who became part of the process: enthusiasts, fishermen, divers, ichthyologists, aquarists, photographers, boat captains and crew members, writers, journalists, magazine and newspaper editors, film producers, and even those who were attacked by sharks and lived to share their experiences with us. Many of the people whose names follow on our individual lists helped both of us: people like Ron and Valerie Taylor, Rodney Fox, Ken Norris, Burney Le Boeuf, Jack Randall, Peter Benchley, Sonny Gruber, Bob Britcher, Mateo Ricov, and Leighton Taylor are friends as well as colleagues. The Megalodon paintings by Charles R. Knight are reproduced through the kindness of his granddaughter, Rhoda Knight Kalt. We thank also Gary Larson, for the use of five of his inimitable cartoons, and Toni Carmichael for permission to use them.

From its tentative beginnings to its final form, the book was shepherded through the contractual and editorial processes by our agent Carl Brandt, and when the stack of manuscript and art finally coalesced into its unformed state, it was turned into a book by the people at Stanford University Press, including Grant Barnes, Director, and Copenhaver Cumpston, Designer. Bill Carver, of Stanford Press, was the editor of this book, and in addition to the nearly overwhelming responsibility of keeping two authors, a photographer, thousands of facts, and hundreds of references and illustrations organized, his most important contribution was that he kept us honest. Instrumental at HarperCollins was Buz Wyeth, Vice President and Executive Editor. Stanford saw to the book's editing, final illustration selection, typesetting, design, and layout; HarperCollins, to its printing, marketing, promotion, and distribution. Victoria Agee prepared the Index.

RICHARD ELLIS: Elga Andersen-Gimbel; Senzo Uchida of the Okinawa Expo Aquarium; Wilbur Garrett and Charles McCarry of the National Geographic Society; David Doubilet; Bob Britcher and Mateo Ricov of the *Nenad*; Larry Stessin; South Australian abalone divers Neil Williams, Herb Ilic, John Kroezen, Don Black, Trevor Garnaut, and Peter Thompson; Rodney Fox; Ron and Valerie Taylor; Jim McKay; Jack Casey, Wes Pratt, and Chuck Stillwell of NMFS; Ricardo Mandojana; Richard Fernicola; Ralph Collier; Jack Randall of the Bernice P. Bishop Museum, Honolulu; Francisco van Uden of Punta Delgado, the Azores; Perry Gilbert of the Mote Marine Laboratory, Sarasota, Florida; Shelton Applegate of the University of Mexico; Genie Clark of the University of Maryland; Leighton Taylor, then of the Waikiki Aquarium and the California Academy of Sciences; Howard Hall; Bob Johnson of the South Florida Science Museum; Frank Mundus; Gordon Hubbell; Elwood Harry and Mike Leech of the IGFA; Rob Lewis and Ken Jury of the South Australian Department of Fisheries; Ernest Palmer; Larry J. Paul of the New Zealand Fisheries Research Center; the South African Tourism Board, which enabled me to visit Beulah Davis, Geremy Cliff, Jeff McKay, and Marie Levine of the Natal Sharks Board; Durban shark fishermen Les Pearce, Reg Harrison, and Ricky Jacobs; Captain Arvid Nordengen; Leonard Compagno of the Shark Research Center at Cape Town; Graham J. B. Ross and Malcolm Smale of the Port Elizabeth Museum; Alan Bowmaker and Rudy van der Elst of the Oceanographic Research Institute, Durban; "Butch" Hulley and Peter Best of the South African Museum at Cape Town; and Stephanie W. Guest, who helped with everything.

JOHN MCCOSKER: John Stevens and Peter Last of the CSIRO Laboratory, Tasmania; Burney Le Boeuf and Kenneth Norris, University of California, Santa Cruz; Timothy J. Tricas, then of the University of Hawaii; Robert N. Lea and Daniel J. Miller, California Department of Fish and Game; Alfredo Cea Egaña, Universidad del Norte, Chile; W. I. Follett and Ray Bandar, California Academy of Sciences; Chico Chingwidden of the *Nenad*; David Ainley, Scot Anderson, and Peter Klimley of the Point Reyes Bird Observatory; Charles Merrill, captain of the *Simba*; Jeffery W. Meyer, captain of the *Grunt*; Jimmy "Meatball" Williams, captain of the *Buccaneer*; Doc White, captain of the *Mirage*; shark attack victims Jack Rochette, Glen Friedman, Curt Vikan, Harvey Smith, Casimir Pulaski, Mike Herder, Paul Parsons, and Frank Gallo; Richard H. Rosenblatt, Scripps Institution of Oceanography; Jim McKibben, Los Angeles; Francis G. Carey, Woods Hole Oceanographic Institute; Greg Cailliet, Moss Landing Marine Laboratory; John Hewitt, Aquarium of the Americas, New Orleans; Ian Gordon, Manly Aquarium, Sydney; Don Zumwalt, then of Marineland of the Pacific; Dave Powell and Steve Webster,

Monterey Bay Aquarium; Tom Tucker, Ed Miller, and Tad Smith, Steinhart Aquarium; shark fisherman Alan Wilson, Bodega Bay, California; and the one person who watched over my work on this project from its inception, Pamela J. McCosker.


AL GIDDINGS: Particular thanks to my friends and colleagues at Ocean Images, including but not limited to Terry Thompson, Rosa Chastney, Kim Dodd, and Margaret Hall. Many others, both above and below water, have made my shark filming both memorable and easier, including: Dewey Bergman, Stan Waterman, Chuck Nicklin, Dr. and Mrs. Stanley Berman, Leighton Taylor, Rodney Fox, Leroy French, Peter Lake, Doc and Ceci White, Richard Mula, Walt Clayton, Pete Romano, Bryan Anderson, Bob Elfstrom, Chuck Bangert, Dave Clark, Art Kempel, Jim Lipscomb, and William Holden. I also owe a great debt to Peter Guber, whose enthusiasm for my work with great whites catalyzed numerous television shows on the subject. And, special thanks to Al Giddings, Sr., my father, who described "Whitey" in frightening detail while I designed my first amateur underwater camera system in the 1950's.


We dedicate this book to all those who contributed their time and expertise, and especially to Peter Gimbel (1928–1987), whose courage and endurance in pursuit of "Whitey" led the way and set the tone for all those who followed and learned from him.

# Contents

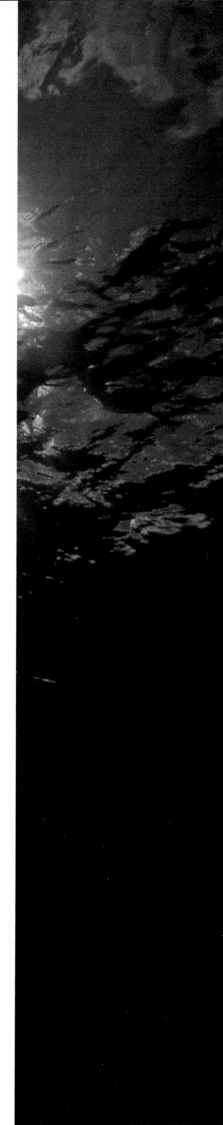

This elusive quality it is, which causes the thought of whiteness, when divorced from more kindly associations, and coupled with an object terrible in itself, to heighten the terror to the furthest bounds. Witness the white bear of the poles, and the white shark of the tropics; what but their smooth, flaky whiteness makes them the transcendent horrors they are? That ghastly whiteness it is which imparts such an abhorrent mildness, even more loathsome than terrific, to the dumb gloating of their aspect. So that not the fierce-fanged tiger in his heraldic coat can so stagger courage as the white-shrouded bear or shark.

HERMAN MELVILLE, *Moby-Dick*

# Introduction

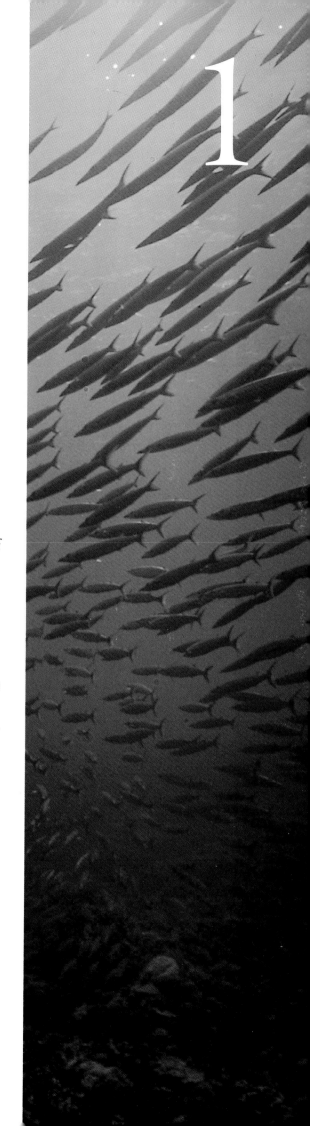

I n the world's oceans are unthinkable numbers of creatures, billions upon billions of them, ranging in size from microscopic bacteria, at the bottom of the food chain, to the blue whale, the largest animal ever to have lived on earth. Some species of marine life are rare; lone representatives turn up somewhere every few years. But many thousands of others number their individuals in the millions or billions. Nowhere on land does one find the sheer tonnage of life that fills the favorable reaches of the sea. Sponges, worms, snails, jellyfish, corals, seastars, urchins, octopuses, giant squids, crabs, big fishes and little fishes, marine mammals and sea birds, and a few species of sea turtles and sea snakes—not to mention forests of kelp, algae, and other plants—call the ocean their permanent home.

We pull animals and plants from the sea. We eat some, and we study them all. But we are kept from knowing the ocean by its very nature; to us it is cold, wet, unbreathable, uninhabitable, often violent and hostile; it is nearly 7 miles deep, and we have only begun to explore its depths. Beyond hurricanes, typhoons, waterspouts, whirlpools, and tsunamis, it offers us a fascinating range of more explicit perils: stinging jellyfish, venom-barbed cone shells, poisonous octopuses, stingrays, electric rays, and knife-edged corals. But most of these are sedentary creatures, asking only to be left alone, and mounting their defenses only when an intruder blunders into them.

Aloof from these passive threats of the reefs and the seafloors, who speak only when spoken to, there is another class of sea creatures, cruising the mid-depths, that are more hostile. These are the animals that *look* for trouble, that *provoke* confrontation, that *attack*. The most notorious of the attackers are the sharks, but only a few of them pose a danger to us. In fact, of the 368 currently recognized species of sharks, only about twenty are known to have attacked humans, and of these, only four—the great white shark, the bull shark, the tiger shark, and the oceanic whitetip—have done so on anything but the rarest of occasions.

There are angel sharks, goblin sharks, crocodile sharks, bramble sharks, monk sharks, carpet sharks, swell sharks, nurse sharks, silky sharks, cow sharks, bull sharks, basking sharks, frilled sharks, cat sharks, leopard sharks, dogfish, hammerheads, porbeagles, and wobbegongs, but the species that comes to mind when we think of attacks *on us* is the great white shark, *Carcharodon carcharias*.

The great white shark is one of the largest and most deadly predators in all the world, whether living now or long extinct. Among living predators on land or in the sea, only the great whales, the sperm whale, the killer whale, the whale shark, and the basking shark grow larger. But if we restrict the idea of predation to a preference for large, warm-blooded prey (a useful distinction when pondering the possibility of being eaten ourselves), only the killer whale, at a maximum length of 33 feet and a weight of 10 tons, grows larger than the white shark.

The sperm whale, or *cachalot*, by far the largest of the toothed whales, reaching a length of 60 feet and a weight of as many tons, is the largest large-prey predator that has ever lived, considerably larger than *Tyrannosaurus rex* or any of the other carnivorous dinosaurs. But sperm whales—Moby Dick was one—feed primarily on squid and other large, cold-blooded invertebrates and fish. Although tales of their violence are legion (and mostly apocryphal, like the reports of their titanic battles with giant squid), we have nothing to fear from an unharmed sperm whale.

Some of the baleen whales, often called the great whales, can reach 100 feet and 150 tons, but these giant cetaceans consume krill—various small shrimplike animals and other small creatures that cannot escape their mammoth mouths. Because the baleen whales—the blue and fin whales, the humpbacks, the right whales, and the others—are toothless, sieving their food from the soup of the sea water with their fringed baleen plates, they present to us a most benign aspect, asking nothing more than to be left alone. (That humankind has not allowed them to fulfill that desire is another, sadder story.) The great whales, like the two big sharks, are predators, to be sure, but they do not seek out and attack large individual animals—and they are themselves subject to the attacks of smaller predators.

The killer whale, actually the largest of the dolphins, is powerful enough to chase and kill the largest of the baleen whales, and on its occasional menu it also lists fishes, sharks, squid, dolphins, seals, sea lions, and penguins.* The killer whale, the most cosmopolitan of all the cetaceans, is found in both polar seas and in virtually all the oceans between, generally traveling in small packs. We can all be grateful that these fast, smart, powerful creatures have completely eschewed human prey. For reasons we will probably never know, they have never attacked humans in the wild.

The white shark, though, infamous for its disturbing inclination to attack and occasionally kill people, is another matter. But although this propensity tends to overshadow its other traits in our thinking, there is a lot more to this giant fish than man-eating. Though its brain is relatively small, compared to that of other vertebrates, the white shark is a skilled hunter, preying chiefly upon seals, sea lions, fish, squid, and whales, and

* In *The Shark*, Cousteau *père et fils'* 1970 book, the authors repeat a story told to them by Dr. Theodore Walker, a researcher on gray whales, of an event that took place off Baja California. Walker saw a group of killer whales playing on the surface of the water, while a half-mile away a 9- or 10-foot shark was swimming lazily:

Suddenly, Professor Walker saw one of the whales plunge vertically into the sea and disappear. About three minutes later, the whale shot up just beneath the shark and leaped clear of the water, holding the shark crosswise in his mouth. The two forms seemed suspended in the air for a fraction of a second, and then disappeared in a shower of spray.

The species of shark is not mentioned, but this account immediately follows a discussion of great whites feeding on the carcasses of gray whales in the lagoons of Baja, so perhaps the Cousteaus meant to imply that it was a white.

employing a battery of sensory devices that might rival the detection systems of nuclear submarines. It is a powerful beast, capable of towing heavy boats for hours when hooked, or straightening out steel hooks the thickness of your thumb.

On the basis of anecdotal experience, circumstantial evidence, and solid scientific data, the white shark is portrayed as a creature that lives almost wherever it chooses to, appearing and disappearing at its whim or with the seasons, usually, but not exclusively, in waters where sea lions and other pinnipeds occur. A single individual operating in such waters is capable of terrorizing an entire seaside community by its actual or suspected presence, and it is not always a solitary hunter.

More than 100 attacks on humans since 1950 worldwide, 22 of them fatal, have been reliably attributed to the great white shark, and—at least in California—the frequency of the attacks seems to be increasing. Human predation on the white shark, however, has been far more successful, and some suspect that the great fish is on its way to becoming an endangered species. We kill the great white for sport (it is a great game fish), for bragging rights (it is a truly gigantic creature), occasionally for food (it is delicious), but usually because we fear that it will otherwise kill us.

Only the sperm whale (which deserves better) has achieved comparable notoriety as a symbol of marine malevolence. If the *cachalot* symbolized the uneasy climate of man vs. beast in the nineteenth century, surely the great white shark is our contemporary Moby Dick. But whereas the white whale merely reciprocates, the smaller beast *initiates* contact. Each of these two sea monsters—the great white whale and the great white shark—has taken its place in the literature of the sea; each has come to represent the times and tides in which its legend was spawned.*

*Just as the white shark is not white, neither was the white whale. Melville described Moby Dick as having a "peculiar snow-white wrinkled forehead, and a high, pyramidical white hump. . . . The rest of his body was so streaked, and spotted, and marbled with the same shrouded hue, that, in the end, he had gained his distinctive appellation of the White Whale." The subtitle of *Moby-Dick*, by the way, is *The Whale*, not *The White Whale*. (And in the title of the book, Melville used the hyphen, but when he is discussing the eponymous whale himself, the hyphen disappears. This confusing distinction is maintained in the earlier editions, but is dropped in later versions.)

A woodcut from Guillaume Rondelet's 1554 *Libri de Piscibus Marinis*, perhaps the earliest illustration of the great white shark.

Although tradition holds that it was a whale that swallowed Jonah, there are those who believe the "great fish" of the Biblical account was a grouper or a shark. In his *Life of Sharks*, Paul Budker not only discounts the likelihood that a whale was the swallower, but actually identifies the shark by species. Basing his arguments on the writings of the French naturalist

Guillaume Rondelet (1507–1566), Budker suggests "that the impossibility of passing a man down the narrow throat of a whale led Rondelet to search for a marine animal capable of swallowing such a large prey and bringing it up whole later on. *Carcharodon*, the white shark, was not a bad choice." Further on, he concludes that "one should, therefore, substitute 'shark' for 'whale' in the story of Jonah, and even, for the sake of complete accuracy, *Carcharodon carcharias*." In his original description of the great white shark, published in his *Systema Naturae* of 1758, Linnaeus, too, had said that the great white is an enormous fish, and probably the kind that swallowed Jonah.

A great white shark bursts from the water, exuding power and purpose. South Australia.

Even though most kinds of sharks had not been identified or distinguished prior to Linnaeus's introduction of scientific nomenclature, we do have a very early record of the capture of a great white shark. Neils Stensen (commonly known as Steno), a Danish geologist and anatomist of the seventeenth century, was one of the first scientists to propose that fossils represent the remains of once-living organisms. He had been studying certain toothlike stones, and was convinced that these glossopetrae ("tongue stones") were really the teeth of giant, extinct sharks.

In 1666, when Steno was 29 years old and employed as scientist and physician to Ferdinand II, the Grand Duke of Tuscany, the head of a large

# In the Cage off South Australia

There is no way of knowing how many people have gone down in cages by now to see the great white shark in its own element. Peter Gimbel was probably the first American to do it, but by the late 1960's several Australians, including Ron Taylor, Rodney Fox, and Henri Bource, had entered the cages to photograph the sharks. Gimbel's film "Blue Water, White Death," released in 1971, was a critical success, but it was "Jaws"—for which Ron Taylor shot the live shark footage off South Australia—that left divers wildly eager to go eye-to-eye with the maneater. Soon after the release of the movie, dive-tour operators began to offer a dive with the great white as "the ultimate diving experience." In 1976, See & Sea Travel of San Francisco sent out a newsletter, offering (for $4,000, air fare not included)

a new series of diving adventures totally unlike anything we have ever offered before. . . . We will have Rodney Fox, one of the first white shark hunters, as our skipper, and we

also hope to have Ron and Valerie Taylor aboard ship with us. There is no guarantee that the sharks will come, but we will be working the precise reef where previous white shark epics were filmed. . . . There's no doubt that with this new program See & Sea will be offering the Mt. Everest of diving thrills.

Other tours followed, and by now hundreds of intrepid (or terrified) divers have experienced the chilling experience of coming face to face with the great white shark off South Australia. In a recent brochure, those who would lay out the

ABOVE: Richard Ellis and Rodney Fox aboard the shark dive-boat *Nenad* off South Australia, 1985. Notice the healed scar under Fox's left arm.

OPPOSITE: Preparatory to a dive in the cage, Rodney Fox (nearest the shark) lures great whites to the boat with chum and hunks of meat and fish.

$7,000 (still not including airfare) are told that "the rewards include enough stories for a thousand cocktail parties and memories and photographs enough to last a lifetime."

In February 1985, I had the opportunity to stock up for the thousand cocktail parties (a prospect, by the way, infinitely more intimidating than diving with a maneating shark). I had been hired by *National Geographic* to do a story on South Australia's fish and fisheries, and this naturally included a visit to South Australia's most famous fish.

I was with Rodney Fox, the survivor of a white shark attack in Australia (pp. 000–00), the ichthyologist Dr. Eugenie Clark, and *National Geographic* underwater photographer David Doubilet, aboard the refitted prawn trawler *Nenad*, out of Port Lincoln. Off Dangerous Reef, in Spencer Gulf, we dumped a smelly slumgullion of ground tuna, chopped horsemeat, and blood into the water to establish a chum slick that we hoped would attract sharks. After three days of anxious waiting, our

first shark appeared, its dorsal fin smoothly slicing the water as it glided silently and ominously toward the 10-pound chunks of horsemeat that we had hung over the side. It was only a "small" specimen, perhaps 12 feet long, but it probably weighed more than a thousand pounds, and to me it looked as big as a limousine.

There was some nervous joking about "having appointments elsewhere," but that shark was the reason we had come to Spencer Gulf, and as Rodney gleefully turned the water blood-red with his ladles of chum, the yellow, elevator-sized, steel-mesh cages were lowered into the water. We then lowered ourselves into the cages, carefully pulling the top hatches closed over our heads.

Even though it was the austral summer, the water temperature was about 55 degrees Fahrenheit, and we wore full wet suits with gloves and hoods, and full scuba gear, in order to be able to watch the sharks at leisure. Some leisure: as the shark approached, I cowered as far toward the back of the

cage as I could get, my tank clanking noisily against the bars. The only other sounds I could hear in this eerie, blue-green silence were the hollow, whistling hiss of my mouthpiece as I inhaled (too often and too deeply) and my own bubbling exhalations. At this rate, I would use up my one-hour air supply in ten minutes.

When I realized that the shark was not trying to bite through the bars to eat me, I relaxed a little, and began to see this fish for what it was—not an underwater homicidal maniac, hellbent on taking huge chunks out of me, but rather a supremely graceful, beautifully designed super-predator who had far more right to be in this Southern Ocean than I did. When I had managed to get my breathing under control, I watched the shark glide effortlessly around the cage, propelled by short thrusts of its powerful tail, steering with minute adjustments of its pectoral fins.

The shark, a male, circled silently, majestically, in a cloud of foot-long tommy-ruffs. The tom-

mies had also been attracted to the gunk we had been throwing in the water, and seemed indifferent to the huge predator that cruised among them. The shark, equally indifferent to the tommies, moved slowly, his hefty solidity perfectly integrated with the liquidity of his medium. He didn't move *through* the water so much as he moved *in* it; it was a part of him just as he was a part of it. However incompressible water is, it offers no apparent obstacle to *Carcharodon*. Time had slowed down underwater; even the tommies seemed to dart a little slower. If a white shark were music, this one would be a solo cello, *molto piano*.

The old wives' tale says sharks are driven to a feeding frenzy by blood in the water, but at no time did this shark appear agitated or excited. We were drenched, bathed, showered, shampooed, awash, adrift in blood, and still the shark swam slowly, implacably, around us. Its black eye was expressionless, a matte-black squash ball punched into the bullet-shaped snout. Close up I could see the tiny black pores on the underside of its prognathous upper jaw: the ampullae of Lorenzini, sensitive receptors of minute electrical charges in the water. Its mouth hung slackly open; just the points of its legendary teeth protruded from its upper jaw, but the lower ones were fully exposed. Though its mouth turned down at the corners, the shark smiled.

The white shark is threateningly beautiful. Even its color, industrial gray above and white below, seems perfect for its function. (It is in fact difficult to imagine this fish any other color; next to this iron-gray and white efficiency, the stripes of the tiger shark appear frivolous.) The white shark is cleanly designed, smoothly contoured, though this one had smears of red anti-fouling paint on its snout where it had rubbed up against the *Nenad*'s keel.

This ancient fish exhibits the best design innovations of the modern nuclear submarine or jet fighter. The solid, muscular body exudes strength. It is conical at one end, flattened at the other, and gracefully tapered in between. The flattened end is bisected by the quarter-moon of the vertical tail, moving in thick, short arcs. The flared pectoral fins, like short wings, are held almost horizontally outward. I noticed the black spot at the axil, where the pectoral joins the body, and something I never saw before: the trailing edges of the pectorals are white. The underside of the pectorals is also white, tipped with black. The broad back is crowned by the great dorsal fin, a high, triangular, gracefully curved sail, rounded and heavy on its leading edge, trailing off to paper thinness toward the rear, like the wing of the jet fighter. A miniature second dorsal fin rises just forward of the massive tail, and on the ventral surface, just forward of the lower lobe of the tail, is another miniature fin, reflecting the shape and size of the second dorsal.

The white shark is composed, as it were, of softened, intersecting triangles. The dorsal fin is the largest of these, but the pectorals too are elongated triangles, rounded at all angles. The caudal fin is a bent triangle—or two smaller ones joined at their bases—with a triangular notch hacked out of the trailing edge of the upper lobe, near the top. The anal fins are rhomboidal, one triangle grafted onto another, and only the two claspers, rolled cylinders of tough cartilage, break the relentless triangularity.

The cone-like snout of this flesh-seeking missile is a rounded triangle, and in its grinning mouth are the most famous triangles of all: the serrated, scalpel-sharp, ivory teeth, the front rows erect and the subsequent interior ranks progressively flattened until they disappear into the roof and floor of the mouth.

Like the deadly jet fighter, the white shark is graceful and powerful, sexy and frightening. (Have a look at p. 16.) It is fear made flesh, a nightmare giant fish with hundreds of teeth, a black-hole death-eye, the strength of a bulldozer, the speed of a fighting bull, and the deft control of a soaring falcon.

Occasionally, we would be showered again with blood, as Rodney dumped more of the chum into the water from the boat ("just to keep it interested," as he told us later). Another white shark emerged from the gloom, and for a while there were two of these silvery, bullet-nosed specters swimming around us. I was by now less afraid than profoundly awed. I was face to face with the most infamous jaws in the world, watching great white sharks do what they are so well-designed to do: swim and eat. (In fact, white sharks do very little else, other than to make little sharks.)

Time didn't stand still long enough for me; I was out of air and had to come out of the cage. There is a moment of fear as you climb out of the hatch: you know there is a maneating shark waiting for you to make a misstep in the awkwardness of your backpack and scuba tank.

We would dive again with the sharks at Dangerous Reef, and also at the South Neptune Islands, but though I hesitate to suggest that I had become blasé about it, the subsequent dives were nothing like the first. The rush that comes from first staring into that empty black eye as the shark mouths the flotation tanks or swallows a 10-pound lump of horsemeat just a foot from your face is unparalleled. And you do this in the shark's element, all the while more frightened by doing it in a bath of blood.

When you are safely back on deck, laughing and re-telling the stories (as you rehearse for the thousand cocktail parties that are to come), you remember the green water, the striped tommies, the silvery web of light flickering on the shark's back, and the teeth, the teeth. If there is one thing that is burned into your mind, it is the image of white teeth in a gaping mouth large enough to swallow a child.

*Richard Ellis*

OPPOSITE, ABOVE: A white shark, surrounded by tommy-ruffs, glides along in a bath of blood dumped from the surface.

OPPOSITE, CENTER: From the safety of the cage, Rodney Fox hand-feeds a huge shark off South Australia. Note the characteristic black spot at the axil, and the black tips of the pectorals.

OPPOSITE, BELOW: A large male all but conceals the diver in the cage.

white shark was brought to the court at Florence, and it fell to Steno to examine it. In a published report, he remarked on the close resemblance of the teeth to the glossopetrae he had been studying, described the gape of the jaws, and described the structure of the eye and the ear, even though by the time he examined it, the head was badly desiccated and many of the teeth were missing. (It was his student, Stephan Lorenzini, who described in detail the mucous-filled tubules in the snout of the shark—sense organs now known as the ampullae of Lorenzini—but Steno was the first to comment on their existence.) Steno eschewed the name *Lamia* for the white shark, which had been used earlier by Rondelet and Conrad Gesner (1516–1565), in favor of *Canis Carchariae*, but this too would change when Carolus Linnaeus, responding to the chaos of names that had always in prior years plagued natural science, devised the system of nomenclature that would be applied to every living thing. Today, that system accords to the great white shark the zoological, or scientific, name *Carcharodon carcharias*.

It was Linnaeus (1707–1778), an eighteenth-century Swedish naturalist, who bestowed the name *Squalus carcharias* on what today, in English-speaking countries, we call the great white shark. In the tenth (1758) edition of his *Systema Naturae*, he named most of the animals known in his time, using the system of binomial nomenclature of his devising—genus name followed by species name—that remains in use today. In naming the white shark, Linnaeus followed another Swede, his student Pieter Artedi (1705–1735), and the illustration he drew upon for his description was one by Rondelet that had appeared 200 years before, in Rondelet's 1558

Engraving of the jaws of a white shark from Ulisse Aldrovandi's 1613 *De Piscibus libri V*.

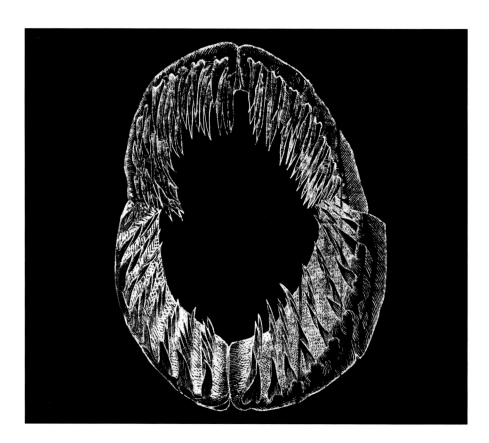

treatise on fishes, *La première partie de l'histoire entière des poissons*. Obviously, Linnaeus could not examine every preserved specimen of every animal he described, and he had therefore to rely on descriptions and illustrations that he trusted. His description of the teeth (*dentibus triangularibus serratis*, "serrated triangular teeth") is quite good; and as is clear from Rondelet's figure (see p. 4), his choice for an illustration for the white shark was a good one. No holotype, or "typical specimen," was designated in his description, and he gave the white shark's habitat as, simply, "Europe."

Linnaeus called the white shark *Squalus carcharias*, but its accepted name is now "*Carcharodon carcharias* (Linnaeus, 1758)." Had Linnaeus had the foresight to have placed the species within the genus in which it now finds itself, he would not be parenthetically surrounded in the fish's name. The rules of taxonomy require that because Linnaeus properly identified the white shark in his original description, he deserves credit for the original authorship of the species—and the species epithet he gave it, *carcharias*, has accordingly been retained. Subsequent authors, however, have felt that the species is more closely related to those within another genus (*Carcharodon*), and have placed it there. (Not many sharks were known in Linnaeus's time, and he in fact placed *all* of them in *Squalus*; but with some 368 species of sharks recognized today, that is no longer a realistic disposition, and *Squalus* is now restricted to the typical dogfishes.)

The genus *Carcharodon* was proposed by Sir Andrew Smith in an 1838 work by the German ichthyologists Johannes Müller and Friedrich Henle, but it was not until 1878 that the generic name was linked up with Linnaeus's specific name. Before that year, the white shark was variously known as *Carcharodon smithii* and *Carcharodon verus*, and even afterwards it was known variously as *Carcharodon lamia*, *Carcharodon capensis*,

A nineteenth-century engraving entitled *Le Requin* (The Shark). The fish is clearly a great white shark, identifiable by its size and the black tips of its pectoral fins. The upper lobe of the tail, however, is much too long.

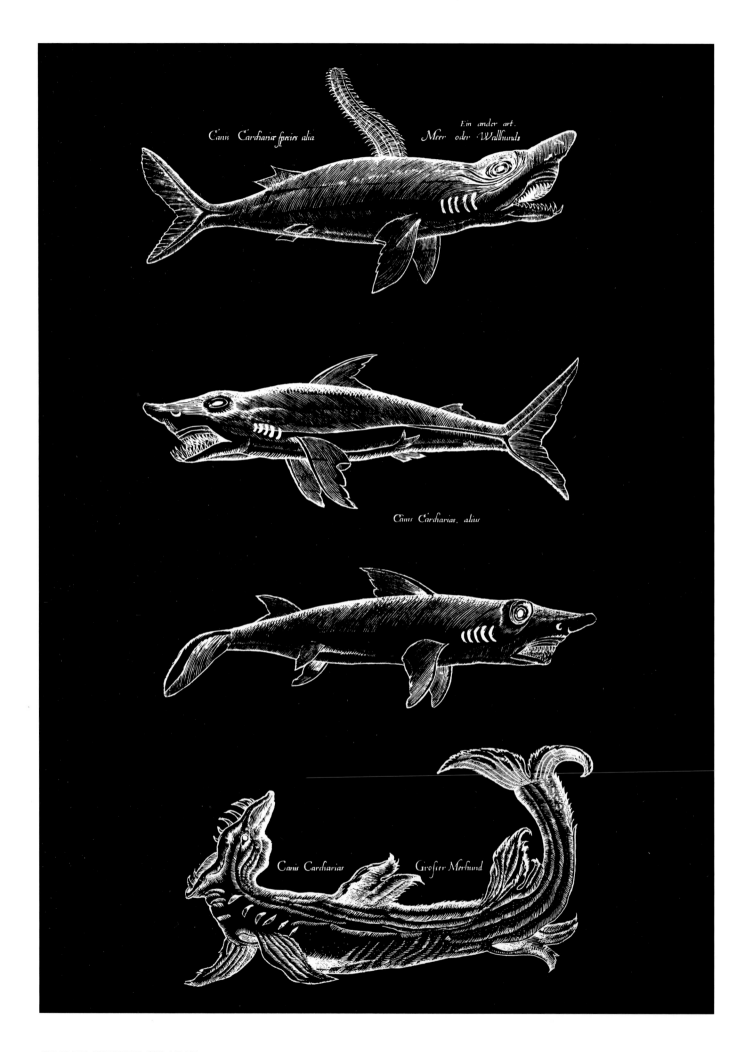

Canis Carchariæ species alia

Ein ander art.
Meer oder Wallhundt

Canis Carcharias, alius

Canis Carcharias          Großer Meerhund

*Carcharodon rondeletti*, and *Carcharodon atwoodi*. But when the taxonomic dust finally settled, it had come to be known as *Carcharodon carcharias*. This crunchy mouthful of names is derived from the Greek words *carcharos*, which means "ragged," and *odon*, or "tooth."

Because various species of sharks have been known by various names, at various times, and in various languages, and because in years past the distinctions among the species were not noticed with much precision, it is difficult, if not impossible, to determine when someone first recognized the white shark as an animal distinct from other sharks. Its evolutionary history obviously predates that of humans by many millions of years, but it has been only within the last few centuries that most of us have attempted to differentiate one species of shark from another. Before that, a shark was a shark—or a *tiburón*, a *requin*, a *tubarão*, a *Haifisch*, a *mano*, a *pescecane*, an *akula*, a *selachos*, or a *squalus*.

According to the *Oxford English Dictionary*, the word "shark" is "of obscure origin. . . . The word seems to have been introduced by the sailors of Captain (afterwards Sir John) Hawkins, who brought home a specimen which was exhibited in London in 1569. The source from which they obtained the word has not been ascertained." (We may note, however, that the word "shark" sounds not unlike *carcharias*, which to modern Greeks means simply "shark," and many etymologists believe *carcharias* is the distant origin of the word "shark.")

The particular creature we know as the great white shark, a.k.a. *Carcharodon carcharias*, goes by many other names in other places. (In some places, "great" is not automatically a part of its name: in their 1989 book, Springer and Gold have demoted it to simply "white shark.") In Australia it is known as "white pointer" and "white death"; the South Africans also know it by those names, but add "blue pointer," "uptail," and "tommy" to the list. In most of the countries where this fish occurs, it has also acquired the exquisitely descriptive name "maneater." But where English is not the mother tongue, the white shark is generally known by a translation of its most common English name; for example, in Spanish it is called *tiburón blanco* (and also *jaquetón* and *devorador de hombres*); in Portuguese, *tubarão branco* and *tubarão-come-homens*; in Italian, *grande squalo bianco*; and in French, *grand requin blanc*. The Germans know this creature as *Weisshai*, the Japanese as *hohojirozame*, and the Russians as *seldevaja akula*. Since people who speak for example Turkish, Chinese, or Zulu may have occasion to refer to this fish in their own language, there must be almost as many names for this shark as there are coastal languages, particularly since the appearance of "Jaws." (But those who, like the Nepalese and the Bedouins, abide deep in the terrestrial hinterlands probably do not call it anything at all.)

Because of this multiplicity of common names, across languages but often even within *one* language, the value of Linnaeus's system becomes abundantly clear: no matter what language the *common* name may be written in, the *scientific* name of the great white shark will appear exactly as you see it here: *Carcharodon carcharias*. This guarantees that anyone reading about this creature, whether the document be in Spanish, Swahili, or Sanskrit, will know from its scientific name exactly which animal is being

OPPOSITE: For *De Piscibus*, published in 1613 in Bologna, Italy, Ulisse Aldrovandi drew (or had drawn) these sharks. The top one seems to have a sawfish saw for a dorsal fin, and the bottom one was probably drawn from a desiccated specimen, which would account for its contorted posture.

ABOVE: The business end of a 4,000-pound white pointer caught off Victoria, Australia.

Only on its underside is the white shark white.

discussed. And although new data or new interpretations of relationships occasionally lead taxonomists to move a species from one genus to another, the name *Carcharodon carcharias* has stood untouched for 113 years.

In discussions of sharks, the language of everyday experience often suffices; in discussions of the great white shark, the language of superlatives predominates. It is the supreme hunter-killer; the largest game fish in the world; the most awesome and dangerous of the sharks; the *ne plus ultra* of predators. A thesaurus of the pejorative would be required to list its real or perceived characteristics: savage, dangerous, fearsome, fearless, mean, vicious, voracious, insatiable, ravenous, pitiless, sinister, dreadful, hateful, horrible, frightening, formidable, terrible, terrifying, menacing, malevolent, ominous, monstrous. But this list does not add up to the great white shark, and does not do it justice. It is both more and less than the sum of its adjectives, more and less than its reputation, and a great deal more than the little we know about it. It may in fact be one of the few creatures that we can never know. The great white shark arrives with its reputation fully developed, yet the truth remains elusive. Which of the stories are true, and which are fantasy fed by fear?

# Close and Distant Relatives

2

T here are many fish—and many fishes—in the sea and in the lakes and rivers. In fact, they are the most numerous of the vertebrates, whether in numbers of individuals or in numbers of living species. Most recent estimates count some 8,600 species of birds, 4,500 mammals, 6,000 reptiles, 2,500 amphibians, and anywhere between 20,000 and 25,000 species of fishes. Of all the vertebrates, fishes are the least known, owing to a habitat generally inaccessible to scientists, and though there is a great deal that we do know, our ignorance is reflected in considerable and ongoing disagreement and uncertainty about fish classification.

Fishes inhabit virtually all the aquatic biomes in the world. They are found in all the oceans, from the poles to the tropics; at every depth, from the sunlit surface to the abyssal trenches where no light ever penetrates; and in racing torrents, placid lakes, crystal mountain streams, and muddy, opaque rivers. They thrive in waters of all temperatures, from almost freezing to hot; and they can breathe and survive in alkaline, fresh, brackish, or salty environments. (There are even some fishes that spend much of their lives out of the water, and others, such as salmon and bull sharks, that are capable of moving from salt to fresh water, remarkable accomplishments that need not concern us here.)

Today, the vast majority of the world's fishes can be assigned to one of two groups: the cartilaginous fishes (sharks and their relatives) and the bony fishes (most of the others.) Prior to the appearance of the bony fishes in the Devonian period some 400 million years ago, the world's oceans were populated by jawless creatures known as cyclostomes or agnathans (represented today only by the hagfishes and lampreys) and several lines of now-extinct creatures with assorted features not encountered at all in today's fishes. In his classic study of vertebrate paleontology, Alfred Romer wrote that

A considerable majority of the fish population of [the Devonian] period, however, belonged to groups now long extinct and peculiar in structure: the arthrodires,

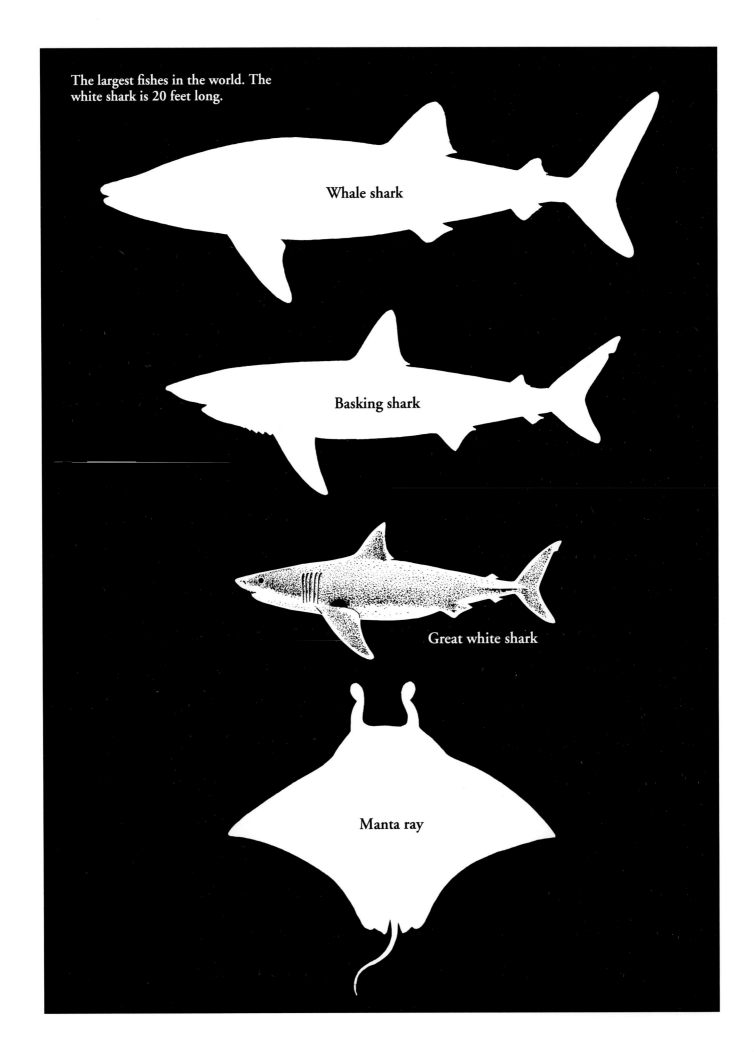

The largest fishes in the world. The white shark is 20 feet long.

Whale shark

Basking shark

Great white shark

Manta ray

SQUATINIFORMES (one family), the angel sharks, flattened sharks that look more like rays but have gill slits on the sides of the head, and a caudal fin in which the lower lobe is longer than the upper.

HETERODONTIFORMES (one family), the bullhead sharks or horn sharks, which have different kinds of teeth within each jaw, including pointed teeth for grasping and pavement-like teeth with which they crush shellfish, shells and all.

ORECTOLOBIFORMES (seven families), the carpet sharks, which have prominent barbels at the edges of the nostrils, and include such diverse species as the zebra sharks, the nurse sharks, the wobbegongs, and the gigantic whale shark. Many of the species are nocturnal, foraging at night and resting on the bottom during daylight hours.

CARCHARHINIFORMES (eight families), known collectively as groundsharks, a varied group characterized by an elongated snout, eyes with a nictitating membrane, and two dorsal fins. This is the largest group of sharks, numbering almost 200 of the 368 known shark species, including the catsharks, the houndsharks, the hammerheads, and the carcharhinids, or requiem sharks.* The carcharhinids include some of the best-known and most familiar of all sharks, such as the blue, tiger, bull, and dusky sharks, the oceanic whitetip, and the reef sharks.

LAMNIFORMES (seven families), the mackerel sharks, another varied assemblage, characterized by ovoviviparous reproduction, mouths that extend back beyond the eyes, and two dorsal fins, typically of different sizes. Included are the ragged-tooth sharks, the basking shark, the goblin shark, megamouth (see p. 44), the threshers, and the mackerel sharks of the family Lamnidae. The lamnids are spindle-shaped, large-eyed animals with bladelike teeth, caudal keels set laterally on the tail stock, and a nearly symmetrical, crescent-shaped tail fin. The great white is recognized as a lamnid, along with its extinct cousins in the genus *Carcharodon*; the shortfin and longfin mako sharks (*Isurus oxyrinchus* and *I. paucus*) and their extinct relatives; the salmon shark (*Lamna ditropis*); and the porbeagle (*L. nasus*).† The threshers (family Alopiidae) appear to be the lamnids' closest relatives.

Somewhere within the past 100 million years, there appeared the first of Lamnidae's bullet-nosed, scalpel-toothed superpredators. From their teeth, we assume them to have been remarkably similar to today's lamnids. The most astonishing of these was *Carcharodon megalodon*, a 50-foot version of today's white shark (see p. 35), which left as evidence of its existence teeth larger than your hand.

Throughout the world, other fossil shark teeth appear, documenting the existence of ancestral lamnids that are less spectacular than Megalodon but equally interesting. In the United States, the sites of these fossil finds are widely separated, and often appear far from existing oceans and even in low mountain ranges, clearly demonstrating the vast changes in the earth's landmass configuration posited by plate tectonics theory. Depending on the mineral content of the seafloor in which the teeth were deposited, they appear in various colors, ranging from beige and ocher to brown and black.

* According to Paul Budker, whose book was originally written in French as *La Vie des Requins* (The Life of Sharks), the word "requin" has nothing to do with a mass for the dead, as is commonly supposed. He wrote that it might have something to do with a "Normo-Piccardian form of *chien*" (French for "dog"), since "the word has long been written as *requien*." In French, the word *requin* means simply "shark," and Budker concludes his etymological discussion by observing that "the derivation of the various words for shark remains baffling and offers an interesting field for study."

† In 1758, Linnaeus had named the white shark *Squalus carcharias*, but in 1810 Constantine Rafinesque, an American naturalist, changed its name to *Carcharias lamia*—which also did not long escape taxonomic revision. The word *lamia* is related to the Greek *lamna*, which can be variously translated as "shark" or "predatory shark," and which in Greek mythology appears as a bloodsucking serpent with the head and breasts of a woman. Although its original usage is obscure, Müller and Henle chose to apply it to a family of sharks, the Lamnidae, in 1838. A lamnid, then, is any member of the Lamnidae. (The word "porbeagle," by the way, has nothing to do with long-eared hounds and may be a combination of two words in the long-extinct Cornish language.)

OPPOSITE, ABOVE: Probably the most wide-ranging of all sharks, the graceful blue shark (*Prionace glauca*) is found throughout the world's temperate and tropical waters. It is a fish- and squid-eater, usually harmless to swimmers and divers.

OPPOSITE, BELOW: The oceanic whitetip (*Carcharhinus longimanus*) is a large, abundant species, capable of attacks on people. Only its pelagic habitat keeps it from appearing frequently in the Shark Attack File.

RIGHT: The tiger shark (*Galeocerdo cuvier*) owes its name to the pattern of stripes on its sides, which are more pronounced in younger specimens.

BELOW: Electrical sensors on the underside of the head of the hammerhead shark (*Sphyrna mokarran*) are believed to assist the shark in locating prey buried in the sand.

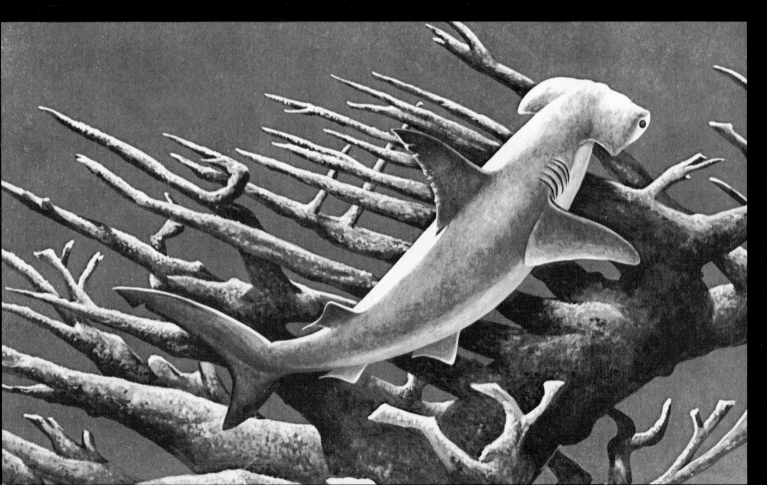

RICHARD ELLIS -75

**OPPOSITE, ABOVE:** The porbeagle (*Lamna nasus*) is the smallest of the mackerel sharks, and its offshore habitat precludes attacks on most swimmers. The origin of its common name is a linguistic mystery.

**OPPOSITE, BELOW:** Second only to the whale shark in size, the basking shark (*Cetorhinus maximus*) can reach a length of 40 feet. Its huge gills enable it to expel vast quantities of water after it has strained out the plankton.

**LEFT:** The shortfin mako (*Isurus oxyrinchus*) is one of the world's premier game fishes, capable of 20-foot leaps out of the water. It is a close relative of the great white.

**BELOW:** One of the most unusual of all sharks, the goblin shark (*Mitsukurina owstowni*) has been found in deep water in scattered locations around the world.

The tail of the thresher shark (*Alopias vulpinus*) is as long as the shark's body, and may be used to stun small prey fishes.

In many localities in the United States, there are places called Shark-tooth Hill, each so-called from an abundance of shark teeth in rich fossil deposits. Not far from Bakersfield in southern California is one of them. There, according to elasmo-paleontologist Shelton Applegate, "the ocean bottom muds and silts have been uplifting through faulting and folding so that we can take a shovel and dig shark teeth out of the hillside in the middle of the San Joaquin Valley." Venice, Florida, on the Gulf coast just south of Sarasota, is another good source of fossil teeth, and in addition to Megalodon teeth, this region also yields the teeth of the ancestral lamnid, *Isurus hastalis*. The teeth of *I. hastalis* resemble those of *Carcharodon carcharias* in size and shape (see facing page), but they have no serrations, and their former owners have therefore been placed in the genus *Isurus* with the makos.

In 1985, de Muizon and DeVries suggested that *Isurus hastalis*, the acknowledged mako ancestor, is likely to be the lineal ancestor of the white shark as well, since weakly serrated teeth discovered in Peru are considered "morphologically intermediate" between *I. hastalis* and *C.*

*carcharias*. In support of this hypothesis, the French paleoichthyologist Henri Cappetta wrote, two years later, "The origin of *Carcharodon* from *Isurus hastalis* seems very likely. . . . It may be added that the teeth of *Carcharodon* whose serrations have been removed by wear look very much like teeth of *I. hastalis*." But because Megalodon did not share this common mako-like ancestor, the argument goes, Megalodon deserves separate generic ranking. The genus name *Carcharocles* (and its synonyms *Procarcharodon* and *Megaselachus*) had previously been proposed for a group of five extinct species from the Middle Eocene (45 million to 2 million years ago), and it is within this group that Cappetta and others feel Megalodon should reside. They have therefore proposed *Carcharocles megalodon* ("minutely jagged giant tooth," a reference to the smaller edge serrations) as the name for the giant shark commonly referred to as Megalodon. We prefer not to enter this nomenclatural wrangle, being content to recognize that white sharks and Megalodon probably occupy proximate twigs of the same evolutionary bramble bush. Until further notice or more convincing evidence, we cautiously follow those who recognize *Carcharodon megalodon* as the correct binomen.

The eastern shore of the United States, from Chesapeake Bay to South Carolina, has surrendered large numbers of large teeth of assorted species of extinct lamnids, including several close relatives of the white shark. These have been differentiated on the basis of tooth shape, and classified as *Carcharodon angustidens*, *C. auriculatus*, and *C. sulcidens*. Dealers in fossils also offer sharks' teeth from such unexpected locations as Belgium, Morocco, Kansas, Nebraska, and Zululand, South Africa. (David Davies found several huge Megalodon teeth at Uloa in Zululand, and at Sapolwana he discovered 136 teeth of *Carcharodon sulcidens*, arguably an ancestor of the white shark.)

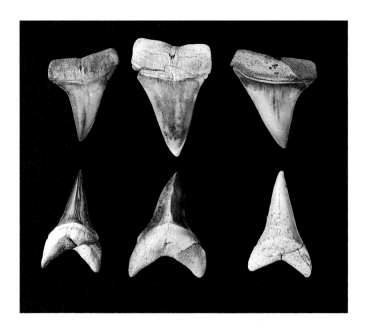 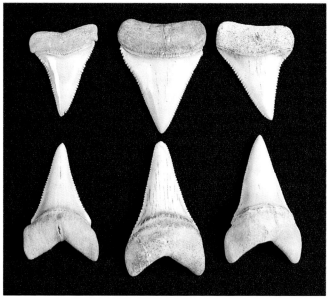

Two series of teeth, from the upper and lower jaws of (LEFT) the fossil mako *Isurus hastalis*, excavated at Aguada de Lomas, Peru, and (RIGHT) the white shark, excavated from a Lower Pliocene deposit at Sacaco, Peru. Although the teeth of *I. hastalis* lack serrations, they bear a remarkable resemblance in shape to the teeth of the white shark. Many paleoichthyologists now believe that the white shark is descended from *I. hastalis*, and not from Megalodon.

Megalodon is extinct, but *C. carcharias* has survived the vicissitudes of time and fate, and its classification—its evolutionary tree—is as follows:

| | |
|---|---|
| KINGDOM: | Animal (all life except plants, viruses, and various one-celled organisms) |
| PHYLUM: | Chordata (vertebrates, lancelets, and tunicates) |
| SUBPHYLUM: | Vertebrata (vertebrates) |
| CLASS: | Chondrichthyes (cartilaginous fishes) |
| SUBCLASS: | Elasmobranchii (sharks, skates, and rays) |
| SUPERORDER: | Selachii (sharks) |
| ORDER: | Lamniformes (mackerel sharks) |
| FAMILY: | Lamnidae (lamnid sharks) |
| GENUS: | *Carcharodon* (the great white and its four extinct cousins) |
| SPECIES: | *Carcharodon carcharias* (the great white shark)* |

* For perspective, your own classification goes like this:

| | |
|---|---|
| KINGDOM: | Animal |
| PHYLUM: | Chordata |
| SUBPHYLUM: | Vertebrata |
| CLASS: | Mammalia (mammals) |
| SUBCLASS: | (none established) |
| SUPERORDER: | (none established) |
| ORDER: | Primates (tree shrews, lorises, tarsiers, marmosets, monkeys, baboons, apes, and hominids) |
| FAMILY: | Hominidae (a dozen hominids, most of them extinct) |
| GENUS: | *Homo* (modern humans and one or two extinct ancestors and relatives) |
| SPECIES: | *Homo sapiens* (modern humans) |

Sharks are defined in part by their reproductive strategies. Although many bony fishes produce large numbers of eggs at each spawning (millions in some cases), sharks are much more parsimonious, producing fewer eggs (dozens per pregnancy) and, in all species, fertilizing them internally. The pelvic fins of all male sharks are modified into claspers (see p. 92), which function as intromittent organs to convey the sperm directly into the genital opening of the female. The sperm is generated in the testes and forced into the clasper groove by fluid pressure from the siphon sac, one per clasper. In many species, hooks or spines on the ends of the claspers give the males additional purchase during copulation. The females of these species often have a thickening in the terminal part of the oviduct, evidently an evolutionary response to the development of hooks and spines in the males.

In the more flexible species, such as the catsharks, the male coils around the female during copulation, but in the more rigid forms like the carcharhinids (the lemon shark has been observed mating in captivity, and the blacktip and whitetip reef sharks in the wild), the male and female swim parallel to one another while the male inserts one of his claspers. Most sharks have managed not to reveal their mating activities to us, although bite marks on the females suggest that the males grasp the females with their teeth during the process. Nothing whatever is known of the mating habits of the white shark.

Many shark species lay eggs, which, like the eggs of birds and reptiles, contain the developing embryos. (In the bony fishes, the eggs remain unfertilized, and contain no developing embryos until the female has released the eggs and the male has showered his sperm onto them.) The egg-laying shark species are *oviparous*, which translates as "egg birth." Shark eggs are often leathery cases, and they are sometimes corkscrewed into crevices for protection from predators. Among the oviparous species are the swell shark, the horn shark, and the whale shark, which lays eggs larger than footballs.

The *viviparous* sharks maintain a "placental" relationship with their developing young, more in the fashion of mammals than of fishes, and the young are born alive, as fully functional miniatures of their parents. No sharks care for their young; on the contrary, the risk is that the mothers will gobble up their babies as soon as they are born. Fortunately for the pups, there appears to be a hormonal factor that inhibits the mothers from feeding during the pupping season. "Once the young sharklet or pup is released from the egg or from the mother," wrote Perry Gilbert in 1982, "it is on its own, for there is no parental care." Species that are known to be viviparous are the hammerheads, the carcharhinids, some of the smooth dogfishes, and the basking shark. Some of the requicm sharks (carcharhinids) give birth to sizable litters: blue sharks (*Prionace glauca*) can produce as many as 60 pups, and Bigelow and Schroeder report a female tiger shark (*Galeocerdo cuvier*) that contained 82 embryos.

But by far the most common method of parturition in the sharks is a combination of the previous two, known as *ovoviviparity*, wherein the young developing in the uterus are nourished not only by the yolk of the egg, but also, when they leave the egg, by fluids secreted by glands in the wall of the oviduct. The eggs hatch within the oviduct, and after the young absorb the nourishing contents of the yolk sac and ingest the nutritive secretory fluids, they are brought forth alive. In some species, the unborn embryos compete for survival, the embryos eating their siblings until only one is left in each of the paired oviducts. This intrauterine cannibalism—known as "oophagy" (egg eating)—was first noticed in sand tigers (*Eugomphodus*), and has subsequently been discovered to occur in threshers, makos, and porbeagles. If the other lamnids are oophagous, it is likely that *Carcharodon* is too. A possible advantage to the birth of a small number of very large babies—a strategy available only to the largest shark species—is that there will be few predators large enough to attack the babies, thus ensuring their survival. (Female white sharks tend to grow

larger than males, certainly an advantage to a mother that gives birth to enormous offspring.) Most bony fishes give birth to very large numbers of very small babies, quite a different strategy for ensuring that at least some will survive.

The sequence whereby animals feed on other animals or plants, and larger animals feed on *them*, and so forth, is commonly known as "the food web," because each organism is linked to so many others in the struggle for survival. Because the smallest organisms, which must supply nourishment to the next smallest, exist in astronomical numbers, they are often represented as the base of a hypothetical pyramid. As we move up this pyramid, we find prey organisms *and* their predators decreasing in quantity and the predators usually increasing in size. (See p. 117 for a discussion of why big, fierce animals are rare.) At the top of the pyramid are those creatures that are the ultimate beneficiaries of all of this eating of smaller organisms: the apex predators that nothing feeds on. (An injured or wounded predator is another matter, and even lions, tigers, and bears, the apex predators of the terrestrial world, can be attacked by smaller creatures if they are incapacitated.) In the sea, the apex predators are the killer whale, the sperm whale, and the great white shark.

But although the white shark is indeed a formidable hunter, and the largest predatory fish in today's oceans, not long ago—geologically speaking—there existed a creature that reached twice the length of the longest white shark known, and probably weighed twenty tons or more. That was Megalodon, the apex of apex predators.

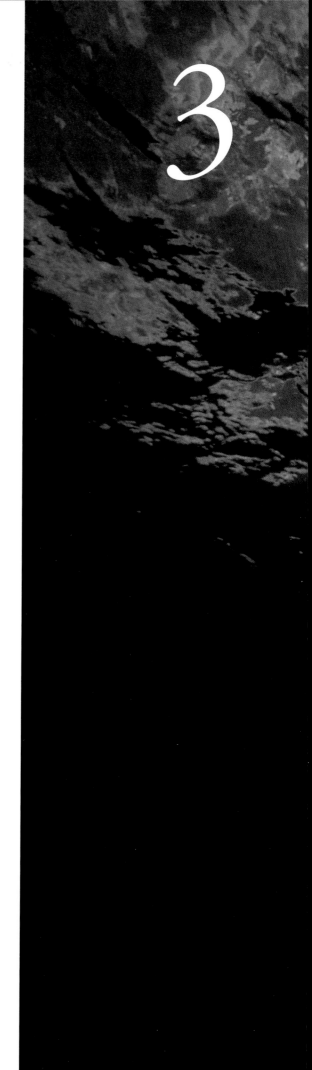

# Megalodon: A Giant Ancient Relative

3

efore there was *Carcharodon carcharias*, there was a very large shark named *Carcharodon megalodon*. Abundant fossil evidence shows that it lived during the Middle and Late Tertiary, as far back as 50 million years ago, and probably wandered the same seas as the modern white shark, plying pretty much the same trade. It was not the direct or immediate ancestor of the white shark, but was surely a close relative—most likely its evolutionary great uncle. At a length of 50 feet or more, it was probably the most terrifying predator that has ever lived.

For convenience, this giant fish is often called simply Megalodon—which translates as "great tooth." Its teeth, our only souvenir of its existence, are often larger than a grown man's hand, but in general form they closely resemble those of its smaller relative. The differences are nonetheless sufficient to justify our separating the extinct and recent sharks as distinct species: besides their obviously greater size, Megalodon teeth have more and relatively smaller serrations and, above the root, a scar or "chevron" that is lacking on the teeth of adult *C. carcharias*. That they are conspicuously different in color, as well, is simply a consequence of fossilization: the teeth of all living sharks are white, whereas the teeth of extinct or fossil species range from light brown to black.

We do not actually know what Megalodon looked like, since all we have to go on are its teeth, but we assume (from good paleontological practice) that it looked a lot like the living white shark, though considerably larger. Their teeth are so similar that the two species have been placed in the same genus by most systematic biologists (but see pp. 30–31). They believe that the two are as close to one another in form and genetics as, say, a lion is to a tiger. The two big cats (which are even more alike internally than externally) are both assigned to the genus *Panthera*—as *Panthera leo* and *Panthera tigris*—and in like manner the two great sharks have most often been placed together in the genus *Carcharodon*.

Hanging in the Hall of Fossil Fishes at the American Museum of

Megalodon, shown alongside a drawing of one of its teeth and, for comparison, a recent *Carcharodon* tooth (erroneously identified as having come from a 36-foot specimen). Drawing by Charles R. Knight, the renowned illustrator of prehistoric creatures.

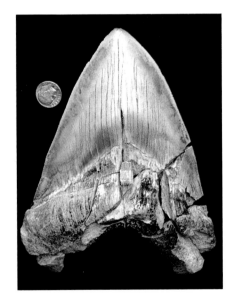

Fossil teeth provide irrefutable evidence for the impressive size of the largest predatory shark in history. This gigantic tooth, measured vertically at 6.8″, may be the largest Megalodon tooth on record. It was collected by Peter Larson of the Black Hills Institute of Geological Research in 1987, in an Upper Miocene deposit at Aguada de Lomas, Peru.

Natural History in New York is a reconstruction of the jaws of Megalodon. Most of the teeth in the reconstruction are the real thing, albeit from a number of different donors, but the jaws that hold them are necessarily a fabrication, scaled up from those of a white shark, for want of a better model. They are large enough for a grown man to stand upright in, and most books about sharks reproduce a photograph of the model, either with a lone man seated impassively within the jaws or with six gents in lab coats positioned so as to demonstrate the enormous size of the jaws. The full text of the label that accompanies these immense jaws, prepared in 1940, reads as follows:

### THE JAWS OF A GIANT EXTINCT SHARK

Most of the oceans during middle and late Tertiary time were inhabited by a giant shark named *Carcharodon megalodon*, a close relative of the living white shark or man-eater.

The jaws suspended above have been restored in plaster to hold the fossil teeth of this giant shark. The size of the jaws was determined on the basis of the tooth-jaw proportions in the modern relative, and the same number of teeth was used in the restoration as in the living form. All the teeth from a single *Carcharodon megalodon* have not been found together, but it is probable that the extinct and living species have about the same number of teeth in each jaw.

As restored, the jaws measure nine feet across. The largest teeth average six inches in height. It is estimated that this giant shark reached a length of approximately forty-five feet.

If we are to accept these jaws as an accurate reconstruction, it is obvious that their owner would have to have been considerably more than 45 feet in length. Someone made a mistake, either in the reconstruction or in the estimated length of the great fish. Others who have observed this inconsistency have simply assumed that the length estimate was in error; in a book called *Shark Safari*, for example, Hal Scharp postulates a length of 120 feet for Megalodon, and breathlessly concludes that the shark "could engulf an entire truck within its gigantic jaws!" But in a 1973 paper in the journal *Science*, Dr. John E. Randall, an ichthyologist with the Bishop Museum in Hawaii, wrote that the reconstruction "has been shown to be at least one-third too large because all the teeth were regarded as nearly the same size as the large ones medially in the jaws." In other words, in real sharks, the teeth are much smaller toward the rear of the jaw, and using teeth all of the same size produces a jaw that is much too big.

Megalodon probably did reach a length of 45 feet or more, but not with these jaws. In fact, because Megalodon teeth up to 7 inches long have been found, we can postulate a maximum size considerably greater than the 45 feet indicated by the American Museum's label. In a discussion of fossil teeth found at Uloa, South Africa, David Davies, the Director of the Oceanographic Research Institute in Durban, wrote: "Estimates of size made from the fossil teeth of this wide-ranging shark obtained in various parts of the world indicate that it may have reached 60 to 80 ft. in total length." *

Given the fearsome reputation of the comparatively small white shark, we are fortunate that Megalodon is extinct. Consider what our

\* Now that the jaws in the American Museum have been shown to be exaggerated—but have not been removed or changed—other institutions have built more accurate models for display. At Sea World in San Diego, Dr. Leonard Compagno has supervised the fabrication of a much more accurately scaled version, only about 4 feet high, but now the teeth are white, not the grayish-brown fossils they ought to be.

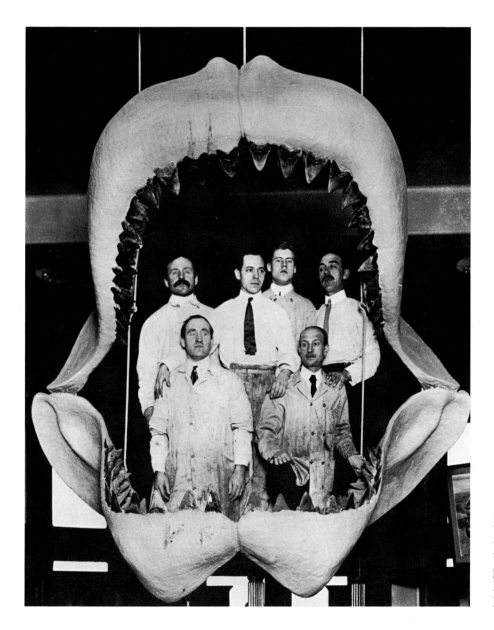

In the most famous of all Megalodon illustrations, ichthyologists pose in the reconstructed jaws of the giant prehistoric shark in the Hall of Fossil Fishes of the American Museum of Natural History, in New York.

attitude toward a day at the beach would be if there were 50-foot carnivorous sharks in our offshore waters—sharks large enough to swallow a cow.

There are, of course, larger creatures in the sea. In fact, there are even *sharks* alive today that rival Megalodon in size, but like most of the larger whales, they are harmless plankton-feeders. The whale shark (*Rhincodon typus*) is the world's largest living fish, reaching a length of 40 to 50 feet and a weight of perhaps 20 tons. Second only to the whale shark is another plankton-eater, the basking shark (*Cetorhinus maximus*), which can attain a length of 40 feet. The sperm whale, which can reach a length of 60 feet, is the largest predator that has ever lived, maybe twice as heavy as the largest carnivorous dinosaur.

Although most scientists have (perhaps reluctantly) assigned Megalodon to the ranks of the extinct along with the ichthyosaurs and pterodactyls, references occasionally surface that suggest that they still prowl the depths. Although most of these references are unadulterated fiction, some are to be found in works that might be taken seriously.

J. L. B. Smith was a respected South African ichthyologist who will be remembered for his identification of the living coelacanth, a lobe-finned fish that had been thought to be extinct for 50 million years. In 1938, a single specimen was caught off the East African coast, a discovery that shook the zoological community to its roots. Not only was this heavy-scaled, 5-foot fish a "living fossil," but it was believed by many to have

A great white, a diver, and Megalodon. The man is 6 feet tall, the white shark is 16 feet long, and Megalodon was about 45 feet long. (The intent of the illustration is to show relative sizes; Megalodon no longer exists.)

The second coelacanth discovered in modern times, on the dock in the Comoro Islands in December 1952. J. L. B. Smith, who described it, has his hand on its head, and Captain E. E. Hunt, the man who found it, is at Smith's right. Holding the fin is P. Coudert, Governor of the Comoros.

been the ancient link between fishes and amphibians. It was thought to have been related to the first vertebrate to crawl out of the water, and thus to have represented a direct link in the evolutionary chain that the determinists believed led from amoeba to fish to amphibian to reptile to bird and primitive mammal, and last, to the crowning glory of the entire process, humans. (Nowadays, this progression is dismissed as being ridiculously anthropocentric: we are not the culmination of a process designed to produce us. There are those who would argue that precisely the opposite is true: that humankind, with the unique capability of desecrating or even destroying the planet, represents not the apex of evolution, but the dark specter who has come to end it.)

Smith's was a voice to be reckoned with, and when he wrote in 1961 that "teeth 5 ins. long have been dredged from the depths, indicating sharks of 100 feet with jaws at least 6 feet across," he seemed to be warning us that Megalodon lived. He went on quickly, however—though not very reassuringly—to add that "These monsters may still live in deep water, but it is better to believe them extinct." Amen.

Despite the hundreds, even thousands, of Megalodon teeth that have been dredged from the ocean floor or found embedded in the chalky cliffs of California, Maryland, Florida, North Carolina, Belgium, and Morocco, *not a single white one has ever been found*. All the teeth that have been unearthed or dredged up are brown or black. Moreover, they are not really teeth at all, but fossils, in the same way that the "bones" of the dinosaurs in various museums are not bones at all, but compacted minerals that have gradually replaced the bones over time, precisely duplicating the finest detail. Should someone, then, dredge up a *white* Megalodon tooth, we would know that the giant shark became extinct quite recently—or is flourishing somewhere in the vastness of the oceans and has simply lost a tooth.

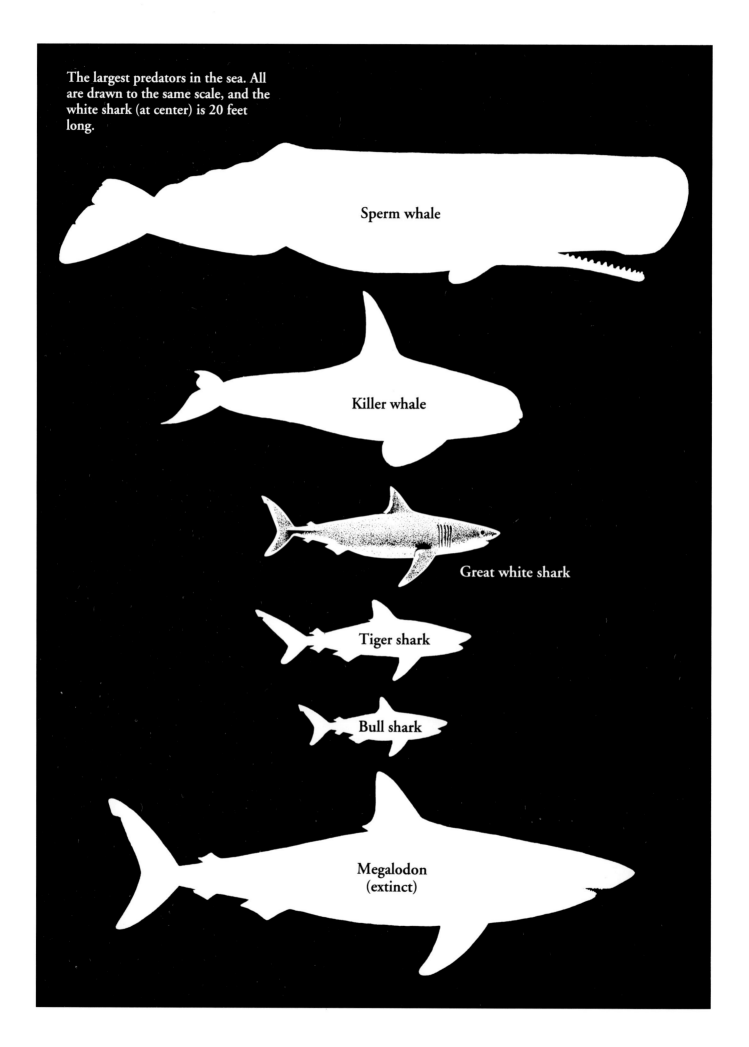

The largest predators in the sea. All are drawn to the same scale, and the white shark (at center) is 20 feet long.

Sperm whale

Killer whale

Great white shark

Tiger shark

Bull shark

Megalodon
(extinct)

A note on sharks' teeth, Megalodon's and others, is in order here. Sharks of all species have multiple rows of teeth; those currently doing the biting are replaced regularly in a process that has been likened to the action of a moving escalator. Behind the functional front rows of teeth, there are other rows, waiting to move forward as those in the front rank fall out or are otherwise dislodged. A shark will therefore have many more teeth in its mouth during its lifetime than would any other vertebrate, the total number from a given animal across a lifetime numbering perhaps in the thousands. One might then suppose that it would not have required many individual Megalodons to have scattered all the teeth ever collected, but not so: we can be certain that hundreds of thousands or even millions more teeth remain in the seafloors or in the ground, most of them never to be seen.

When fossilized shark teeth were first discovered on land, long before any were dredged from the oceans' depths, their origin was a complete enigma. Pliny, the great Roman student of nature, believed that they had fallen from the sky during eclipses of the moon. They were later thought to be the tongues of serpents that St. Paul had turned to stone while he was visiting the islands of Malta, and in consequence they acquired the name *glossopetrae* ("tongue stones"). They were believed to have magical properties, especially as counter-agents to the bites of poisonous snakes, and to that end they were often worn as talismans. By the middle of the eighteenth century, however, their origins were understood, though people believed they came from particularly large specimens of the familiar white sharks. In his 1766 *British Zoology*, Thomas Pennant wrote that "Teeth of this fish [the great white] are very frequent in Malta, some of which are four inches long."

There are many references to gigantic teeth dredged from the ocean's depths, but not one of these described a tooth as white. The *Challenger*, the first vessel dedicated to oceanographic research, dredged up several of these manganese-encrusted teeth in 1873 (see Murray, 1891), but only later did their origin become clear. (Manganese nodules form very slowly, but they exist on the ocean floor in uncountable millions. Not all of them are formed around sharks' teeth, of course. According to Heezen and Hollister's *The Face of the Deep*, "ice-rafted debris, pumice, the earbones of whales, the teeth of sharks, and other nearly indestructible projectiles become the nuclei of the golf-ball to grapefruit-size manganese nodules which litter much of the deep-sea floor.")

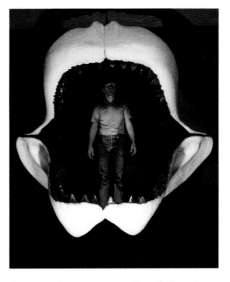

Among the most popular of all paleo-ichthyological exhibits is a set of the jaws of Megalodon. This one (only the teeth are real) is in the Smithsonian's Museum of Natural History in Washington.

Depending on the mineral content of the sea floor in which they are found, fossil teeth of Megalodon range in color from cream to black.

We know by inference that the great ancestral sharks fed on whales, because their remains have been found together, the whale bones often tooth-scarred. But why Megalodon, with its 7-inch teeth and a mouth large enough to accommodate an upright piano, should have disappeared remains a mystery.

There were once giant ground sloths, enormous bisons, huge turtles, and even 50-foot crocodilians, all of which are extinct, and in all cases we have complete skeletons that confirm the giants' existence. But although the modern counterparts of these giants are all much smaller, gigantism does not necessarily lead to a reduction in the size of descendants; the earliest horse-like mammals, for example, were the size of fox terriers, their descendants increasing in size over the ensuing millennia to yield ultimately the horse, the zebra, and other modern equines.

Scientists now regard extinction as an oft-repeated event along a continuum, not as the "failure" of an individual species. Still, there has to be a reason—or a set of reasons—for the disappearance of a given animal over a particular period of time, particularly when the animal's adaptation to its environment appears still roadworthy. As far as we know, there is no cosmic stop-watch that ticks off the time of *Eohippus* or *Stegosaurus*, and closes it out forever when the animal has lived out its allotted, unrevealed purposes. Except that we have not found one, there appears to be no reason why Megalodon should not be flourishing today.

In a paper entitled "Serpents, Sea Creatures and Giant Sharks," submitted to Bio 130 at Harvard University in 1968, James F. Clark contended that a "giant shark of the magnitude of *C. megalodon* presently inhabits the deep sea. This beast, ranging between 60 and 120 feet, is intimately related to the living *C. carcharias*, if indeed it is not simply a gigantic representative of that species." It is not the intention of this discussion to dissect the excesses of an undergraduate paper, but Clark's essay came to the attention of Peter Matthiessen, who referred to it in *Blue Meridian*, his popular (and otherwise excellent) 1971 book about Peter Gimbel's search for the great white shark. Matthiessen acknowledges Clark's contribution (assigning him to the staff of the Museum of Comparative Zoology at Harvard, though he only did his research there), and thanks him for "permission to paraphrase his arguments in support of the hypothesis that the white shark's giant relative *Carcharias* [sic] *megalodon* still exists." We can forgive Matthiessen for assuming that the maximum known length of the white shark is 36.5 feet, for his book predates Perry Gilbert's 1973 revelation that the 36.5-foot "Port Fairy" white shark in the British Museum was a typographical error (the specimen was actually no more than 16.5 feet in length, as we shall see in the next chapter). But when Matthiessen follows Clark in his argument that "it seems much more correct to recognize but a single species of *Carcharodon* on the basis of tooth morphology," he makes a serious error. The teeth of the two species *are* distinct, distinct enough that some paleontologists believe the two species do not even share the same ancestor.

Several scientists, too, have postulated the continued existence of giant maneaters. One was the late Gilbert Whitley, an Australian ichthyologist whose 1940 publication *The Fishes of Australia, Part I: The Sharks*, contains this statement:

Large flat triangular teeth with serrated edges have long been known to geologists from the various divisions of the Tertiary formation throughout the world. They are the remnants of sharks which must have attained enormous dimensions, and which were evidently similar in general form to "The Great White Shark" (*Carcharodon carcharias*) of present times. This recent species attains a length of forty feet, at which size it has teeth about three inches in length; since the fossil teeth are sometimes six inches long, it has been assumed that the extinct species reached a length of eighty feet. Fresh-looking teeth measuring 4 by 3¼ inches have been dredged from the sea-floor, which indicates that if not actually still living, this gigantic species must have become extinct within a recent period.

Although he refers to "fresh-looking teeth," Whitley does not come right out and say that this gigantic fish exists, only that it "must have become extinct within a recent period."

Probably the most spectacular citation in all the literature can be found in David G. Stead's *Sharks and Rays of Australian Seas*, published in 1963. This book (also cited by Matthiessen) contains a description of "the most terrible monster that the seas of Mother Earth have produced"—and here he is referring only to the great white. Like everyone else who wrote before 1973, including Whitley, Stead assumed that the 36.5-foot Port Fairy shark was accurately measured, and includes it as "the largest recorded in Australian waters." He lists other known specimens that ranged from 16 to 20 feet, but then he launches into what he calls "the most outstanding of all stories relating to the gigantic forms of this fish ever to come to light—I mean, of course, accounts which really appeared to be founded on fact." Here is the story, as told by Stead:

In the year 1918 I recorded the sensation that had been caused among the "outside" crayfish men at Port Stephens, when, for several days, they refused to go to sea to their regular fishing grounds in the vicinity of Broughton Island. The men had been at work on the fishing grounds—which lie in deep water—when an immense shark of almost unbelievable proportions put in an appearance, lifting pot after pot containing many crayfishes, and taking, as the men said, "pots, mooring lines and all." These crayfish pots, it should be mentioned, were about 3 feet 6 inches in diameter and frequently contained from two to three dozen good-sized crayfish each weighing several pounds. The men were all unanimous that this shark was something the like of which they had never dreamed of. In company with the local Fisheries Inspector I questioned many of the men very closely and they all agreed as to the gigantic stature of the beast. But the lengths they gave were, on the whole, absurd. I mention them, however, as an indication of the state of mind which this unusual giant had thrown them into. And bear in mind that these were men who were used to the sea and all sorts of weather, and all sorts of sharks as well. One of the crew said the shark was "three hundred feet long at least"! Others said it was as long as the wharf on which we stood—about 115 feet! They affirmed that the water "boiled" over a large space when the fish swam past. They were all familiar with whales, which they had often seen passing at sea, but this was a vast shark. They had seen its terrible head which was "at least as long as the roof of the wharf shed at Nelson's Bay." Impossible, of course! But these were prosaic and rather stolid men, not given to "fish stories" nor even to talking at all about their catches. Further, they knew that the person they were talking to (myself) had heard all the fish stories years before! One of the things that impressed me was that they all agreed as to the ghostly whitish color of the vast fish.

Summarizing, Stead writes that he has "little doubt that in this occurrence we had one of those rare occasions when humans have been vouchsafed a glimpse of one of those enormous sharks of the White Death type, which we know to exist or to have existed in the recent past, in the vast depths of the sea. While they are probably not abundant they may yet be so." Even the smaller of Stead's figures (115 feet) offers a sense of the captivating fascination of the giant shark.

Zane Grey, the western novelist and big-game fisherman, never caught anything in that range, but he firmly believed that such monsters

# Megamouth:
# A Bizarre Recent
# Discovery

In November 1976, Peter Benchley called to tell me he had heard that "they found a Megalodon." In a state of near-hysteria, I tried to substantiate this incredible claim. If true, that news—so fitting that it would come from Benchley, the author of *Jaws*—would change the world's swimming habits forever.

It seems that the *AFB-14*, a naval research vessel operating in deep water off the northern coast of the Hawaiian island of Oahu, had deployed two orange-and-white parachutes as sea anchors, and when they hauled them in, the crew discovered that one of them had been swallowed by a very large shark. Parachute-eating sharks are remarkable enough, but this creature was more than a little unusual: it was of a type totally unrecognizable to the crew. Over 14 feet long, the huge-mouthed creature weighed three-quarters of a ton. It had thousands of tiny teeth, and its rubbery lips make it look more like a seagoing hippopotamus than a shark. The sea anchor had been deployed at about 500 feet, which

suggests that this was a deepwater plankton-feeder, and therefore a fish that would be most unlikely to have ever taken a baited hook. Were it not for the pure coincidence of the ship and the shark being in the same place at the same time—and the bizarre inclination of the shark to swallow the 'chute—this animal might never have been discovered.

I had just seen the appearance of my *Book of Sharks*, in which I had written, "For every species that is synonymized, there is probably a new one already discovered or waiting to be discovered." Still, I hadn't expected a major new species to be discovered within a month of the book's publication. It turned out that the new shark had been nicknamed "Megamouth," and this had led to someone's thinking they had heard "Megalodon." It was subsequently described by Drs. Leighton Taylor, Leonard Compagno, and Paul Struhsaker, who determined that it was not only a new species, but the basis for a new genus and family as well. It was christened *Megachasma pelagios*,

which means "deep-water big-mouth." It was not until 1984 that a second specimen, also a male, was caught off southern California. A third male washed ashore in Western Australia in 1988, and a fourth, a badly decomposed male, was discovered, washed ashore, in Japan, in 1989.

The first *healthy* megamouth was not seen until October 21, 1990, when a commercial fisherman snagged one in his gillnet, 7 miles off Dana Point, southern California. He brought the 15-foot male into the harbor, where ichthyologists marveled at it and television crews filmed it for science, for posterity, and for publicity. Since no aquarium had the facilities to exhibit this creature, the authorities wisely (and sensitively) decided to release it. On October 23, the shark, dubbed "Mega" by the media, was returned to the Pacific. A radio transmitter attached to its hide allowed the scientists to track it for several days.

So the scientists have seen five of these amazing fish, but no Megalodons.          *Richard Ellis*

Charles R. Knight painted Megalodon several times. In this lunette, the giant shark is shown chasing some spotted eagle rays, while smaller sharks scatter.

* David Stead (1877 – 1957) predicted 80-foot sharks in a little book published in Australia in 1933, *Giants and Pygmies of the Deep*. In the section devoted to the white pointer he wrote: "It reaches at least 40 feet, as far as observed specimens have been recorded, but teeth of a similar kind have been seen by me, which must have come from a specimen not less than 80 feet in length. Such a sea devil as this could comfortably accommodate one hundred humans at one meal!" Stead's recounting of the story of the 1918 "115-footers" is found in a 1963 publication, edited after his death by Gilbert Whitley, in which Stead referred to his friend Zane Grey as "one of the doughtiest hunters of the Great Fish ever known."

exist. He cited Stead's account to prove it: "Dr. David Stead, of Sydney, a scientist of international reputation, corroborates my claim that there are white sharks up to eighty feet and more. If there are not, where do the shark teeth, five inches across the base, come from? . . . The waters around Australia are alive with many species of sharks. Why not some unknown species, huge and terrible? Who can tell what forms of life swim and battle in the ocean depths?" *

The fascination with giant sharks continues unabated. In 1981, obviously in the wake of the enormous success of "Jaws," Robin Brown wrote a story called *Megalodon*. In this thoroughly silly book, 200-foot sharks with 24-inch teeth occasionally come out of their abyssal caves to gobble up nuclear submarines. After many chilling adventures, the narrative concludes with an airlift of a trained sperm whale to dispatch the giant sharks—as if even a sperm whale would be a fit adversary for such monsters.

In 1987, Vantage Press (a vanity press) issued *Carcharodon*, a tale written by a man named George Edward Noe. If Brown's *Megalodon* is silly, then *Carcharodon* is a howler. It seems somewhat unfair to carp about a book that the author paid to have published, but the subject matter begs at least a mention here. The book begins with an 80-foot shark, "having survived millions of years frozen in a thick wall of ice near the polar ice cap," suddenly finding itself alive and hungry. It goes on a carnivorous rampage, gobbling up manta rays, fish, whales, boats, and, of course, practically every human being that it encounters. In the end, the hero, a cantankerous marine biologist not surprisingly named George Edward *Benson*, kills it with a harpoon shot from the bow of a borrowed Norwegian whaling ship.

All evidence suggests that Megalodon no longer exists, except perhaps in the minds and writings of Robin Brown, George Noe, J. L. B. Smith,

David Stead, Gilbert Whitley, or James F. Clark. On the basis of an analysis of the manganese layer on two of the teeth dredged up by the *Challenger*, W. Tschernezky concluded that Megalodon "became extinct in the latest Pleistocene or even survived until the Holocene period." Now the Holocene Era incorporates approximately the last 10,000 years, right into our own century, and perhaps those who would postulate giant sharks living at great depths—or off Australia—are not so far from the truth. All the evidence seems to point to their fairly recent disappearance, and it is not inconceivable that *Homo sapiens*—we have been around unchanged for a good 40,000 years—actually saw the 6-foot dorsal fin of *Carcharodon megalodon*.

Because we need mysteries—and because the sea so readily provides them—Megalodon will remain the *bête noir* (or, more accurately, the *bête blanc*) of the monster hunters. To date, no concrete evidence has surfaced to substantiate the continued existence of these giants. But there will always be those who keep hoping that one will appear. Let us hope we are not in the water when it does.

# 4 The Size of the Great White Shark

There is something morbidly fascinating about a giant shark, something that touches a chord in all of us. Many things frighten us, but the fear of sharks (is there such a word as "elasmophobia"?) is somehow unlike most of our other fears. It seems more profound, more deep-rooted, and it often manifests itself as *revenge*. We run from snakes or shudder at spiders, but we *hunt* sharks. In the water, we imagine imminent attacks, particularly when something unseen brushes past us in the surf. Perhaps something in our distant past has imbued us with a primordial fear of being eaten. Or perhaps it is not so complicated: perhaps the thought of being eaten alive is so palpably and rationally terrifying that we do not need to search our anthropological history. Regardless, there is something about the shark that has caused humankind a communal frisson ever since we first had the temerity to invade its domain.

The great white shark is not the largest fish in the world, nor is it the largest shark. That dual distinction belongs to the whale shark (*Rhincodon typus*), a harmless tropical plankton-eater. But the white shark is the largest fish, shark or otherwise, that attacks large prey, and that puts it into very select company indeed. Some of the billfishes can reach enormous size; the world's record black marlin, for example, weighed over 1,500 pounds. There have been recorded instances where swordfish or marlin have stabbed vessels with their bills, but we cannot attribute these incidents to ferocity, for these giants prey exclusively upon smaller, schooling fishes and little squid, and pose no threat to people at all. Similarly, the giant bluefin tunas, which can also reach weights in excess of 1,000 pounds, feed on fast-swimming fishes like mackerel. The only other sharks of significant size that have been known to attack humans are the tiger, *Galeocerdo cuvier*, which averages about 12 feet in length full-grown, the bull shark, *Carcharhinus leucas*, maximum length about 10 feet, and the 12-foot oceanic whitetip, *C. longimanus*.

At its largest recorded size, *Carcharodon carcharias* is considerably larger and heavier than any other predatory shark. (The next largest is the tiger shark, the record for which is an impressive 18 feet, but this svelte specimen weighed a mere 1,780 pounds.) All sharks are carnivores, and in that sense even the plankton-eating whale shark and basking shark can be classified as predators. But it is the *method* of hunting that distinguishes the white; the other two giants feed on minute zooplankton, with none of the chasing, slashing, and biting associated with carnivorous predation. (In due time, we will get to all that chasing, slashing, and biting, as experienced occasionally by humans, routinely by fishes and marine mammals.)

Because it is the largest predatory fish and also the largest fish ever taken on rod and reel, there has been great interest in the maximum size of *Carcharodon carcharias*. (Even though the gender is rarely mentioned— especially in the early accounts—the larger white sharks are almost always females.) In the literature there are repeated (but unverified) references to gigantic specimens, such as the following footnote from a 1935 publication: "According to the information of V. D. Vladykov [the senior author of the paper], a 37-foot maneater was found dead in a herring weir on White Island (near Grand Manan) in the middle of June, 1930. From the liver 210 gallons of oil were obtained." In *The Guinness Book of Animal Facts & Feats*, Gerald Wood tries to validate Vladykov's claim by some rather circuitous reasoning ("Would the Canadian ichthyologist, a man of high reputation, have included hearsay data unless he was positive it was accurate?"), but he cannot document the size of this shark. His attempts to contact Vladykov "proved fruitless"—Vladykov has since died—but still, Wood maintains that "an unbelievably huge carcharodon died in Canadian waters [Grand Manan Island is in the Bay of Fundy, close to the Maine-New Brunswick border] in June 1930."

Through Don McAllister, ichthyologist of the National Museum of Natural Sciences in Ottawa, the indefatigable John Randall managed to obtain a tooth of this shark, and in a 1987 study, he concluded that it actually came from a shark that was 16 to 17 feet in length. But then McAllister, evidently intent upon claiming the record for Canada, located a 95-year-old fisherman named Linwood Carroll who not only had a larger tooth, but actually recalled the incident (in a piece McAllister published in 1987):

I well remember the shark; the weir was near Bill's Island, it was a monster and a bad one. . . . Two fellows were in a dinghy—without warning it bit the side and crushed it like an egg shell. Other boats were there and many was trying to get a running bowline on its tail and we finally did. Then they put it in tow of a big boat with a lot of power to tow it to White Head and at times it would stop the boat. They tied it to the breakwater, where it died.

Mr. Carroll had kept a tooth, which he finally donated to the Museum. It was 1.7 inches in height, about 1.4 inches of which was enamel. Although larger than the tooth examined by Randall, its shape suggested that it came from the upper jaw rather than the lower, and Randall's estimate of the size of the shark still holds. *Sic semper gigantibus.*

*The Guinness Book of Animal Facts & Feats* is full of fascinating speculations and unproven "facts." Wood includes a 43-foot blue pointer (great

* The actual reference is found in a
1958 book by a popular South
African writer named Lawrence
Green. In a chapter of *South African Beachcomber* entitled "Fangs
of the Sea," Green wrote: "I have
discovered a record of a carcharodon forty-three feet long caught in
False Bay many years ago. A ship
had come in with plague on board,
there had been a number of sea
burials, and the sharks had followed her all the way into False
Bay." Green himself died many
years ago, and although much
of his research can be verified
(though he provides no references)
the "forty-three-foot carcharodon"
will probably remain permanently
unidentified and unconfirmed.

A mysterious "photograph" that
purports to show a 30-foot white
shark caught in the Maldive Islands, but carries no other confirmation. The loop alongside the
shark's head looks suspiciously
like a paper clip.

white) that ran aground in False Bay, South Africa, but writes that "it
would be impossible to give the date of the 43-footer {because} newspapers
of those days gave little or no space to such events," and he "drew a blank"
when he tried to document the existence of this monster. * Wood also
mentions a 26- and a 25-footer also trapped in Canadian nets; a 20-footer
that had been harpooned in 1758 after it had swallowed a sailor that had
fallen overboard; and a couple of 20-footers harpooned in Twofold Bay,
New South Wales, Australia, by whalers. For all these "records," Wood
cites a Cuban 21-footer as "the largest great white shark actually to be
weighed." (With that one, he begins to approach reality. We will shortly
be discussing each of these sharks.)

Almost buried in the musty stacks of ichthyological literature, we
find the September 1891 issue of *The Mediterranean Naturalist*, which
contains a report on climatic changes in the form of higher temperatures
and humidities. The anonymous naturalist then reported on some strange
fishes that had come into the Mediterranean from the Indian Ocean (presumably by swimming through the Suez Canal), in response to changes in
water temperature:

> The fauna too, is undergoing remarkable changes and it is not unusual to find the
> Great White Shark of the Indian Seas, which was until lately quite unknown in
> these regions, disporting itself in the waters of the Eastern basin of the Mediter-
> ranean. The waters of the Adriatic are especially favoured by these unwelcome
> intruders, owing no doubt to the more equable temperature of the waters. During
> the late naval manoeuvres, a specimen of the white shark was caught that weighed
> four tons and measured 33 feet in length.

In the collection of the British Museum of Natural History, there is a set
of white shark jaws that for many years bore the information: "Port Fairey,
36.5 feet." In an 1870 catalog of fishes in the British Museum's collections, ichthyologist Albert C. L. G. Günther made the following entry on
p. 391: "Jaws from specimen 36½ feet long, Port Fairey (?) Australia."
(The question mark is probably a reference to the misspelling of Port Fairy,
a small coastal town in Victoria, Australia.) Subsequent publications—
including Bigelow and Schroeder's then-definitive 1948 work, *Fishes of the
Western North Atlantic*—adopted this figure as correct (their reference reads
"The largest teeth of a specimen 36½ feet long were about two inches
long"), and it was soon considered authentic.

Because a 36-foot white shark so far exceeded any other known specimen, conservative scientists questioned it. In a 1964 publication on fossil
sharks, for example, David Davies wrote, "The record for the largest specimen of *C. carcharias* obtained by Bigelow and Schroeder (1948) measured
36½ feet in length—there is, however, some doubt as to the authenticity
of the length measurement of this specimen."

Although he actually examined the British Museum jaws in July
1962, Cornell University shark biologist Perry Gilbert did not publish his
findings until 1973. In an article called "Sharks and Shark Deterrents" (co-
authored by his wife, Claire Gilbert), he wrote:

> Among the dangerous species, the great white shark, *Carcharodon carcharias*, is
> reputed by Bigelow and Schroeder to be the largest, with a total length of 36.5

feet or 11.1 m. There is reason to question this figure, for on July 4, 1962, one of us (PWG) examined and measured the largest jaws and teeth of a great white shark present in the collections of the British Museum. Although there were no data on the jaws, the curator in charge believed them to be from the shark reputed by Günther to be 36.5 feet long. Thirteen days later I examined and measured the jaws of a 16.5 ft (about 5 m) great white shark in the collections of the Oceanographic Research Institute at Durban, South Africa, and was struck by the fact that the jaws and teeth of the Durban and British Museum specimens were approximately the same size. I concluded that the figure of 36.5 feet, so widely quoted, was probably a printer's error, and should have read 16.5 ft. If this be true, the largest great white shark that has actually been measured was taken off Havana, Cuba, and reported by Luis Howell-Rivero to be 21 ft or 6.4 m long.

The jaws of the 16.5-footer that Perry Gilbert had been examining in Durban when he concluded that the "Port Fairy" 36.5-footer in the British Museum could not have been so long.

In other words, the 36.5-footer is a typo. Perry Gilbert measured the jaws at the Oceanographic Research Institute in Durban in the presence of David Davies, the Director. According to Gilbert, the conversations they had in 1962 regarding the similarity of the Durban jaws to those in the British Museum were probably the inspiration for Davies' 1964 statement. (Because Davies died in 1965, we have had to rely on Perry Gilbert's recollection of that meeting.)

The Cuban specimen mentioned by Gilbert is also discussed by Bigelow and Schroeder in their discussion of *Carcharodon*. In the section devoted to size, the authors mention the Port Fairy specimen, asserting that it was never actually measured; note a 30-footer that also was not measured; and then write, "The three next largest actually measured have been 21 feet and 17 to 19 feet in length." The 21-footer is mentioned in two footnotes, which read as follows:

> 12. Taken recently off Havana, Cuba, and reported to us by Luis Howell-Rivero.
> 16. We have received a good photograph, apparently of this specimen, with a weight stated at 7,302 pounds, from Ollyandro del Valle.*

For years this Cuban 21-foot *devorador de hombres* was believed to be the largest white shark ever measured. This 1945 photograph (whereabouts now unknown) appeared in the magazine *Mar y Pesca* in 1974.

For many years, this was the only information about the Cuban shark, and because it appeared (in 1948) in Bigelow and Schroeder's respected and influential work, it was accepted as gospel. Dario Guitart-Manday, a Cuban ichthyologist, in an article co-authored by J. F. Milera for the Cuban journal *Mar y Pesca* in 1974, reproduced photographs of the shark on the dock and a full-sized photo of one of its teeth, which measures a little more than 2.8 inches. The article describes the capture of this *devorador de hombres* in 1945. It had taken a baited hook attached to a floating oil drum, and after a considerable struggle, had been towed to shore at Cojimar. According to this article, the shark was measured at 21 feet, but was never accurately weighed. ("The weight of the animal was never ascertained, since there were no facilities in the area, but fishermen hazarded a guess at more than 7,000 pounds.") Since the demolition of the 36.5-foot record, this fish has been held to be the longest white shark ever actually measured.

In a 1987 study, however, Randall "refutes" the size of the Cuban shark. He compares the photograph (reproduced in the article by Guitart and Milera) with a photograph of a 16-foot 7-inch specimen taken in

* When one of us (Richard Ellis) wrote to the Museum of Comparative Zoology at Harvard (where the papers of Henry Bigelow and William Schroeder are housed), trying to find this photograph, he was told that it could not be found, and was "probably a lost cause." According to a letter (to John McCosker) from Jorge del Valle, the name of his father should be Alexandro, not "Ollyandro."

# Shark Spotting from the Air

During the summer of 1978—just a couple of years after the publication of *Jaws*—a giant shark was photographed from the air off Block Island, east of Long Island. Since the whole country (particularly the East Coast) was still in the grip of "Jaws-mania," the shark received enormous publicity. A photograph of the shark appeared on the front page of New York's *Daily News*, then the largest-circulation daily in the country. Biologist Jack Casey, trying to keep the thing in perspective, was quoted as saying that it "was over 20 feet, probably considerably larger than the largest on record, which is 21 feet," and he added, "Very, very few large great whites have ever been photographed."

During the course of that summer, I was flying over Long Island Sound, looking for a reported school of sperm whales. I never saw the sperm whales, but I did spot what appeared to be a very, very large great white shark. Russ Kinne (the pilot) and I were wild with excitement, and I shouted over the engine noise that this must be the "monster" that everyone was talking about. Russ brought the plane in as low as he could, and we both photographed the shark for all we were worth.

Now it is not a little unsettling to find your pilot hanging out the window of the plane as the stall-horn sounds, indicating that you're flying at a dangerously slow speed. There is never a time when you want your plane to fall into the ocean, of course, but if you had to choose the absolute *worst* time to have it happen, it would probably be when there is a 30-foot great white shark swimming below you.

When we'd had our photos processed, and had taken a look, it was obvious that we had indeed photographed a very large shark. What was *not* evident, however, was whether or not it was a *white* shark. We hadn't measured it, of course, but we'd been close enough, often enough, to be able to estimate its length fairly accurately, and there was no question in Russ's mind *or* mine that it was at least 25 feet

long, longer than any white shark ever measured. That alone should have given us pause; after all, if someone is going to spot the largest white shark ever seen, it is unlikely, at best, that it would be people who are actually looking for it. (It is usually people who are *not* looking for such things who find them, as was the case when Megamouth was discovered in 1976, or the coelacanth, in 1938.)

So I examined my photographs carefully, trying to convince myself and anybody within earshot that I had indeed photographed the world's largest white shark. Certain aspects of the photographs, like the excessively pointed snout and the great breadth between the eyes did bother me. And no matter how fervently I wanted to believe my fish was a great white, I was having trouble with the very thing that would differentiate my photographs from any others ever taken of white sharks: the size. Nevertheless, I plowed ahead. I sent blow-ups to the NMFS lab at Narragansett, so that my friend Casey would corroborate my triumph.

FINAL

Vol. 60. No. 33

DAILY ◉ NEWS

New York, Wednesday, August 2, 1978

Variably cloudy today, 80. Partly sunny tomorrow. Details page 103

Price: 20 cents

Is This THE Shark? Wanna Bet a Fin on It?

By BRIAN KATES

Unfortunately, Casey and his colleague H. L. ("Wes") Pratt had decided that their original identification (the one reported in the *Daily News*) was incorrect, and that the monster fish was really a basking shark. (It was Wes Pratt who, a couple of years earlier, had taken *National Geographic* photographer David Doubilet diving with basking sharks in an area very close to the one we had overflown.) The basking shark is of course nothing to sneeze at, at least as far as size is concerned, but for ferocity, it doesn't have a patch on the great white. *Cetorhinus maximus* (which, interestingly, translates roughly as "great whale-shark"), is a great, dark, plankton-eating shark, second only to the whale shark for the title of world's largest fish. Basking sharks, which are found in temperate waters around the world, feed on plankton, which they filter from the sea water with their fringed gill rakers. They have only microscopic teeth, and although they can reach a length of 40 feet or more and a weight of five tons, they are considered harmless.

I suppose I thought our shark was a white because I *wanted* it to be a white. What shark researcher *wouldn't* want to be the one who spotted and photographed the largest white shark in the world?

*Richard Ellis*

Senzo Uchida, Director of the Okinawa Expo Aquarium, alongside the carcass of the 16.5-foot, 3,938-pound female that was caught on a longline off Okinawa in June 1981. Notice the bite marks on the head and side of the shark, most likely inflicted by other sharks after it had died on the line.

Okinawa in 1986, and says that the Okinawan shark seems larger. The article by Guitart and Milera also reproduces photographs of a vertebral centrum and a tooth of the Cojimar shark, and Randall writes that *their* size, too, indicates a shark of some 16.5 feet. * He concludes by saying, "Undoubtedly *Carcharodon carcharias* exceeds 20 feet (6.1 m) in length, but as yet there is no authenticated record of such a size."

Measuring sharks is not as simple as it sounds. Of course you put one end of the tape on the tip of the shark's nose, but where do you put the other end? Fishermen, always interested in maximum lengths, are likely to look for a way of obtaining the longest possible measurement, but biologists are more interested in a reliable standard that can be universally applied. Because, on the one hand, the tail might be bitten and thus shortened, and because, on the other hand, it is possible to bend the upper lobe of the tail so that the total length is artificially greater, biologists insist (whenever possible) on more standard measurements. The "standard length" of ichthyology is that measurement made from the tip of the snout to the upper side of the base of the caudal fin. Another measurement, appropriately called the "fork length," is from the snout tip to the *fork*, the deepest part of the angle formed by the intersection of the upper and lower lobes of the tail. The lack of a system of measurement common to fishermen and people who study fish is one of the factors that account for so much disorder in the size records for large fishes.

In May 1987, a gigantic white shark was netted by a fisherman named Peter Riseley off Kangaroo Island, South Australia. Unnamed "experts" quoted in the magazine of the South Australian Fisheries Department "say that it would be in excess of 7 metres [23 feet] long and weigh somewhere between 3,500 and 4,000 pounds." Even though the ship's winch was capable of lifting 4,000 pounds, the fishermen could not get the shark aboard. They hacked off one of its pectoral fins and spent four and a half hours cutting off its head, which was brought to shore. (Why they did not tow the entire shark to shore has not been explained.[†])

* But tooth size may not be a reliable indicator of total length. Some ichthyologists support the remote possibility that there might be two species of white sharks: a large-toothed variety and a small-toothed variety. A more likely reading of this conundrum is that there is substantial variation in the tooth size of individuals, and tooth size may not accurately reflect age or overall size.

† McCosker recently had an opportunity to examine the jaws of this specimen, now on display at the Manly Aquarium, near Sydney. The teeth are large but misshapen, and not large enough to support the 23-foot allegation convincingly.

In a 1984 television program on the adventures of Australian Vic Hislop ("The Shark Hunter"), we learn of his dedication to cleansing the seas of maneaters. His technique is to attach a bait—usually a living shark—to a floating oil drum, in hopes that something will come to eat it. Off South Australia, we see Hislop hauling in one white shark, and then he appears towing two of them. The first one was measured at 17 feet 4 inches, and the second is said to measure 20 feet 4 inches, but "it will never be weighed." The cable that was to hoist the shark to weigh it snaps, and the narrator tells us "that since the cable was tested to withstand two and a half tons, the shark has to weigh more than that."

Hislop had already been in the news in 1978, that time claiming to have landed the largest white shark ever. Off Phillip Island, south of Victoria, Hislop caught a female great white that was, according to newspaper reports, "7 metres long, with an estimated weight of 2.25 tonnes." The catch was heralded in the local papers as "the world's record . . . larger than the boat used to catch it." Indeed this was an enormous shark, but the measurements of "7 metres and 2.25 tonnes" are clearly imprecise, and presumably rough estimates. Converting 7 meters to feet and inches, however, turns the figure into a precise-sounding 22′11″, which instantly makes it appear that the shark was measured very carefully. *

Under careful scrutiny, shark information often shrinks along with the shark. In the Chilean newspaper *La Tercera*, a headline read "*¡Gigantesco tiburón en Iquique!*" In the accompanying article (the photograph showed the *tiburón* to be a white shark), the fish was described as being *siete metros y mil kilos*, about 23 feet and 2,200 pounds—which is much too slender for such a length. In response to an inquiry about this *tiburón*, we received the following response from Dr. Louis H. DiSalvo of Coquimbo: "On the big shark. I called up the fishery that caught it, and after two days of waiting for a return call, they sheepishly answered that the papers were wrong and that it actually measured closer to 5.8 meters (19′) and weighed 1,300 kilos (2,865 pounds), measured on a truck scales. . . . Apparently the crew squabbled over the thing and it was cut up in pieces and parceled out."

White sharks have been found in the Mediterranean, but over the centuries the depletion of its marine mammals has eliminated the white sharks' major food supply, and they are exceedingly rare. In 1987, however, off the island of Malta, an enormous white shark was captured. John Abela, a Maltese shark enthusiast reported (in a letter to McCosker) that a 23-foot, 5,000-pound specimen had been caught by local fisherman Alfred Cutajar, nicknamed "Son of God" for his sharkfishing prowess. (Evidently, this was the third such monster that he had caught within the decade.) The accompanying photographs show a very large shark indeed, and Abela, who measured it himself, claims also to have the jaws of the two others Cutajar had caught within the past decade: a 13-footer and a 20-footer.

The waters and the literature are full of monsters. There is no way of verifying or refuting some of the more outlandish stories, such as the 25-footer mentioned in Cousteau's *The Silent World*, or the 32-footer that David Webster says was caught off Santa Monica, California. In *Sportfishing*

Crew member Andrew Brochoff aboard Peter Riseley's boat with the head and pectoral fin of the roughly 22-foot white shark that Riseley caught off Kangaroo Island, South Australia. The fish was too heavy to bring in whole.

ABOVE: According to the Melbourne *Herald & Weekly Times*, this white shark weighed 5,000 pounds. It was caught on hooks suspended from a floating oil drum by Vic Hislop ("The Shark Hunter").

RIGHT: Possibly the largest white shark ever measured: reported as a 23-footer, it was caught by Alfred Cutajar off Malta, in the Mediterranean, in 1987. Its stomach contained a 6-foot blue shark, an 8-foot dolphin, and a sea turtle. The hand on the shark's flank (at base of photo) affords a sense of scale.

*for Sharks*, by Frank Mundus and Bill Wisner, the authors sum up—but do not document—many of the exaggerated records: "There's one authenticated capture of a 30-footer. Reported lengths up to 20 feet, chiefly in commercial fishing annals, are by no means rare. At least a couple of 21-footers are on the books, a 24-foot specimen is recorded for the Caribbean, and there have been periodic references to 25-footers."

Without some sort of documentation, most of these monsters must be dismissed. This is not to imply that only scientists can produce accurate records; many of the record white sharks have been caught and measured by fishermen. The most-quoted weight for any fish in the world is probably the 2,664 pounds of Alf Dean's rod-and-reel world's record fish, and the record has stood since 1959. Frank Mundus, the prototype for Captain Quint in "Jaws," but very far indeed from being an obsessed madman, fishes out of Montauk, Long Island, and has probably caught or supervised the catching of more white sharks than any other man or woman alive. (More on Mundus on pp. 192–95.) His best-known trophy, hanging in a saloon at Montauk, is the mounted head of a 17.5-foot female that was harpooned in 1964 and estimated to weigh 4,500 pounds.

This seems a rather inflated figure, and indeed, Mundus admits that the shark was never weighed. Starting with the Cuban 7,000-pounder (also never weighed), the recorded weights of white sharks fluctuate wildly, often being totally out of proportion to the length of the fish. There are records of 16-footers at 1,500 pounds, and 16.5-footers at 3,500 pounds. A lot of this probably has to do with what (if anything) the shark was eating before it was caught. If the fisherman has been chumming up his shark with chunks of horsemeat, do you add the weight of the chum to the total weight?* Obviously, some fishermen do. Or if the shark has been feeding on a dead whale, taking 25-pound bites out of the carcass, do you add the whalemeat? When fishermen in Monterey Bay, California, harpooned a 16-foot 9-inch white shark that had been feeding on a dead basking shark, they removed a 27-pound chunk of basking shark from its throat. In W. I. Follett's 1966 discussion of this incident, no mention is made of the amount of basking shark meat in the stomach of the white, whose total weight was said to be 2,820 pounds.

It is likely that white sharks can weigh as much as 2 tons. In a 1963 essay on the sharks of the Florida-Caribbean region, Stewart Springer, a highly respected student of sharks, wrote, "The power of a large white shark is difficult to estimate. In the fishery these sharks were able to break wire rope or chain having a breaking strength of approximately 3,800 pounds. Since many white sharks weigh as much as 3,800 pounds, this does not seem unreasonable."

Off Albany, Western Australia, in April 1976, Clive Green caught a 16-foot female *Carcharodon* that was weighed at 3,388 pounds. Although considerable publicity attended this feat of angling (a line manufacturer again hailed it as "the largest fish ever caught on rod and reel"), it was not allowed as the world's record. One of the rules of the International Game Fish Association (IGFA), which superintends world-record catches, is that a catch will be disqualified if "the flesh, blood, skin, or any part of mammals" is used for chumming or bait. (The idea is to discourage such illegal

* The verb "to chum," whose origins the dictionary finds obscure, means to spread on the surface of the water a mixture of fish oil, ground fish, and other attractants. The mixture itself is also known as "chum," and the trail it leaves in the current is known as a "chum slick." In Australia the mixture is called "berley," and in England they know the stuff as "rubby-dubby," as used in Trevor Housby's book about shark fishing in British waters, *The Rubby-Dubby Trail*.

# In Search of the Azores Giant

Early in 1981, I received a letter from Gerald Wood, the editor of *The Guinness Book of Animal Facts & Feats*, published in England, to the effect that there had been a 29-foot 3-inch white shark caught off San Miguel Island in the Azores in July 1978.

Some years earlier, in my *Book of Sharks*, I had written that the largest known white shark, a female captured in Cuba in 1948, was 21 feet long. When I heard that there was a fish that was more than 8 feet longer than the Cuban specimen, my ears pricked up. If this was true, it would completely revise our estimates of white shark size, and would essentially confirm the existence of giant sharks, making the killer in *Jaws* terrifyingly possible. (Though no one ever actually measures it, the shark in Peter Benchley's novel is estimated at 20 to 25 feet.)

With Wood's letter was a photograph of a very large, very dead shark, which he maintained was the 29-footer. (The photograph was subsequently reproduced in Wood's

book, with this unequivocal description: "The enormous bulk of the 29 ft 6 in great white shark harpooned by Azorean fishermen in 1978.") There is nothing in the photograph that would confirm the actual size of the shark, so I decided to investigate it for myself.

A new magazine had been started in New York a couple of years earlier, and I wanted very much to write for them. Owned by a German conglomerate, *Geo* was an exciting magazine, and I proposed an article on my search for the monster shark of the Azores.

(When I was asked if a photograph of a tooth would suffice to demonstrate the shark's size, I responded by saying that any unscrupulous person could easily carve one out of a bar of soap, and to demonstrate, I did just that.) The editors finally accepted my proposal, and I began the laborious process of setting up a trip to the Azores, a group of nine islands some 800 miles west of Portugal. I wrote to the Department of Tourism. I wrote to the Museum in Ponta Delgada. I called the American Consulate. I contacted a local fisherman who agreed to act as my guide and interpreter. I learned from Gerald Wood the name of the "well-known European big-game fisherman" who had photographed the shark at the quayside in 1978, and I called him too. (The fisherman, Trevor Housby, lived in Lymington, England, and had written several books on shark fishing.) Armed with a sheaf of letters, notes, and high hopes, I left for the Azores (via Lisbon) in April 1982.

With the help of my guide, Francisco Van Uden, a big-game fishing captain of San Miguel Island, I began a search of the island for evidence of the 29-foot *tubarão branco*. We visited people who knew of someone who had reportedly seen the shark, but were told that the person either was on some other island or had died. I offered a $100 reward for a tooth from this shark, but no one seemed to have one. I spoke on the phone to a man on the island of Graciosa (no mean feat if you don't speak Portuguese and he doesn't speak English) who said he had a 3-inch tooth—which would have indeed been longer

than any known tooth—but he had lost it. I looked at many photographs of dead sharks, and in the museum at Ponta Delgada there was a wrinkled, mummified specimen of a white shark that was approximately 15 feet long. (It was certainly not the 1978 *tubarão*, since this dusty carcass looked as if it had been hanging in the museum for 50 years.) When I brandished poor photocopies of the photograph that Wood had originally sent me, people told me that the folks in the photo were in fact them, or their friends, or their children; that the photo had been taken in 1978, or 1948, or 1953.

I went to the island of Fayal, where the sperm whalers put out to sea in small boats, the way their ancestors did a hundred years ago. Gerald Wood had told me that the whalers often harpooned white sharks, so with my trusty interpreter by my side, I questioned the whalers about the 29-footer or any other large sharks they might know about. They had no idea what I was talking about, and suggested that they had better (and

ABOVE: A simulated tooth of a white shark alongside an actual fossil Megalodon tooth. The simulated tooth, carved from a bar of soap, would have been, if real, from a white shark larger than any that has been recorded.

OPPOSITE: The 29.5 feet initially accorded this Azorean shark eventually proved to be a wild exaggeration.

In the Museu Carlos Machado in Ponta Delgado, on the island of São Miguel in the Azores, there is a mounted 15-foot great white shark, known locally as *tubarão branco*.

less dangerous) things to do than to harpoon giant sharks.

Finally, I went to the offices of *Correio dos Açores*, the daily newspaper of the Azores. I looked through every single newspaper from 1970 until the day of my visit, and although I found a couple of records of shark *attacks*, I found absolutely nothing about a shark—giant or otherwise—that had been harpooned in Vila Franca, Caloura, or any of the other places that I had been told the shark had actually appeared. The only mention of a giant shark that I found in the newspaper was a reference to my search for it: on May 7, a headline asked, "*Maior tubarão do Mundo capturado em Vila Franca?*" ("The largest shark in the world captured in Vila Franca?").

The "Great Tooth Hunt" ended in a most ignominious fashion, some six years after my visit to the Azores. While I was collecting the illustrations for this book, I wrote to Gerald Wood to ask him for a print of the photograph he had sent me a photocopy of in 1982. He willingly obliged, and then proceeded to unravel the mystery of the Azores Giant. Although the photograph in question was furnished by Trevor Housby, it had been taken, not by him, but rather by a professional photographer named Silvano. (Housby originally claimed that he had only had time to snap a couple of shots before rushing off to catch a ferry, but this rang false because I had *been* in the Azores and there *are* no ferries from Vila Franca or Caloura.) A biologist who claimed to have measured the shark didn't really do so either; everyone connected with this sordid affair seems to have lost touch with the truth.

It is difficult to decide what all of this means. Trevor Housby is a respected author of books and magazine articles about shark fishing, and of *The Hand of God*, a book about whaling in the Azores. Why would a man risk his reputation by fabricating such a story? How could he expect it to be believed? The urge might have more to do with the subject than with the writer. The durability of the story of the Port Fairy 36-footer is testimony to how well the white shark lends itself to (and encourages) exaggeration and hyperbole. The alluring combination of fisherman and giant fish is too much for any but the most honorable fisherman to resist. Add to that the probability that the Azorean shark was never measured or preserved, and you have a whopping "fish story" just waiting to be told.

*Richard Ellis*

use of dolphins or other mammals.) Since Green used whalemeat as bait, his record was disqualified.

In August 1986, Donnie Braddick, fishing out of Montauk with Captain Mundus, caught another white shark that a line manufacturer also proclaimed as "the largest fish ever taken on rod and reel." The fish does not appear in the 1987 IGFA record book, although the line manufacturer's ad does. According to the ad, the fish was 17 feet long and weighed 3,427 pounds. There seems to be no question about the shark's size, but a question about the way in which it was caught resulted in its disqualification. The fishermen had tied their boat to a whale carcass, which meant that they too were guilty of using "any part of mammals . . . for trolling or casting," and like Green's, Braddick's giant fish did not enter the official record book. (Alf Dean's 1959 world-record 2,664-pound white shark was caught with "porpoise" as bait, but this record has been allowed to stand because the shark was caught before the rule concerning mammals was introduced.)

What, then, is the largest white shark on record? In his 1987 "Refuta-

Fishing out of Albany, Western Australia, Clive Green hauled in this 3,388-pounder. It did not qualify as a world's record because whale meat had been used as bait, illegally.

Donnie Braddick (left) and Frank Mundus with the head of a 3,427-pound white shark caught in August 1988, off Montauk, Long Island. Though this is probably the largest fish ever taken on rod and reel, it failed to qualify for the record because the wrong line weight was reported to the IGFA.

tion," John Randall quotes Gordon Hubbell (a Miami veterinarian and collector of white shark teeth, jaws, and data) as saying that the largest white shark he knows of is a 19-foot 6-inch female caught off Western Australia in 1984. This monster weighed 3,324 pounds, and was neither caught on rod-and-reel nor harpooned. It was *lassoed* by Fisheries Officer Colin Ostle off Ledge Point, near Albany.

There are several other verified records of 19-footers, such as the South African specimen mentioned by David Davies in his 1964 study of fossil sharks:

A large specimen of *C. megalodon*'s nearest living relative the Blue Pointer *Carcharodon carcharias* was harpooned in the whaling grounds, approximately 100 miles off Durban, on 29 June 1962. The largest teeth in the upper jaw of this specimen measured 55 mm. in total length, the total length of the shark was 19 ft. and the estimated weight was 3,000 lbs.

This is the shark harpooned by pirate whaling captain Arvid Nordengen that brought Peter Gimbel to Durban during the "Blue Water, White Death" expedition, but the figure of 19 feet is obviously the measured length from nose to tail tip, whereas the "fork length," used in the record books, is actually 16.5 feet.

In the waters of Canada's Maritime Provinces, the white shark is considered "not uncommon." Off Cape Breton Island, in 1953, a white shark (identified by a tooth fragment it left behind) rammed and holed a fishing dory, and in 1966, a 12-footer was trapped in a fishing net in the Minas Basin of Nova Scotia. Then, too, there is the "37-footer" from Grand Manan Island (see p. 49), whose size, identity, and existence were never verified.

In the summer of 1983, on Prince Edward Island, in the Gulf of St. Lawrence, a very large female white shark was trapped in a herring net. Although it was never measured, the shark was estimated at between 17.5 and 20 feet in length. Fisheries officers allowed only a couple of pictures to be taken before the shark was whisked off to be buried, to avoid the media blitzkrieg that might have attended the appearance of a maneater off a tourist beach.

The number of very large white sharks said to have been caught or sighted is enormous, but some of these are apocryphal, some are imaginary, and some are simply wild exaggerations. (Bigelow and Schroeder recount the story of "an Australian specimen, reported in the local newspapers as 16 feet long, [that] actually measured only eight feet six inches.") Quite often the size of the shark is exaggerated beyond all rational bounds, probably because the viewer has no idea of how large this fish is supposed to get. When the maximum size of the white shark was generally accepted as exceeding 35 feet, sightings of 25-footers did not seem that remarkable. In his *Living Fishes of the World*, Earl Herald—a respected ichthyologist whose book was published in 1961, before Perry Gilbert examined the Port Fairy jaws in the British Museum—wrote that

The largest maneater ever caught measured 36½ feet in length and was taken at Port Fairey, Australia. Although it dates back more than ninety years, the jaws have been preserved intact in the collection of the British Museum. In contrast with this giant, most of the maneaters caught today are in the 20- to 25-foot range. Because of the thickness of the body, these sharks are massive fish. For example, a small shark 17 feet long can weigh as much as 2,800 pounds.

We know now that a 17-foot white shark is anything but "small," and in fact is fairly close to the maximum confirmed length. We know, too, that there have been 17-footers that have weighed more than 4,000 pounds. Until the Port Fairy jaws were actually measured, however, 35 to 40 feet

When this monster was caught in a fishing net off Alberton, Prince Edward Island, Canada, in 1983, city officials quickly disposed of the carcass to avoid unwanted publicity.

# The Smallest White Shark

How *small* can a self-sufficient white shark be? Because it is not hatched from an egg, but rather born fully developed and completely functional, not very small.

During the summer of 1975, when I was living in Rhode Island, I received a call from one of the local fishermen, telling me that they had a shark on the dock. (I had asked that they call me if any sharks were brought in.) I asked what kind of shark it was, and was told, "It's just a gray shark." At that time, I was working on the text for my *Book of Sharks*, and I was interested in all types of sharks, but I confess that I was not too interested in seeing a blue or a sandbar, sharks that were fairly common in Rhode Island waters. I almost didn't go to the docks at all.

But because I had asked them to call me, I did go, and when I got there, I recognized the fish immediately as a white shark, although it was certainly not great. It was 4 feet 2 inches long, a perfectly

formed miniature of the adult that it would have become had it not drowned in the fishermen's nets. I told the fishermen that it was a great white, and they assumed I was joking—after all, this was the summer of the release of the movie "Jaws," and it can be said that most of the country (certainly most of the country where people swam in the ocean) was in the grip of what can accurately be described as "shark hysteria." When they asked me to get serious and *really* iden-

tify it, I assured them that it was indeed a white, and proceeded to point out its salient characteristics: conical snout, black eyes, lunate tail with almost equal lobes, black spots at the axil, and, finally, its triangular, serrated teeth.

A baby white shark is a miniature version of an adult, and even in death it exudes strength, power, and menace. It doesn't look like a baby shark—it doesn't look like a baby *anything*. At 4 feet in length a newborn white shark is larger than most other species of sharks full-grown. A crowd gathered as I proceeded to dissect this 4-foot baby (I had called my friends at the Narragansett Lab of the National Marine Fisheries Service and asked them what they wanted, and they told me "stomach contents"), and after I told them that it was indeed a baby white shark, people nervously asked me, "Where's its mother?"

This shark was one of the smallest great whites ever measured, and its capture in a net indicates that it was free-swimming. In his 1984 report, Leonard Compagno has given 127 centimeters (49.5 inches) as the smallest known to him. The Narragansett NMFS Lab has one in its freezer that is 122 cm (47 inches) long and weighs 26.7 pounds, a good bit less than Victor Springer's estimate of 36 to 60 pounds for white shark neonates. Four-foot-long *babies* suggest something considerably larger along the growth curve, and that expectation is satisfied at the upper end, where some of the largest fish in the world lurk. *Richard Ellis*

ABOVE: Chuck Stillwell of the National Marine Fisheries Service poses with one of the smallest white sharks ever caught. Captured in a fishing tournament off Bayshore, Long Island, it was 41 inches long and weighed 28 pounds.

OPPOSITE: Richard Ellis dissects a baby white shark that had got trapped in a fisherman's net off Narragansett, Rhode Island, in the summer of 1974.

In the summer of 1989, fishermen off Okinawa snagged another big female white shark and brought it to Uchida-san. The shark looks even larger when compared to a small person.

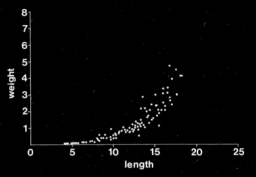

Relationship of total length (in feet) to weight (in thousands of pounds) in 127 white sharks. As the data points make clear, there is a clear pattern in the relationship (for those who care, the equation is $W = 0.447L^{3.084}$, where $W$ = weight in pounds and $L$ = length in feet).

One of the very large female white sharks brought ashore at Kintown, Okinawa, in 1985.

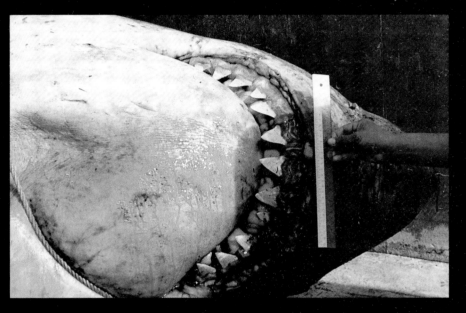

seemed to be the accepted maximum length, and 25-footers were seldom questioned.

In *Tigers of the Sea*, Hugh Wise refers to a white shark that was enmeshed in the nets of the Ocean Leather Company of Cape Lookout, North Carolina, in June 1918: "This shark was credited with a length of twenty-two feet and a girth of eighteen feet and so could have weighed two and a half tons." A careful reading of the source of this allegation (an article by Russell J. Coles in the journal *Copeia* for 1919) reveals that the shark in question "escaped during its death struggle," and the author writes that his "carefully noted observations justify the following claim of dimensions for it." In other words, Coles's identification of a 22-foot shark (with a circumference of 18 feet) is only a guess, made as the shark was, by his own description, fighting violently.

The largest white sharks accurately measured range between 19 and 21 feet, and there are some questionable 23-footers in the popular—but not the scientific—literature. These giants seem to disappear or shrink when a responsible observer approaches with a tape measure. Until someone verifies anything over 21 feet—a record that has stood since 1948, and even this one is subject to question—we shall accept that figure as the maximum known size for the great white shark. But even at a paltry 19 feet, a great white can weigh as much as a rhinoceros, and that is a very big fish indeed.

In 1973, John Randall published a discussion of the size of the great white shark, wherein he reproduced a photograph of the infamous Port Fairy jaws. Randall, too, measured the jaws at the British Museum, and using measurements of the jaws and teeth—and comparing these measurements to jaws and teeth in various other collections—he concurred with Gilbert's conclusions. From examinations of the width of bite marks on the carcasses of whales, Randall also postulated the existence of sharks larger than the 21-foot specimen caught in Cuba in 1948, and wrote, "It seems likely that white sharks more than 21 feet long swim in our seas today and remain to be captured."

On August 23, 1988, a sensational story appeared in *Weekly World News*, a checkout-stand tabloid. It revealed that a Soviet nuclear submarine had been "ATTACKED BY 120-FOOT SHARK" in the South China Sea. Alongside the photograph of a shark's gaping maw, the newspaper quoted Soviet marine biologist Alexei Pedko's observation, "There is much about the ocean we don't know."

About the great white shark, too, there is much that we do not know, but there is also much about it that we do know.

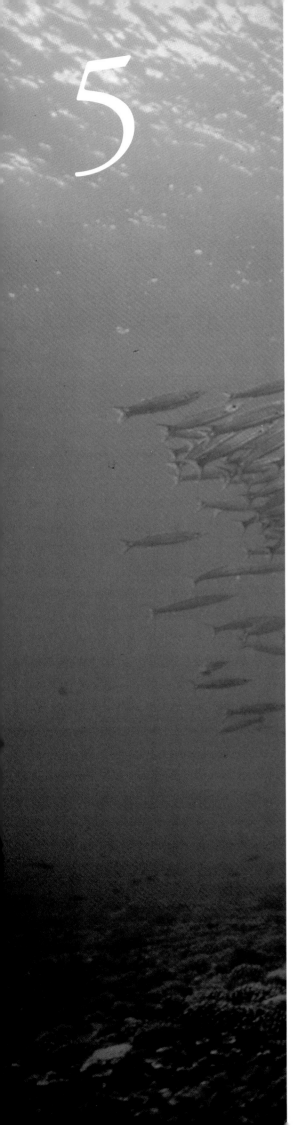

# 5

# Morphology and Biology, or Form and Function

Perhaps more than any other creature, the white shark seems more than the sum of its parts. A package of cartilage, guts, hide, and teeth has somehow become one of the most feared animals on earth. Both the exterior and the interior of *Carcharodon* exhibit unique and highly specialized developments, and in concert these developments yield some remarkable kinetic possibilities.

In his 1852 *Treasury of Natural History, or, A Popular Dictionary of Animated Nature*, Samuel Maunder summed up what was known about the white shark at the time:

The white shark, in size and voracity, the most formidable of all the species, is an inhabitant of most parts of the globe, though much more frequently seen in the warmer than in the colder latitudes. It is believed to reside principally in the depths of the ocean, rising at intervals in order to pursue its prey. It sometimes attains a length of from twenty to thirty feet, and its mouth is sufficiently wide to enable it to receive the thigh, or even the body of a man. The head is of a depressed shape and broad, terminating in an obtusely pointed snout; the margin of each jaw is furnished with from three to six rows of strong, flat, triangular, sharp-pointed and finely serrated teeth; the tongue is broad, thick, and cartilaginous, and the throat extremely wide; the eyes, as in most of the genus, of a bluish or greenish cast. The pectoral fins are large, strong, broad, and pointed; the first dorsal fin {is} falcated behind, and pointed; the second is situated near the origin of the tail, which is slightly lengthened and of a bilobate shape. The general colour is a pale or whitish ash, but darker on the upper parts. The internal parts of the Shark present many remarkable particulars: the brain is small; the throat is very short, and of a diameter not greatly inferior to that of the stomach, which is of vast size, and dilatable to a great degree; the intestinal canal, instead of forming a mere continued tube, consists rather of a large series of meshes or divisions, placed in a spiral direction throughout its length. During the breeding season, which takes place at different periods in different climates, the Sharks are observed to approach the shores, in order to deposit their young in the most favorable situations. The length of a newly hatched shark does not exceed a few inches.

Though all of this reads well enough, nearly all of it, except for the description of the visible, physical characteristics, is wrong. In what follows, we will try to present a correct picture of the functional anatomy of the great white shark. We cite Maunder's text not so much to ridicule a nineteenth-century natural historian as to emphasize how difficult it is, even today, to discover how something works, and—what is even more complicated and mysterious—*why* it works that way.

What will *not* be dealt with, in terms either of form or of function, are questions about how old a white shark can get, how fast it can swim, all-out, or how deep it can dive. To the best of our knowledge, none of these questions has been answered—at least not to our satisfaction. For example, on the question of depth, Leonard Compagno wrote that white sharks inhabit "continental and insular waters from the surf line to the outer shelves and rarely down the slopes to at least 1,280 m." Probably following Compagno—or perhaps using the same unidentified source— Springer and Gold wrote that "the white shark may occur in offshore waters of great depth (up to 1,280 m)," but there is a significant difference between swimming *to* a depth of 1,280 meters and swimming (at whatever actual depth) in water that is 1,280 meters deep.

The obvious way to begin a discussion of the morphology of the white shark is with its outer covering, that which keeps the innards in and the water out. Whereas most fishes are covered with scales, the shark's body is covered with fine, rough, toothlike prickles, from the tip of its snout to the end of its tail. So small as to be invisible to the naked eye, these dermal denticles ("skin teeth") explain the sandpaper-like roughness of shark skin, a texture particularly noticeable when one's hand is rubbed from stern to stem. (The skin of the basking shark differs in that the denticles grow in every direction, and the skin is abrasive no matter which way you rub it.) Dermal denticles provide all sharks with protection from both minute parasites and hungry predators. They also reduce water turbulence by increasing the laminar flow along the shark's surface. They differ in shape at various points along the body, but they also differ from one shark species

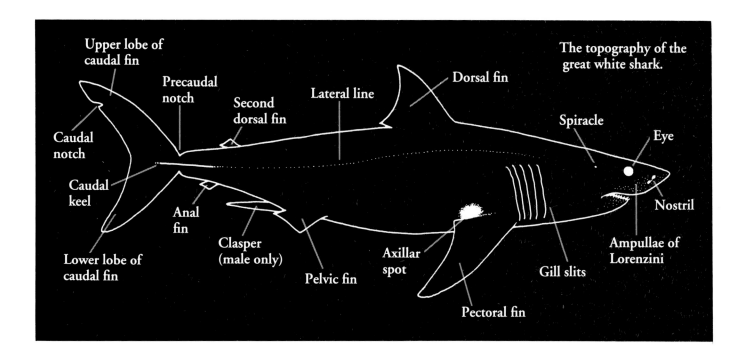

The topography of the great white shark.

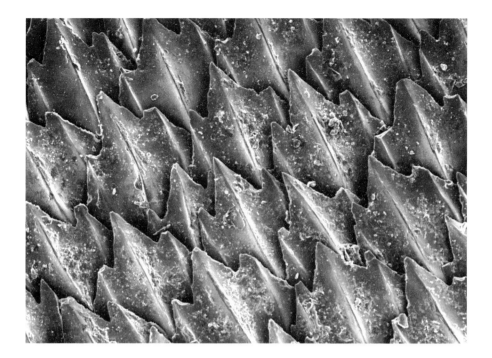

Electron micrograph of dermal denticles on the skin of a great white shark. The shape of each denticle is characteristic, varying from species to species and even at various points along the body.

to another, sufficiently to allow precise species identification. Under a microscope those of the white shark appear like miniaturized horseshoe crabs with three longitudinal ridges, the middle ridge the longest.

At its forward tip, the snout, or rostrum, of the white shark is conical, but less pointed than the artillery-shell nose of its close relative the mako. The snout is not a perfect cone, but blunt at the tip and somewhat flattened on the dorsal surface, allowing the eyes a bit more binocular vision and reducing the resistance of the water to the characteristic lateral head-swinging motion as the fish swims.

Just behind the eye is the spiracle, an accessory respiratory opening by which those sharks that sit motionless on the bottom are able to pass oxygenated water into the gill cavity. In the great white and the other free-swimming sharks, the spiracle is either lost or much reduced.

On the underside of the snout are two widely separated troughs. These are the nostrils, and their function is strictly olfaction; unlike the nostrils of higher vertebrates, they serve no respiratory function. Each nostril is divided by a skin flap on the leading edge, effectively separating the water into an inflowing current and an outflowing current. As the shark's head swings laterally during the normal swimming motion, water enters the nostrils and passes through a nasal capsule containing a series of petal-like lamellae. These lamellae increase the surface area over which the water passes, in turn increasing the shark's sensitivity to chemical odors in the water. The olfactory cells are attached directly to the lamellae, which in turn are connected by the first cranial nerve to the olfactory bulb that constitutes the forward portion of the brain. It is the remarkable development of the olfactory bulb in the forebrain of the shark that has led to the shark's characterization as a "swimming nose"; and indeed, a substantial portion of the shark's brain is devoted to the sense of smell.

Because sharks have always been considered "primitive," they were presumed to have simple brains, simpler than those of other vertebrates. This supposition perhaps reflects the sequence of dissection that most comparative anatomy students pursue, beginning with a shark or a lamprey and progressing "up" through frogs and turtles, eventually ending up with a cat on the dissection table. (Seen against the others, the cat's brain is pretty impressive.) As pointed out by Dr. Glenn Northcutt of the Scripps Neurobiology Unit, an additional bias results from previous studies having been based on the spiny dogfish (*Squalus acanthias*) or the spotted dogfish (*Scyliorhinus caniculus*). These sharks *are* primitive compared to other shark species, and studies of the more advanced sharks have demonstrated that the shark's brain is more complex than was previously assumed.

Unlike the brains of the higher vertebrates, where everything is rolled into a ball, the brain of an elasmobranch is articulated longitudinally, each process separated from the others. Anteriormost (forwardmost) in the topography of the shark's brain are the olfactory bulb and olfactory lobes, which connect to the forebrain; posteriormost (aftmost) is the hindbrain or medulla oblongata, which connects to the spinal cord. The anterior portion of the forebrain, or telencephalon, consists of a pair of large hemispheres that connect the olfactory organs. Rearward in the forebrain from there is the diencephalon, to which the optic nerves attach. On the underside of the diencephalon is the hypothalamus, the seat of the pituitary gland; much of the shark's endocrine function is controlled by this gland, and laboratory experiments indicate that even the feeding and biting responses are affected here. The diencephalon also contains the thalamus and epithalamus glands, and connects the midbrain via a fluid-filled cerebrospinal cavity. The midbrain consists primarily of a pair of optic lobes, which are important in analyzing information received from

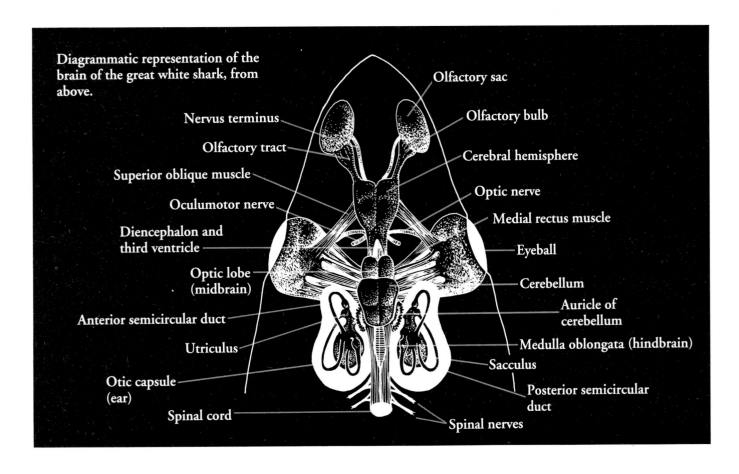

Diagrammatic representation of the brain of the great white shark, from above.

Nervus terminus
Olfactory tract
Superior oblique muscle
Oculumotor nerve
Diencephalon and third ventricle
Optic lobe (midbrain)
Anterior semicircular duct
Utriculus
Otic capsule (ear)
Spinal cord

Olfactory sac
Olfactory bulb
Cerebral hemisphere
Optic nerve
Medial rectus muscle
Eyeball
Cerebellum
Auricle of cerebellum
Medulla oblongata (hindbrain)
Sacculus
Posterior semicircular duct
Spinal nerves

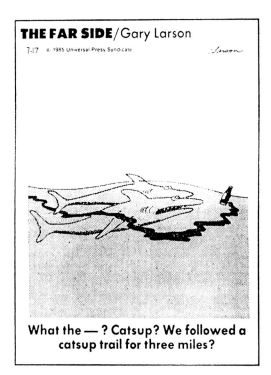

What the — ? Catsup? We followed a catsup trail for three miles?

the eyes. Behind the midbrain is the cerebellum, considered by anatomists to be the coordinating center for much of the shark's muscular activity. And finally, hindmost in the shark's brain is the medulla oblongata, which receives information from cranial nerves that advise the shark of the state of two additional receptor systems—its lateral line (which we shall return to later) and its ampullae (to which we turn now).

The second of these remarkable receptor systems is manifested as a curious pattern of dark holes peppering the top and underside of the snout, rather like a sparse five-o'clock shadow. These are the ampullae of Lorenzini, tiny, jelly-filled capsules beneath the skin that are sensitive to electrical discharges as minute as .005 microvolt. (The jelly-like substance filling the capsules will exude from a fresh shark specimen when the area around one of them is squeezed.) It has been calculated that an elasmobranch is sensitive enough to detect an electrical field distributed throughout a 1,000-mile-long copper wire hooked up to a size D flashlight battery. The pores that open to the capsules are distributed around the head and mouth in a pattern that is different in, and appropriate for, each elasmobranch species. The ampullae contain sensory cells that lie within saclike alveoli, and the alveoli are connected to the brain by the cranial nerves. Not long ago it was thought that the ampullae were sensitive to changes in hydrostatic pressure or temperature change, but now we know that sharks and rays use these extremely sensitive organs to detect the presence of predator or prey underwater, sensing the faint electric field generated by the beating heart, gill action, or swimming muscles of another animal.

Aquatic animals produce direct current from the electrical-potential differences where their skin meets the water. The mucous membranes lining the mouth and gills of a fish also give rise to steady DC fields, and these fields are modulated by the animal's breathing actions. The more rapidly the animal's gills beat, the greater the current generated, and if there is damage to the skin surface, which creates ionic leakage, the current is even greater. (Imagine, then, what a bleeding, struggling human swimmer is advertising!) Dr. Adrianus Kalmijn, now with the Scripps Institution of Oceanography, pioneered experiments in this field during the 1970's, and demonstrated that sharks can find their prey in the dark, even when the prey is buried in the sand, so long as it is not electrically insulated from the predator.

Not only can the ampullae of Lorenzini be used to detect prey, but— at least in theory—they can also be used by elasmobranchs to navigate and orient themselves with respect to the earth's magnetic field. This field, and the seawater currents that move through it, create voltage potentials that can be detected by the ampullae. Stingrays have been taught in experiments to distinguish compass direction on this basis.

One of the most prominent manifestations of the electrical sensitivity of elasmobranchs is the curious shape of the head of the hammerhead shark; since the hammerhead feeds on stingrays and other prey items that may be buried in the sand, it must be able to find them, and the flattened, sideways-extending lobes of its head are believed to relate directly to greater electrical sensitivity.

The black, circular eyes of the white shark are unquestionably eerie and even sinister in aspect, perhaps because they appear to have no pupils. Unblinking and cold, the white's gaze is unforgettable to anyone who has confronted it through the bars of a diving cage. Some species of sharks, and many other animals, like the cat, possess an eyelid-like nictitating membrane beneath the outer eyelid, but the white shark has none, and instead rolls its eyes back into its head to protect them when any sort of contact or collision is imminent (it has been speculated that its ampullae help it to maintain contact with the prey at that moment, when it is otherwise sightless). Many people think of sharks as having poor eyesight, but modern researchers have discovered that certain species, primarily those that inhabit shallow tropical and temperate waters, have considerable visual acuity and an ability to discriminate colors. The microscopic examinations of white shark retinas by Drs. Samuel Gruber and Joel Cohen have demonstrated several anatomical correlates to the behavior that has been observed underwater. For example, *Carcharodon* eyes possess both rods and cones, with the cone photoreceptors concentrated at the center of the retina, indicating that the eye is extremely sensitive to daylight. The decrease in cones at the periphery of the retina suggests that its vision in dim light is poor, and its nocturnal vision poorer still. The relatively small size of the white shark's eye, as well as other internal differences, demonstrates that it is a surface feeder. (Deepwater sharks, needing to capture more light, usually have larger eyes.) Further evidence of the white shark's dependence on daytime vision is provided by the moderate development of its tapetum lucidum ("clear layer"), a series of mirror-like surfaces inside the eye that reflect light back through the retina and thereby improve vision at low light levels. That these surfaces are not as well-developed in the white shark as they are in other shark species is further demonstration that the white is primarily a diurnally active animal.

Valerie Taylor, Australia's most celebrated woman diver, and the snout of a dead white shark. The photo shows clearly the shark's nostrils and the ampullae of Lorenzini.

As the shark attacks the cage, it rolls its eyes back for their protection.

Sharks have ears and can hear, but just how well has not been determined. The anatomical structure and location of the two labyrinths (ears) afford them directional detection of sound waves underwater, which, in effect, is hearing. From the vantage point of the shark cage, we have seen white sharks react to loud underwater noises, but for the most part they appear unresponsive to the usual clatter of shipboard activity. Tropical clearwater sharks, such as the gray reef shark (*Carcharhinus amblyrhynchos*) and the lemon shark (*Negaprion brevirostris*), respond quickly to low-frequency vibrations produced by wounded or struggling fish, which in experimental situations have been more than 820 feet distant.

There is, in any case, some disagreement about what constitutes hearing underwater. Richard Backus of the Woods Hole Oceanographic Institute defined hearing very broadly as "any perception of sound, not by means of the ear alone but by any mechanism whatever," and suggests that sharks hear by means of both the labyrinths and the lateral line, or acoustico-lateralis system. This system (clearly visible in many bony fishes as a long line down the side) is a network of pressure-wave detectors that we as creatures of the air have difficulty in comprehending. Through it, sharks and bony fishes are able to sense (feel or hear, as you like) water currents and pressures as well as sounds, and through the mechanical displacement of water they can sense their own posture and muscle response as they swim. In sharks, the system consists of sensory cells embedded in the skin and interconnected by a fluid-filled canal along the midlateral flanks. Movement created by the turbulence or vibrations of other fishes (or by the shark itself) displaces water through openings in the canal. That entering water then displaces (moves) the sensory-cell hairs, resulting in nervous impulse transmissions to the brain via the network of lateral line nerves. (This assertion presupposes that the white shark responds similarly to other, smaller shark species that *have* been investigated.) Whether the movement of energy through water occurs as vibration (the "near field") or as pressure (the "far field"), it displaces the pressure-sensitive hairs of the lateral-line system, producing a pattern and rhythm of nervous impulses.

Beginning on the snout and connecting with the lateral line are the neuromast cells, which are probably responsible for detecting marine currents as well as the water waves reflected from other creatures or solid objects. It has been suggested in studies of other shark species that these receptors are responsible for the "bumping behavior" so often seen prior to the shark's feeding on a prey item. Some even suggest that the bumping behavior of some shark species allows external taste receptors to sense the edibility of the next meal. But until *Carcharodon* proves to be more amenable to captivity, experimental verification of this ability in this species remains a goal for the future.

Sharks do have, on their tongues and on the floor of the mouth, numerous taste buds that seem to work in conjunction with the olfactory system, much as do our own.

Knowing now that the white shark's snout is packed with a complex array of electrical, mechanical, and chemical detectors, it is easy to understand why old mariners suggested a sharp rap on the nose as a way of de-

Miami shark enthusiast and jaw collector Gordon Hubbell, D.V.M., with the jaws of an 18-foot white shark.

flecting an attack. And perhaps the advice has some merit in confrontations with smaller species of sharks. But a person close enough to a great white shark to punch it in the nose is probably unlikely to report the results.

Protecting himself with a broomstick, Al Giddings leaves the cage. This photograph shows clearly the shark's lateral line and caudal keel.

Beneath all the white shark's detectors is the mouth, broadly rounded, slightly downturned at the corners, producing somehow an almost child-like grin. A grin on the face of a maneating shark immediately translates into something demonic, and when the shark opens its mouth, and the tooth-studded upper jaw is fully extended, the grin is converted into a malevolent maw. When the mouth is open, 26 upper and 24 lower teeth are exposed in the front ranks, and many more lie in reserve in succeeding ranks. The teeth not only are responsible for the scientific name *Carcharodon carcharias*, but they also offer a diagnosis of the animal's evolutionary lineage. The finely serrated, triangular, nearly symmetrical teeth are shared only by other species of the genus *Carcharodon*, including Megalodon, now extinct.

Behind each tooth of the front rank is a row of replacement teeth, lined up like a dental conveyor belt so that when one of the outermost functioning teeth is lost, a new tooth moves forward to replace it. At any one time, approximately one-third of the teeth are being replaced. The white shark loses and replaces hundreds or thousands of teeth during its lifetime, and because of their number and durability, the teeth of sharks (of all species) are the most common of vertebrate fossils. In a 1977 article, Steve Lissau wrote that sharks' teeth are "about as hard as granite and as strong as steel."

Sharks' teeth consist of apatite crystals embedded in a protein matrix. (Apatite is calcium phosphate, the substance of bone in all verte-brates.) The apatite crystals form fibers that bend toward the cutting edge of the teeth, providing the strength, and the gelatinous protein matrix prevents them from becoming too brittle. Of all sharks, white sharks have the most complicated arrangement of these apatite crystals—and probably the strongest teeth. The teeth are covered with enameloid, a substance similar to enamel, but different in that it originates from both the dermal *and* epidermal cells.

The largest teeth in the white shark's jaws are not the central pair but the adjoining ones, and the two to the outside of *those* are considerably smaller, though why these should be smaller remains a mystery. The teeth of the upper and lower jaws interlock quite nicely, even though the upper jaw teeth are somewhat broader in shape than the narrower, more pointed lower ones. The benefit of this design can be seen when one examines the shark's feeding behavior in slow motion, as we were able to do through the use of Al Giddings' dramatic high-speed photography. The lower teeth serve to pin the prey while the upper teeth, with their razor-sharp serra-tions, sever the flesh like a saw blade. A more effective mechanism for taking large chunks out of a gristly, muscular mammal would be difficult to envision. Shrewd indeed, of Peter Benchley, to name his novel *Jaws* and thereby establish the business end of the great white shark as a permanent fixture in the language of fear.

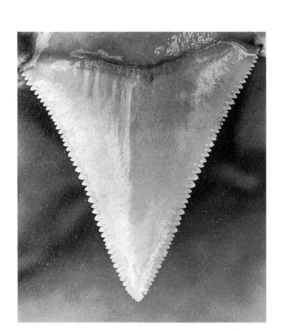

An upper tooth of the white shark, showing the sharp serrations that en-able the shark to bite through tough cartilage and muscle.

Like all fishes, the lamnid sharks maintain a body temperature that is just slightly higher than the external environment, but they have added a twist to poikilothermy (cold-bloodedness). Through evolutionary modifications of the circulatory system, the white shark, its relatives the mako and the porbeagle, the thresher shark, and even the unrelated tunas have become functionally warmer-blooded animals, as implanted thermometers have demonstrated. An examination of the blood chemistry and circulatory anatomy of these sharks and tunas discloses the marvelous inventiveness of natural selection, since although the roads to blood-warming taken by these otherwise unrelated fishes are quite different, in this instance they converge with the same results: improved performance in the pursuit of prey. Warm muscles are more responsive than cold muscles.

To understand how the white shark, the mako, and their kin achieve this marvel of elevated body temperature, it is necessary to understand the circulatory pathway of a more typical shark. The blood, which is produced by the spleen, is distributed from the heart to the muscles and viscera via the gills. The gills are connected to the heart by the ventral aorta, and in most sharks the blood that has been oxygenated by the gills leaves via the dorsal aorta, a large artery that proceeds from shoulders to tail, deep within the body and tucked beneath the spinal column. This artery, via smaller arteries and capillaries, supplies the needs of the tissues, and a corresponding network of veins then gathers the oxygen-spent blood and returns it to the heart via the postcardinal and abdominal veins.

But the circulatory pathways of lamnid and thresher sharks are dramatically different from those of typical sharks. The dorsal aorta of the lamnids and threshers is considerably reduced in size. Oxygenated blood from the gills is instead fed to the muscles via large, subsurface cutaneous arteries. There, the blood enters the internal musculature via the rete mirabile ("wonderful net"), a capillary bed of small arteries and venules that operates as a countercurrent heat exchanger. The blood is warmed as a result of contact with the swimming muscles, and the blood vessels on the way to the heart contact blood vessels from the gills. Heat is thereby passed from venule to artery, and body heat is retained rather than lost at the gill filaments. (Heat is diffused much faster than oxygen when it reaches the gills.)

It is important to realize, however, that the aquatic medium is an infinitely capacious heat sink, and this process is available only to those animals that have an appropriate ratio of body surface to body volume. In small fishes, thermal diffusion is so great that no amount of circulatory rearrangement would save body heat. But the mass of a white shark is such that its core is distant from the cold environment. Similarly, other large, cold-blooded animals, such as giant leatherback turtles and, presumably, large dinosaurs, are or were able to live in habitats ranging from the tropics to the temperate regions because they could retain the heat energy created by the flexing of their own muscles. Dr. Frank Paladino of Purdue University and his colleagues recently coined the term "gigantothermy," which they define as "the maintenance of constant, high body temperatures by means of large body size, low metabolic rate, and use of peripheral tissues as insulation."

Another aspect of this adaptive juryrigging is the enlargement of the pericardial arteries, only modestly developed in other sharks and in bony fishes, so that warmed blood may be supplied to the viscera.

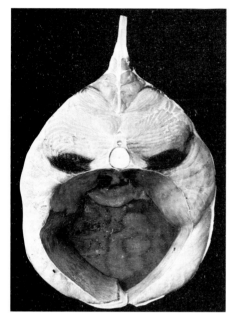

Cross section of a 500-pound white shark, cut at the level of the dorsal fin. The dark bands at 10 and 2 o'clock are the red-muscle bands that heat the blood.

Magnified cross section of the red muscle of a porbeagle (*Lamna nasus*, a close relative of the white shark). The thicker-walled arteries surround the thinner-walled veins. Blood is warmed by muscle activity and transported to the heart by the veins.

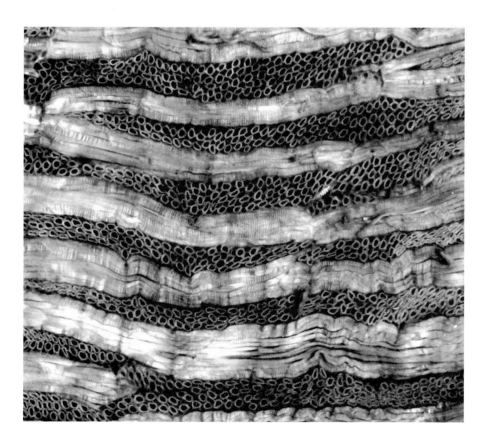

# The Massively Destructive First Bite

It is always easier (and a lot more comfortable) to analyze white shark behavior in the laboratory than from the gunwale of a pitching boat or in a cage submerged in 50-degree water. But the sharks won't cooperate, and during our expedition to Dangerous Reef with Al Giddings in 1980, Tim Tricas and I attempted to discern patterns of feeding behavior, and to discover how the shark's separate anatomical elements were orchestrated as it fed. To analyze the above- and below-water footage that Al had shot, Tim returned to Al's studio to review, frame by frame, the separate components of a shark bite. The results of that study were published in 1984 by Tricas and McCosker in a paper on the predatory behavior of the white shark.

Tricas selected 36 exemplary "feeding events" and analyzed the 16-mm footage on a film-editing table, which permits freezing any individual frame and advancing the film a frame at a time. (Most of the research had consisted of observing sharks feeding on blood-dripping burlap bags of tuna or horsemeat suspended from ropes hung over the side of a boat off South Australia. The same actions had been filmed by Stan Waterman in 1979 while sharks fed on whale carcasses off Long Island.) Because Giddings had shot the film with the camera turning at a rate of between 24 and 200 frames per second, Tricas was able to analyze continuous events that took place (in real time) in less than .005 second.

Tim began to realize that the biting action was not a haphazard series of chomps, but rather a predetermined, five-step progression (see the illustrations). First (1), while keeping the axis of its body on an even plane, the shark lifts its snout to provide a suitably large mouth opening for the food item, setting the snout at an angle as great as 40 degrees above the longitudinal axis of its body. This action requires about 0.2 seconds. At the same time (2), the lower jaw is depressed in order to fully extend the gape, an action that also takes less than 0.2 second. Then (3) the palatoquadrate (the upper jaw)

**THE FAR SIDE/Gary Larson**

Andy! Look what you're doing to your fork! Tuna salad doesn't require seven tons of pressure per square inch

The white shark, which usually does its biting under water, shows the power of its massive jaws.

is protruded, resulting in the startling—and terrifying—image of the white shark's upper jaw, teeth, gums, and connective tissue exposed and thrust forward from the roof of the mouth. (The projection of the upper jaw from the skull, as opposed to its being fused to the skull, is what makes possible its extension, and is one of the wonders of cartilaginous fishdom.) This event and the lifting of the lower jaw (4) jointly consume only the next 0.2 second, and fix the prey so that it cannot escape the completion of the biting sequence, in which the upper jaw retracts and the snout drops (5), applying the force necessary to remove a large mass of flesh.

A typical carcharhinid reef shark tears off small pieces of flesh, but the white shark removes a large chunk of its prey by pinning it with its lower jaw teeth and at the same time moving its head laterally to shear the chunk free with the upper jaw teeth. The films show that white sharks employ their great weight for leverage, and occasionally shake their head savagely, in an exaggerated version of the smaller species' feeding behavior. After a single-bite feeding bout, the white shark's snout returns to its normal position, but

In a remarkable series of photographs, a 14-foot great white demonstrates its jaw movements. As the shark engulfs the bait, its snout is lifted and the upper jaw begins to move forward.

The upper jaw (the palatoquadrate) rotates forward and downward, exposing the upper teeth.

With the bait engulfed, the snout begins to drop and the jaws return to their normal position.

prior to each successive bite of a multiple-bite bout, the snout remains partially elevated, resulting in a shorter interval between bites.

In eleven successive complete feeding events, the entire bite interval was between 0.75 and 1.78 seconds. Since on the average it takes *less than a second* for a great white shark to complete what an ethologist would call its "modal action pattern" (and a scientific or lay observer would call one of the most frightening sights imaginable), one may well contemplate one's own behavior in the presumably hypothetical situation of finding oneself face to face with an attacking white shark. Forget "striking it on the snout," as a Navy pilot's manual once said. A hungry ton-and-a-half shark will not be deterred by an underwater punch in the nose from a 150-pound swimmer. The best way to avoid having to test the bite-and-spit theory (see p. 110) is to categorically avoid being in the water with a white shark. Look at the movies. Read the book.

*John McCosker*

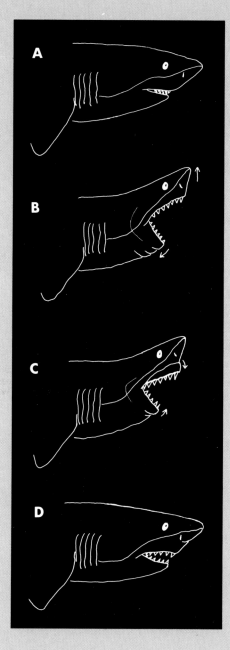

Jaw movements in a surface attack: **A**, the jaws prior to the attack; **B**, the snout lifts and the lower jaw drops; **C**, the upper jaw protrudes, exposing the upper teeth, and the lower jaw drops, exposing the lower teeth; and **D**, with the bite complete, the snout drops and the jaw returns to its normal position.

As a result of these major departures from the pattern of other species of sharks, the white shark and its relatives have been able to elevate their muscle temperature as much as 5 degrees Fahrenheit, and their stomach temperature more than 7 degrees above that of the water through which they swim. The advantages of warm-bloodedness are intuitively obvious to humans, for we are warm-blooded and generally prefer not to be cold. But to ectothermic vertebrates, a 5-degree rise in temperature can increase the rate of chemical reaction two to three times over, and allow the muscles to contract more swiftly and more powerfully. The increased visceral temperature allows more rapid digestion—a necessity for a large, fast-swimming shark, and beneficial to a predator whose prey is abundant but sporadically encountered and equally swift.

But body warming does not stop there. Recent studies of lamnids by Dr. Francis Carey of the Woods Hole Oceanographic Institute and his colleagues have indicated that lamnid brains and eyes are also warmed, by a network that fills the suborbital sinus. This warming improves the stability and performance of these vital organs as the shark moves into different thermal regimes. Interestingly enough, this structure is similar to the carotid rete of birds and mammals, which are warm-blooded, but serves to heat rather than cool the temperature-sensitive nervous tissues.

The remainder of the plumbing of the great white is similar to that of other sharks. The heart, larger than the heart of most other species, is found where you would expect to find it, in a chamber behind the gills and forward of the liver. All sharks have a heavily muscled, two-chambered heart.

*Carcharodon* also has a relatively enormous, bilobate, chocolate-colored liver that constitutes as much as one-fourth of its total weight. In addition to serving the normal hepatic functions and storing fatty energy reserves, it helps to keep the shark afloat by its great buoyancy. Liver oil is five to six times more buoyant than sea water, and according to David Baldridge's 1970 studies of the function of the liver in sharks, "Success of predatory sharks in feeding upon agile prey depends largely upon their ability to maintain optimum maneuverability, and this is determined by static and dynamic interrelationships between the fish and the water in which it operates." Water, contained chiefly in the muscles and cartilage, accounts for almost 75 percent of a shark's body weight, and it is the liver that enables the shark to reduce its specific gravity.

The digestive tract of the shark, like that of other carnivorous creatures, is quite short when compared to that of omnivores (bears or humans, for example) or herbivores (sheep or elephants, for example), both of which require additional surface area for the digestion of tough plant material. Behind the stomach is the duodenum (the beginning of the small intestine, and standard issue for vertebrates), but inside the duodenum is the spiral valve, a structure unique to elasmobranchs and such primitive bony fishes as the sturgeon. Variously compared to an enclosed spiral staircase or a carpenter's auger, it too is a device for increasing the surface area upon which final digestion takes place.

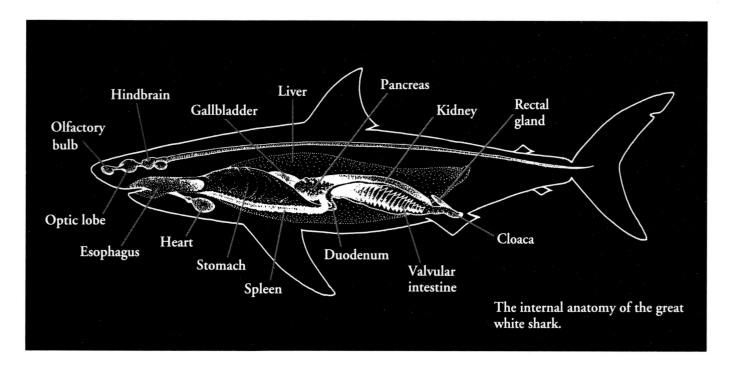

The internal anatomy of the great white shark.

In both sexes, a pair of dark-red, longitudinal, fleshy kidneys lies along the vertebral column, one on each side. The two drain into the urinary sac and ultimately the cloaca, via separate ureters. The kidneys are undifferentiated by sex, but the gonads, not surprisingly, are dramatically different. The male's testes are large whitish sacs that lie beneath the liver. The sperm they produce are conveyed by means of ducts to the claspers, a pair of external, intromittent organs by which the males fertilize the females. In the female, in the same location as the testes of the male, are the ovaries (the right usually well-developed, the left vestigial). When ripe, the ovaries expand and occupy most of the visceral mass. Eggs, released primarily from the right ovary, pass through a tract to the oviducts, the long tubes within which the embryos develop.

Until recently, the birthing or parturition process of the great white shark was another of its great mysteries. This huge fish, so long the object of concentrated sport and commercial fisheries, had never been seen in a gravid or pregnant state. (That females achieve a greater length and weight than males has also meant that the fish the fisherman chooses to battle, from among those attacking the bait alongside the boat, is more often than not an older female.) True, there were occasional reports of pregnant females, but these were either undocumented or so outlandish as to be rejected as fabrications. For example, Norman and Fraser, in a volume published in 1937, recounted an unconfirmed story of a 2.5-ton, 14-foot female that was caught at "Agamy, near Alexandria in the Mediterranean," in 1934: "It was only after a struggle lasting several hours that it could be landed by three boatloads of Egyptian fishermen. When it was cut open, 9 young were discovered inside, each 2 feet long and weighing 108 pounds. Judging from the published photographs of the mother, and from the size of her babies, there can be little doubt that this was a Great White Shark, which is well known in these waters. . . ." Attempts to locate the "published photographs" in the British Museum have proved fruitless, but in order for a 2-foot-long shark to weigh a hundred pounds,

# Taking the Shark's Temperature

In 1979 Dr. Francis Carey of the Woods Hole Oceanographic Institute had discovered that the lamnid sharks were capable of elevating their own body temperature. By equipping makos and porbeagles with transmitting thermometers, he and his colleagues had shown that the action of the *rete mirabile* (a fine network of capillaries) is of considerable physiologic benefit to these species, by enabling them to raise their body temperature significantly above that of the ambient water. To complete his studies, he needed data on *Carcharodon carcharias*, the largest and the most uncooperative of the largely uncooperative mackerel sharks.

When Al Giddings invited me to join him on his first South Australian film expedition in 1980, I placed the white shark body-temperature experiments at the top of my list of research goals. I contacted Tim Tricas, then a capable and enthusiastic graduate student at the University of Hawaii, and invited him to join us. Tricas had designed and assembled small elec-tronic transmitters that could be attached to reef-dwelling butterflyfishes. (Radio waves do not transmit under water, hence the difficulty of communicating with submarines at depth; instead, acoustic pulses must be transmitted, pulses that are both short-ranged and short-lived.) Tricas's small, epoxy-encased transmitters allowed him to monitor the depth and position of the individual fishes on the reef by listening to the various frequencies on a directional hydrophone. For butterflyfishes, the amount of information that can be transmitted is limited by the size of the package; a butterflyfish is about the size of your hand, and can carry a transmitter and battery pack no larger than a hearing aid. Because a white shark could probably manage as large a package as we needed, Tricas designed a flashlight-sized transmitter. Several of the instruments he built were sensitive to water depth, water temperature, and body temperature and could broadcast their information as a function of the acoustic pulse rate.

In the summer of 1979, as we were preparing to leave for South Australia (our trip was scheduled for January 1980, the middle of the austral summer), Frank Carey got the opportunity he had been waiting for. A dead fin whale off Montauk serendipitously provided him with the setting (see p. 109 for a more detailed account of the incident). He implanted a temperature probe in one of the white sharks that was feeding on the whale carcass, and discovered that its muscle tissue was as much as 9 degrees Fahrenheit warmer than the surrounding seawater. His findings eloquently confirmed the presence of working heat exchangers in *Carcharodon*, and effectively closed the circle: all the lamnids are homoiothermous, or warm-bodied. We pressed on with our plans for South Australia, hoping to be able to corroborate Carey's data and pose some additional questions to the sharks.

We arrived at Dangerous Reef aboard the *Nenad* in January. After only 24 hours of chumming, several white sharks began slowly and

majestically circling the boat. As Rodney Fox dangled great slabs of horsemeat from the rails, Tim and I assembled our tagging and tracking gear. When an 11- to 12-footer was tempted into range, we managed to slap two ultrasonic transmitters onto him. One of the transmitters told us the temperature of the surrounding water, while the second gave us the temperature of the swimming shark's musculature. As it swam through 70-degree (Fahrenheit) surface seawater, the shark maintained a body temperature of 77 degrees. After several hours, the shark swam off into cooler, thus presumably deeper, water and its body temperature dropped slightly. The dif-

ference between body temperature and water temperature was significant, and the higher of the two is more desirable for muscle contraction.

We had attached the transmitters to the shark's hide by means of small, breakaway harpoon points, to be inserted either underwater, from a cage, or from alongside the boat, as the shark was feeding. Was this cruel or painful to the shark? I don't think so. The implantation of the barb never caused the feeding sharks to flinch or to interrupt their activities for a moment. (Although the sharks didn't complain, some other photographers did. They had traveled halfway around the world to get pic-

Aboard the *Nenad* off Dangerous Reef, South Australia, John McCosker harpoons a shark to implant a radio tag.

The telemetric package, ready to be inserted into a tuna. When the tuna is then fed to a shark alongside the boat, the shark can be tracked and its internal temperature monitored.

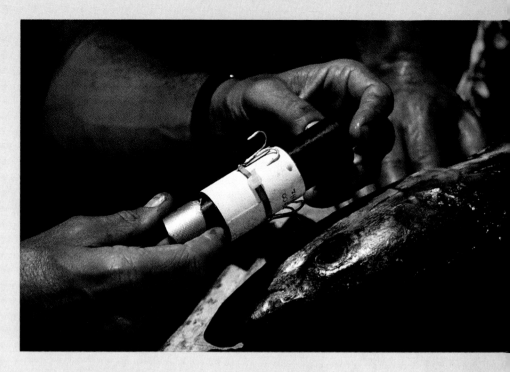

tures of great whites, and they were annoyed by the "electronic costume jewelry" worn by some of the sharks. Evidently, the inclusion of this paraphernalia in their slide show for the folks at home risked destroying the impression of wild, free-swimming sharks, threatening to life and limb.)

But we weren't finished. Another piece of the puzzle was needed to understand the shark's energetics, and for that, we had to measure its engine temperature. Because the rate of digestion and the action of the particular enzymes involved are both temperature-linked, we surmised that if we combined that information with estimates of swimming speed and feeding capacity, we could estimate how often a white shark must feed.

In 1985 I was back in South Australia, this time looking for a shark that would *swallow* a thermometer. Taking a shark's temperature is not easy, particularly when the patient has not been informed of the importance of the experiment. When we were in suitable waters, I prepared one of

our temperature-sensitive transmitters by removing the magnet that acts as an on/off switch, and began to hear its weakly pinging sound. Because the lithium batteries would last only about a week, I had been eager to begin the experiment from the moment we arrived. I attached large treble fishing hooks to the surface of the transmitter and tucked the entire package into the carcass of a southern bluefin tuna. With the apparatus in place and the tuna in the water, I waited for the shark. And waited. A shark arrived, but evidently wasn't hungry. After two days of unremitting tension, a slender male arrived and immediately took the loaded bait. (The treble hooks were attached so that they would pass through the throat and the esophagus, and then lodge in the shark's stomach for the duration of the experiment. In a few days' time, the strong acids of the shark's stomach would dissolve the hooks and the transmitter would pass harmlessly through.) With earphones in place and stopwatch in hand, I quickly found that my

experiment had worked. The shark's stomach was digesting away at 12 degrees Fahrenheit above the temperature of the ambient seawater.

The shark came back to feed on two occasions, and each time it did, I could hear the reduction of the pinging rate indicative of the swallow of cold water that accompanied each chunk of tuna into its stomach. We watched the shark circle the *Nenad* for three hours, but then it moved off. For the next 31 hours I listened to a metallic "poing, poing, poing," and as I sat there, under the earphones, I was reminded of those old submarine movies like "Run Silent, Run Deep." (Not a bad title for a white shark movie, I thought. . . . Too bad they've used it.) I heard the last of the shark the next evening, as its stomach temperature dropped dramatically, by nearly 5 degrees. Had it completed digestion? Had it fed again? We hadn't fed it in the meantime, so if it *had* taken a great gulp of seawater, the gulp might have been accompanied by a struggling seal.

*John McCosker*

LEFT: Tim Tricas exults as he hears the first sounds emitted by the transmitter he and McCosker have attached to a shark.

BELOW: Unconcerned by the transistorized tag in its flank, a white shark cruises in its usual implacable fashion.

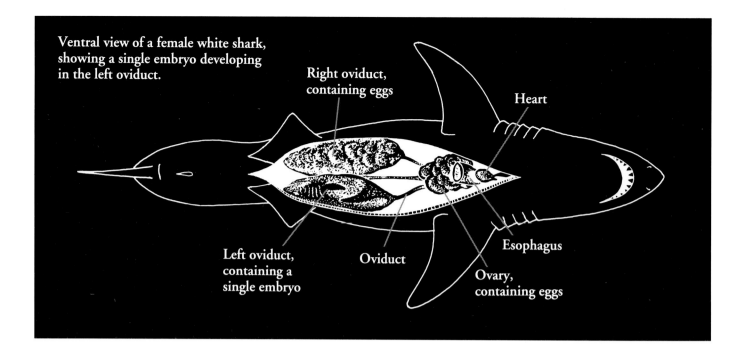

Ventral view of a female white shark, showing a single embryo developing in the left oviduct.

**Right oviduct, containing eggs**

**Heart**

**Left oviduct, containing a single embryo**

**Oviduct**

**Esophagus**

**Ovary, containing eggs**

it would have to be made of iron. Bigelow and Schroeder include this report in their 1948 work, but do not take it seriously, saying that "No account of the developmental stages has yet appeared," and that "the stated weights of these embryos . . . were evidently in error." Perhaps something was lost in the translation from the Arabic.

Many of the small white sharks that have been taken (see p. 65) are thought to have been neonates (newborns) at a length of 48 inches and a weight of around 50 pounds, but it was not until recently that a gravid female was examined. Two prospective mothers were caught in Japanese waters, one off Kin-town, Okinawa, in February 1985, and the second off the whaling port of Taiji in April 1986. Both were brought to the attention of Senzo Uchida, the Director of the Okinawa Expo Aquarium. The Okinawa specimen, the larger of the two at 18 feet, had 192 egg cases in the left uterus. The Taiji female—which was butchered by the fishermen who caught her and had her embryos discarded—was examined and photographed by a Mr. Wakabayashi, and the pictures and data were passed along to Dr. Uchida.

Uchida subsequently presented his findings,* and while acknowledging that they were not based on first-hand observation, he suggested that the white shark, like the unrelated sand tiger and ragged-tooth sharks (of the genera *Eugomphodus* and *Odontaspis*), is oophagous (from *ovum*, for "egg," and *phagein*, "to eat"): in the uterus, the hatched but unborn white sharks are cannibals, eating their weaker brothers and sisters until only the stronger survive—the ultimate in sibling rivalry. It would be hard to imagine a more appropriate debut for the fish that will eventually mature into the most feared predator in the ocean.

* As of this writing, Uchida (with his co-authors Yasuzumi, Toda, and Okura) has presented his observations orally, but has not published the results in a scientific journal. The information we report here was obtained from Uchida's letters to Ellis and McCosker, and from the abstract of his presentation to a Japanese elasmobranch symposium in 1987.

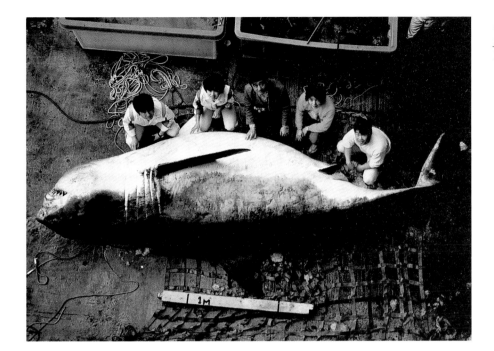

A female great white shark (*hoho-jirozame*) captured by fishermen at Kin-town, Okinawa, Japan.

When the Kin-town shark was cut open, she was found to contain several near-term embryos, each about 40 inches long and weighing about 3 pounds. (The white sacs are embryonic membranes.) This was the first time a gravid female *Carcharodon* had ever been examined.

Let us now depart the controlled vantage point of the anatomist, and step back long enough to ponder the great white as its fellow marine creatures might see it. Depending on the location of the shark, the position of the sun, the bottom topography, and the condition of the sea surface, the great white shark may not be all that easy to see. First of all, the white shark is not white; it is pale only on its underside. Its dorsal surface, the top surfaces of its paired pectorals, and its flanks, beginning roughly at mid-body, are some shade of gray; the color has been variously described as lead-gray, slate-brown, or dull grayish-blue. Such coloration is typical of sharks that habitually swim above the sea bottom; viewed from above, the muddy dorsal coloration tends to blend with the sea floor. This coloration probably functions as camouflage. And from beneath, because it shows only its light belly and lower flanks, the shark is not easily distinguished from the sunlit waters above. Because in daylight the light-colored undersides are in shadow, the contrast between the upper and lower body tones tends to be neutralized, making the shark appear more or less indistinct. This pattern, known as countershading, is standard in military aircraft operating low over the ocean—with the same effect and for the same reasons.

Like the markings of the tiger or the leopard (the cats, not the sharks), the camouflage of the white shark is designed to hide it not from potential predators (there are none), but from the creatures it intends to stalk by stealth. It therefore lacks any obvious marks or signal patterns, and its only distinguishing marks are the black tips of the underside of the pectoral fins and the black smudge at each axil, where the pectoral joins the body. These black marks are obvious when the shark lies dead on the wharf, and biologists have long pondered their function in nature. Are they intraspecies signals, like the color-coded wing patches in many species of ducks? Not likely, and the proper explanation for the smudges becomes obvious when the shark is viewed in its natural habitat. From a shark cage, under water, the black markings can be seen to be fine tunings of the camouflage pattern. Because the fins are not rigid, they flex as the shark banks and turns, and the black smudges compensate for the flash of white that might otherwise alert a potential victim, perhaps a seal basking at the surface.

As for fins, the white shark has the usual elasmobranch complement: a high triangular dorsal, a pair of pectoral fins, a smaller second dorsal fin, a pair of pelvic fins, a tiny anal fin situated below the laterally flattened caudal keels (on the sides, just forward of the tail), and a large tail fin, technically known as the caudal fin. As with all the other elements in the composition of this superbly designed predator, each of these fins and keels performs a particular function in the complex business of being a great white shark.

The fins are supported internally by cartilaginous blocks, called basal elements, that connect the fins to the segments of the vertebral column and to the pectoral or pelvic girdles. Variations in fin structure in living and fossil sharks are numerous, but the white shark is quite generalized in having the base of each pectoral fin include three major elements: propterygium, mesopterygium, and metapterygium. The pelvic fin differs only in lacking a mesopterygium and in having the metapterygia of the males extend backward into the claspers.

Extending outward from the basal elements of the pectoral and pelvic fins are the basal radials, fingerlike internal structures that support the fins. Toward their ends, the radials are overlapped by fringed elements called ceratorichia, meaning "horny hairs." The more recently evolved bony fishes have taken this development further by ossifying these cartilaginous elements (converting them to bone) and affording them muscular attachments. These bony rays afford the teleosts a dextrous maneuverability denied to the cartilaginous fishes.

Whereas most sharks have a heterocercal tail (one with an elongated upper lobe and a more modest lower lobe), the great white and the other

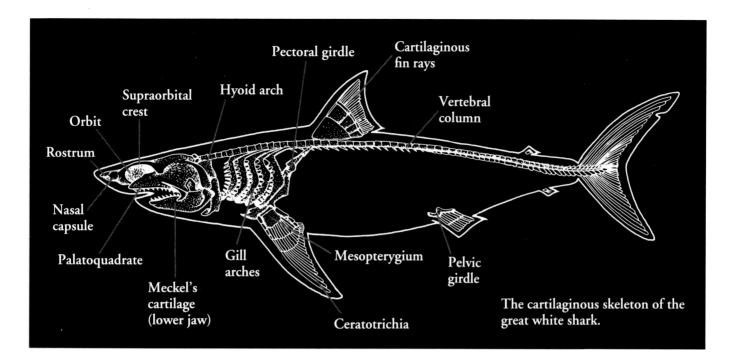

The cartilaginous skeleton of the great white shark.

Labels: Pectoral girdle · Cartilaginous fin rays · Supraorbital crest · Hyoid arch · Vertebral column · Orbit · Rostrum · Nasal capsule · Palatoquadrate · Gill arches · Meckel's cartilage (lower jaw) · Mesopterygium · Pelvic girdle · Ceratotrichia

mackerel sharks have a nearly symmetrical caudal fin, with the two lobes nearly equal in shape and area. This tuna-like tail provides fast-swimming sharks with characteristics that are well-described by resorting to automotive terminology: the tail imparts low-speed torque, and its high-stall-speed shape makes acceleration difficult, but once the shark is under way its forward movement is almost effortless. The white shark does not get off the mark quickly as a drag racer does, but once in motion it maintains a good pace with little effort, like a formula race car.*

The analogy to mankind's machines does not stop at automobiles, however. David Baldridge, a Navy scientist, described shark swimming in aeronautical terms in his 1982 article, "Sharks Don't Swim—They Fly":

The swimming of the shark is very much akin to the flight of an aircraft. As with aircraft, sharks are essentially of a fusiform shape. Their crescent-shaped, vertically oriented tails . . . are almost symmetrical in some species. . . . No matter what the tail configuration, snakelike movements of the body, along with thwartwise, sculling motions of the caudal fin propel the shark forward. Roll stabilization and attitude control result from coordinated movements of the erect first dorsal fin and the horizontal pectoral fins. Sharks have no reverse gear, for, unlike many bony fishes, they cannot elevate the leading edges of their pectoral fins and "flap" them in a way to generate any significant reverse thrust. . . . Being inherently heavier than seawater, sharks must constantly swim, otherwise they sink. The lift required to maintain depth during level swimming is provided by a balance between the airfoil-shaped pectoral fins (which are forward of the shark's center of gravity) and the thrust of the downward-directed sculling motion of the more flexible lower lobe of the caudal fin. Because a shark's center of buoyancy is forward of its center of gravity, if it does not push hard enough to maintain sufficient headway, it will assume a head-up attitude even to the point of being vertical as it sinks through the water column. . . . Likewise, in the manner of flying machines, a shark also has a stall speed—the forward velocity below which there is insufficient force to allow level movement. It makes good sense for a predator to patrol at a speed just comfortably in excess of stall speed.

The very reduced anal fin and small second dorsal fin of *Carcharodon* are homologous with the much larger median fins of more primitive sharks. It has been speculated that in the white shark they serve to im-

*Keith Stewart Thomson, who had conducted detailed studies of the mechanics of the shark's tail, has concluded that the heterocercal tail of most sharks (the upper lobe much longer than the lower) "is a highly refined adaptation for the control of thrust in the vertical plane." In a 1990 article, he wrote, "Evidently an asymmetric tail gives a real advantage *to all but the very high speed fishes* [our italics], where a symmetric tail offers other hydrodynamic advantages. . . ." Among those "very high speed fishes" with a symmetric tail are the great white, mako, and porbeagle sharks.

Seen from this angle, the wide caudal keels of the white shark are clearly evident.

prove the laminar flow of water across the tail, much like the trim tabs on a jet fighter. A careful examination of these "tabs" suggests a function shared not with most other sharks, but with fast-swimming, more recently evolved fishes like the marlin and the swordfish. Another trait shared with the billfishes is the presence of caudal keels along the horizontal margin of the caudal peduncle. The peduncle, or caudal base, is therefore twice as wide as it is deep, and the keels serve both to strengthen the tail fin and to function as cutwaters during rapid tail beats. (Dolphins and whales have also perfected this device; but in their case the entire empennage is rotated 90 degrees to satisfy the up-and-down, rather than side-to-side, motion of the cetacean tail.) Two more white shark details are worthy of inspection: the notch in the trailing edge of the upper lobe of the tail speeds up the water that flows over the tail, and the deep notch that precedes the upper and lower base of the caudal fin allows an improved efficiency in the sculling movement. Both of these adaptations fine-tune this hydrodynamic marvel to a high level of efficiency.

Just how fast *do* great whites swim? Although white sharks have often been observed in the wild, we have no accurate information on their maximum swimming speed—but can suppose that 15 miles per hour is probably attainable. (We do have Frank Carey's calculation from an implanted transmitter, of an average speed of 2 miles per hour over 118 miles in three and a half days—168 miles, including zigzags—but that says more about endurance than about speed). Most often, white sharks have been observed circling boats or feeding on dead whales, activities not likely to encourage or require high-velocity swimming. What we have otherwise are chiefly impressions. During a dive in South Australia, for example, Valerie Taylor reported an eerie silence around her; the sea lions departed, and as she huddled on the bottom, a great white shark zoomed over her "like an express train."

In a journal entry for February 1983 (made available to the authors), Valerie recounts the story of a young sea lion that teased a group of five white sharks by swimming around them, "zipping around and having a fine time." The sea lion then drifted along the bottom, apparently unconcerned by the presence of the sharks:

The 16-footer made a rush at him, but he slipped aside, probably laughing. The white, jaws snapping, was in a fury. Along comes whitey number two, 12 feet long and innocent of the recent events. 16-footer with incredible speed lunged for his gills. 12-footer tried to swerve away but found his belly in his comrade's mouth. The big shark held the smaller shark in his mouth for a second, then in a panic the smaller shark made a dash for freedom, his belly ripped open. Blood poured out as he swam away very fast. . . . his aggressor made no attempt to follow, though he did gnash his teeth a few more times. We never saw him again.

Valerie managed to snap a couple of quick shots of this event (see photo on p. 117), but they were not sharp, and she later wrote, "a 60th of a second cannot stop a charging white shark."

Even though the heavy-bodied white shark swims slowly for the most part—especially when feeding on floating carrion—its design would indicate a capability otherwise. Its muscles are heated by the same heat-exchange mechanisms that enhance the speed of its cousin the mako, probably the fastest of all sharks. For the white shark to have developed the same shape and internal modifications *and then not use them* would seem to be an egregious evolutionary miscalculation. The smaller whites, unencumbered by the great heft of the larger, are probably the faster swimmers, but *all* great whites presumably put on some decent speed when circumstances warrant. Although great whites are certainly not as fast as makos or marlin, they are extremely *efficient* swimmers. In an article on the relative efficiency of certain wing and tail shapes, a professor of aeronautical engineering named Cornelis van Dam wrote that "the most effective form of aquatic propulsion for sustained swimming [of the sort Frank Carey tracked] is achieved when forward thrust is generated almost exclusively by a stiff, crescent-shaped fin mounted on the slender aft portion of the body, as it is in . . . fast-swimming sharks [such as] the mako and the great white." And as it is in swordfish, marlin, sailfish, and tuna—all of them greyhounds of the sea.

When asked if he thought white pointers were fast, big-game fisherman Alf Dean replied, "Like everything, that's comparative. In normal circumstances, they would have no hope of catching seals or dolphins, but for all that, they are fast compared with men. They can go like a streak if they want. But on the other hand, when they're cruising they tend to move slowly, sometimes so slowly that they're hardly moving at all."

So again, we have only impressions. Similarly, no one as yet knows how far into the depths a white shark might descend, or how long one might live, though 20 years or so seems not unreasonable.

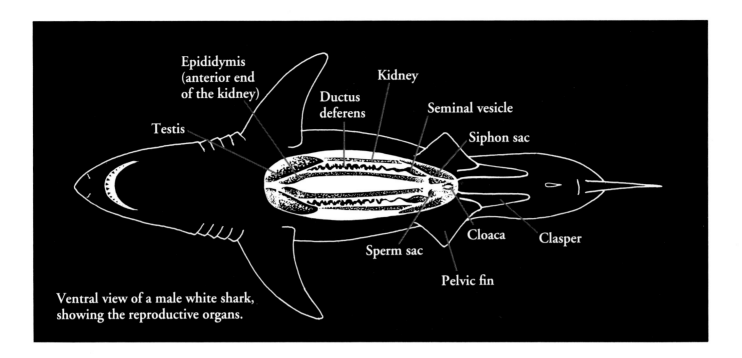

Epididymis
(anterior end
of the kidney)

Testis

Ductus
deferens

Kidney

Seminal vesicle

Siphon sac

Sperm sac

Cloaca

Clasper

Pelvic fin

Ventral view of a male white shark,
showing the reproductive organs.

Just as the pectoral fins and pectoral girdle of the white shark are homologous to the foreleg and shoulder girdle of the more advanced vertebrates, so too are the pelvic fins and pelvic girdle the homologues of the hindlegs and pelvis. In female sharks, the pelvic fins are fleshy rhomboids, but in males the pelvic fins differ from those of other fishes in serving less for swimming than for sexual purposes.

Unlike most other fishes, the cartilaginous fishes all practice internal fertilization; elasmobranchs and the related chimaeras are unique among the vertebrates in having the male intromittent organs derived from the inner edges of the paired pelvic fins. Called claspers, or myxopterygia (from the Greek *myxa*, meaning "mucus," a reference to the sperm, and *pterygion*, meaning "fin"), these elongated, paired devices are used, singly, to fertilize the female internally. Just how this is achieved, underwater and without hands, requires a creative imagination. However it is accomplished, it benefits from the presence of hooks and spurs at the ends of the claspers, as well as some not so subtle foreplay, which consists mostly of biting. The claspers of a juvenile male are nothing to brag about, being little longer than the fin itself, but the organs of an adult male white shark are quite impressive, approaching the length and weight of a pair of Louisville Sluggers. Each clasper is not a hollow tube, but rather a roll of flesh with a central groove that carries the seminal products from the internal testes to the forward tip of the clasper. Movement of the seminal fluid is assisted by pumps known as siphon sacs, which fill with water and then contract, sending the sperm to their ultimate destination with considerable authority. A muscular assistance directs the claspers, one at a time, in a forward direction to achieve insertion while the sharks remain in a missionary-position embrace. Because actual mating has not been observed in white sharks, the foregoing is based on accounts of other, more available species, and upon the known anatomy of male and female great whites.

Its long claspers identify this great
white as a mature male.

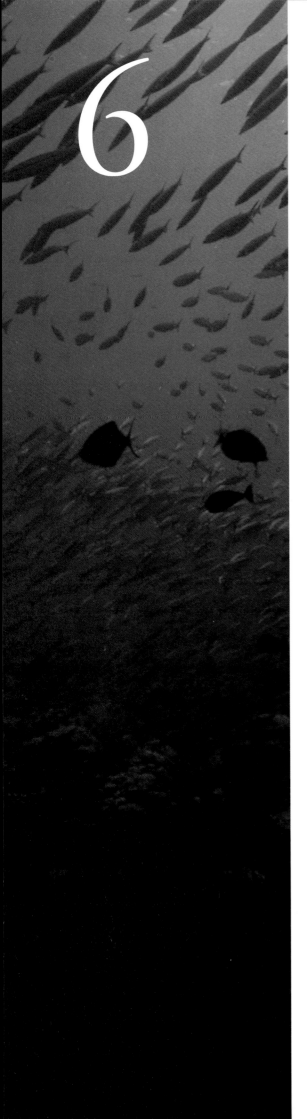

# 6 Food and Feeding

All sharks feed upon moving prey—there are no grazers among sharks—but some are more ostentatious about it than others, crippling very large animals in very violent attacks. Some, too, tend to specialize. The gigantic whale shark and basking shark consume huge mouthfuls of plankton, which consists of small to minute plants and animals and requires little agility or tactical skills. Some species, such as the horn sharks (family Heterodontidae), feed on shellfish and sea urchins, as do many of the skates and rays. Most of the smaller sharks feed on small fish and squid, but there is at least one species, known as the "cookie-cutter shark" (*Isistius brasiliensis*), that makes a living taking scooplike bites out of various large fishes, such as billfishes and tuna, and even out of some species of whales. Hammerheads seem to prefer stingrays (their lobed heads evidently enable them to locate the rays under the sand by sensing the rays' weak electrical field); the Greenland shark feeds on fish and marine mammals (one was found with an entire reindeer in its stomach, but it is assumed that the deer was already dead when the shark encountered it); tiger sharks eat almost anything, but demonstrate a preference for sea turtles; and mako sharks, among the fastest fishes in the sea, can chase down and immobilize such speedsters as bluefish and swordfish, but they also eat smaller fishes and squid. For the most part, however, sharks are opportunistic feeders, eating whatever comes along, including other sharks.

Sharks are the sea's dominant large predators (it has been suggested that the oceanic whitetip, *Carcharhinus longimanus*, is the most numerous large animal—over 100 pounds—in the world), and the hundreds of species utilize an amazing range of sensory systems to fine-tune their hunting skills. Hornsharks can locate shellfish buried in the sand; the enlarged eyes of the deepwater species enable them to see better in reduced light; pelagic species use hearing, smell, sight, and other senses to find fishes and squid in the open ocean; and the great white and the other mackerel sharks, among the most beautifully streamlined animals in the

world, combine all these sensory systems with an efficient hydrodynamic design.

Depending on prey availability and attack success, white sharks eat everything from small fish to large fish (including other sharks), from harbor seals, sea lions, and elephant seals to dolphins and whales. There is evidence that they attack, but for some reason may not eat, sea otters. Off South Africa, they take penguins. They attack living animals, but they also feed on carrion—a predilection that is exploited to attract them to a place where people can dive with them, study them, film them, harpoon them, or catch them on rod and reel. Often, of course, they produce their own carrion, by so grievously wounding a large animal that its demise is only a matter of time.

Throughout the centuries that men have been catching white sharks, a certain amount of excitement has always attended the opening of the stomach. We probably *expect* to find human remains, in order to confirm our characterization of *Carcharodon* as an anthropophage, but there are in fact few instances where a white shark was even suspected of containing human remains, and discoveries of human flesh or bones in a white shark's stomach are exceedingly rare. Biologists still debate the validity of the 8.5-footer that was captured in 1916 off Raritan, New Jersey, after the stunning series of shark attacks discussed on pp. 139–44. In this case, the

As it chomps down on a hunk of horsemeat, the white shark displays its formidable feeding equipment.

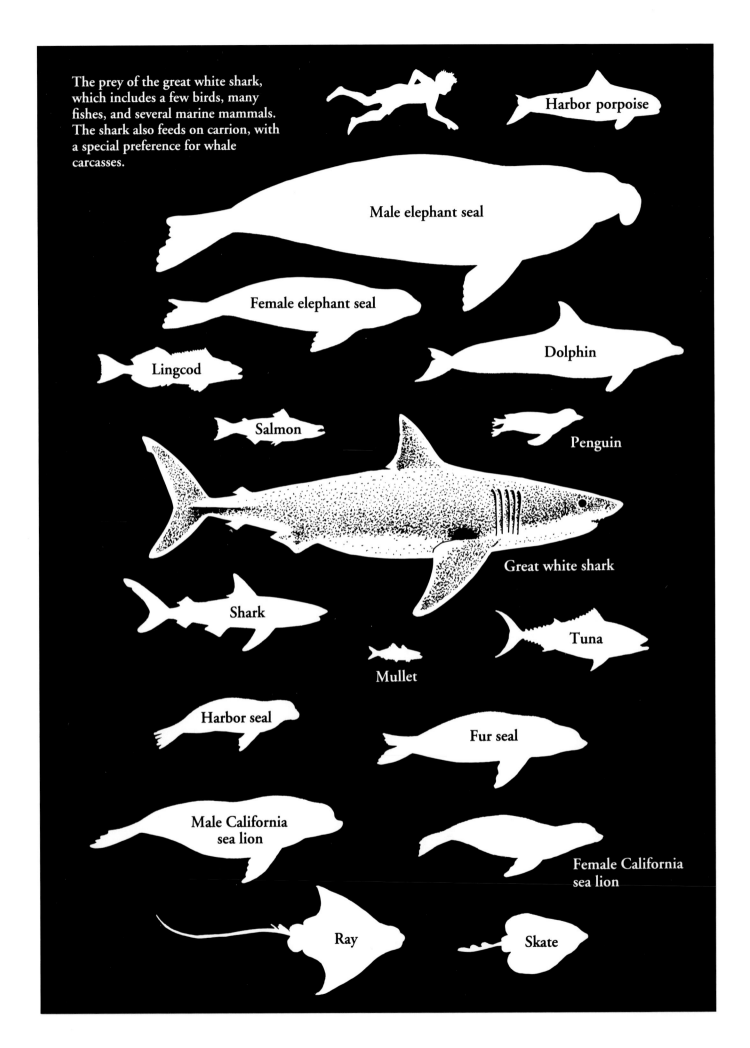

The prey of the great white shark, which includes a few birds, many fishes, and several marine mammals. The shark also feeds on carrion, with a special preference for whale carcasses.

Harbor porpoise

Male elephant seal

Female elephant seal

Dolphin

Lingcod

Salmon

Penguin

Great white shark

Shark

Tuna

Mullet

Harbor seal

Fur seal

Male California sea lion

Female California sea lion

Ray

Skate

flesh and bones were recovered and identified as human, but there was no professional confirmation of the findings.

If a formidable and catholic feeder like the white shark has a "normal" diet, it probably consists of fish, squid, other sharks, cetaceans and pinnipeds of all shapes and sizes, and penguins. But this is only the beginning of the list. In 1867, in his four-volume *History of the Fishes of the British Islands*, after describing the white shark as "the dread of sailors, who are in constant fear of becoming its prey when they bathe or fall into the sea," Jonathan Couch wrote:

> The White Shark is to sailors the most formidable of all the inhabitants of the ocean; for in none besides are the powers of inflicting injury so eagerly combined with the eagerness to accomplish it. They usually cut asunder any object of considerable size, and thus swallow it; but if they find difficulty in doing this, there is no hesitation in passing into the stomach even what is of enormous bulk; and the formation of the jaws and throat render this a matter of but little difficulty. Ruysch says that the whole body of a man, and even a man in armour . . . has been found in the body of a white shark; and Captain King, in his survey of Australia, says he caught one which could have swallowed a man with the greatest ease. Blumenbach says a whole horse has been found in it; and Captain Basil Hall reports the taking of one in which, besides other things, he found the whole skin of a buffalo, which a short time before had been thrown overboard from his ship. Happily the visits of this fish to our coasts are too rare to expose our sailors to its depredations.

In various records (some certainly apocryphal), the following items have been reported from the stomach of the white shark: sea turtles, sea gulls, a whole sheep, a bulldog, a cuckoo-clock, glass, glasses, bottles, tin cans, a straw hat, lobsters, lobster traps, parts of horses, and a Frenchman in a suit of armor. * There is even a story of a thirst-crazed elephant in Kenya that charged into the Indian Ocean and was attacked and eaten by a pack of white sharks, but other African whites seem to be more orthodox in their choice of food. In the stomachs of the 591 white sharks caught in the gill nets set off the coast of Natal between 1974 and 1988, the only unusual item discovered was seaweed.

In Norman and Fraser's 1937 book *Giant Fishes, Whales and Dolphins*, J. R. Norman includes this story of a white shark at Port Philip, Australia:

> A specimen between 15 and 16 feet long had been observed for several days swimming around the ladies' baths, looking through the picket fence in such a disagreeable manner that the stationmaster had a strong hook and iron chain made so as to keep the rope out of reach of his teeth, and this, being baited with a large piece of pork made to look as much like a piece of lady as possible, was swallowed greedily, and then, with the aid of a crowd of helpers, the monster was got on shore. On opening the stomach, amongst a load of partially digested objects, a large Newfoundland dog was found, with his collar on, identifying him as one lost the day before, no doubt swallowed while enjoying a swim in comparatively shallow water.

Sharks have an extraordinary sense of smell; they are extremely sensitive to movements, low-frequency sounds, and electrical charges in the water; and they see much better than we once thought they do. They lack hands, however, and cannot pick up things to examine them. It is therefore likely that a shark encountering a strange object will mouth it to test its edibility, and this might result in the object's being swallowed. It does

* For some reason, biologists rarely find these unusual items, even though they may be particularly interested in the stomach contents of their subjects. It seems that the authors of "popular" (non-scientific) books are always finding weird things in surprising quantities. In *Shark!*, Thomas Helm lists the stomach contents of a single blue shark (a much smaller species than the white and with a proportionately smaller mouth): "Two soft-drink bottles, an aluminum soup kettle with a broken handle, a carpenter's square, a plastic cigar box, a screw-top jar partly filled with nails, a two-celled flashlight, several yards of one-quarter-inch nylon line, a rubber raincoat, a worn-out tennis shoe . . .[and] a three-foot-wide roll of tar paper with about twenty-seven feet of heavy black paper still wound on the spool."

not suggest that sharks, white or otherwise, are random feeders that simply gobble up whatever they encounter. In fact, far from being a random feeder, the white shark has developed a methodology of feeding and prey selection that is unique.

Because they are born as miniature adults, baby white sharks are efficient hunters almost right from birth. In fact, their presumed prenatal cannibalism (the eating of eggs or developing siblings *in utero*) classifies them as efficient hunters *before* birth.

Great whites taken from California waters had eaten benthic sharks such as leopards, smoothhounds, spiny dogfish, and soupfins; stingrays, batrays, and skates; and numerous bony fishes such as cabezon, white sea bass, lingcod, and halibut. These creatures typically frequent shallow bays and sandy coastal habitats, at depths of 10 to 150 feet. The cabezon (*Scorpaenichthys marmoratus*) and the lingcod (*Ophiodon elongatus*) are relatively sedentary species, and depend on their disruptive coloration for protection in nearshore rock-and-sand habitats. Early naturalists may have wondered how a white shark could detect such inconspicuous prey items, but the sharks' recently discovered sensitivity to weak electrical fields is probably integral to prey detection.

John Bass and his colleagues at the Oceanographic Research Institute in Durban have found that *Carcharodon* in South African waters is quite like its California relatives in feeding habits, eating other sharks, skates, rays, and bony fishes. Like their North American cousins, South African white sharks shift their preferences to warm-blooded prey as they mature. And the warm-blooded prey items in the two locales are similar in habits and morphology, with one interesting exception: South African whites demonstrate a particular fondness for the black-footed penguin (*Spheniscus demersus*), an aquatic avian item that is not available on any Northern Hemisphere menu. (Gulls and gannets have occasionally been found in the stomachs of Northern Hemisphere white sharks, but whether they were caught alive or not is not known.)

As they grow longer and heavier, white sharks take larger and larger prey. Off the Natal coast of South Africa, for example, young white sharks prey heavily on small dusky sharks (*Carcharhinus obscurus*)* and the foot-long pilchards that appear in great numbers every year. Studies conducted by the Natal Sharks Board indicate that the white sharks trapped in the nets had fed primarily on smaller sharks, secondarily on bony fishes, occasionally on dolphins. (Small white sharks may not be powerful or quick enough to kill a dolphin, but since dolphins also become trapped in the shark nets, the sharks may feed on the trapped mammals, dead or alive.) Until the Union Whaling Company of Durban shut down in 1975, offal and blood had been used to attract much larger sharks to the same area, particularly for a sport fishery for great whites that flourished off the Durban pier. To the south and west, around the Cape coast, some of the largest white sharks ever recorded have been taken, and there they feed primarily on the plentiful Cape fur seals.

In those areas where there are large pinniped populations—and where other acceptable conditions obtain—seals and sea lions appear to be the diet of choice of adult white sharks. The only region that supports a

* According to a recent study, the shark nets of Natal, which are designed to reduce the numbers of large, dangerous sharks in the area—and thus the number of potential attacks on swimmers—may in fact be contributing to an overall *increase* in the number of sharks. Rudy van der Elst (1979) has postulated that as the larger sharks are fished out (or netted out) of a given area, the reduced predation by the larger ones promotes a pronounced increase in the numbers of smaller ones. (From numerous studies, it appears that the prey most often taken by sharks is other sharks.)

A great white shark chases a sea lion through the curl of a wave in the California surf.

white shark population without a corresponding pinniped supply (though it may once have had one) is the New York Bight off Long Island and New Jersey. Where there are few or no pinninpeds, the sharks must find something else to eat, and what they find seems to be other sharks, bony fishes, and occasionally a whale carcass.

Because the pinnipeds play such an important role in the lives of most populations of white sharks, it will be useful to introduce this large and diverse group of amphibious mammals. There are 30-odd species of pinnipeds—the word means "fin-footed"—and they are found from one pole to the other. Since white sharks do not favor Arctic or Antarctic waters, it is primarily the seals and sea lions of temperate waters that interest us— and them.

Science differentiates two of the three major groups of pinnipeds by the presence or absence of visible ears and by their method of locomotion. (The lone member of the third major group is the walrus, but its high-Arctic habitat renders it largely unavailable to white shark predation.) The earless seals, known collectively as the Phocidae, or phocids, have no external ear but only a small opening in the region of the ear; they propel themselves in the water by sculling with their hindflippers; and they hunch themselves along on land using only their foreflippers. The eared seals, collectively the Otariidae, or otariids, have a visible earflap; they swim chiefly with their foreflippers; and because they can rotate their hindflippers forward when they are on land, they are terrestrially much more mobile than their cousins. Most of the phocids are known as seals of one sort or another, but the otariids may be sea lions or fur seals, which often proves confusing, especially when seals and fur seals occupy the same habitat.

Eagerly sought by sealers for their luxurious fur, the sharp-nosed otariids known as fur seals (genus *Arctocephalus*) are found throughout the Southern Hemisphere, both on various sub-Antarctic island groups and on the southern Australian, South African, and South American mainlands. (An animal known as the northern fur seal, *Callorhinus ursinus*, not closely

LEFT: Southern fur seal (*Arctocephalus pusillus*)

RIGHT: Australian sea lion (*Neophoca cinerea*)

related to the southern varieties, occurs primarily in the Pribilofs and the Aleutians—a habitat that is too cold for it to figure significantly in the diet of *Carcharodon*.)

Along the southern coast of Australia, the Australian fur seal, *Arctocephalus pusillus doriferus*, is found at both ends of the continent, but not along the central coast. Almost all of this coastline—the longest east-west coastline in the world except for that along ice-choked northern Siberia—comprises cliffs fronting on the great Australian Bight, lacking any haul-out spots for the pinnipeds. (Pinnipeds feed in the water, but they breed and raise their pups on land.) In Western Australia the fur seals are found from Eclipse to the Recherche Archipelago, and in South Australia and Victoria their range—by no small coincidence—is exactly that of the white shark. In Judith King's *Seals of the World*, one of the maps of the distribution of the Australian fur seal shows the Spencer Gulf–Adelaide region, long the favorite locale in all the world for those who would seek the white shark.

In these same waters is another pinniped, the Australian sea lion, *Neophoca cinerea*. (Fur seals and sea lions differ chiefly in the shape of the skull, the fur seals having more pointed noses, and in the underfur, which is denser in the fur seals.) Australian sea lions, sometimes called "hair seals" by the Aussies, were hunted extensively by the early settlers and are much less numerous than the fur seals. Of the 6,000 or so that remain today, about 700 make up a breeding colony on Dangerous Reef, of which King wrote, "Many sea lions bear wounds, sometimes of a curved shark-jaw shape with impressions of the triangular teeth, and missing hind flippers show evidence of escape from the shark."

The South African fur seal is morphologically so similar to the Australian that they are considered conspecific subspecies. Unlike its Australian cousin, *Arctocephalus pusillus pusillus* is far from rare: it is so numerous throughout the waters of the Cape that fishermen consider it a serious nuisance. (In a 1981 study of the southern fur seals, Nigel Bonner quoted estimates of 850,000 South African animals, with an annual production of over 200,000 pups, contrasted with a *total* of 20,000 Australian fur seals.) South Africa supports a harvesting program in which several thousand fur

LEFT: Southern sea lion (*Otaria flavescens*)

RIGHT: California sea lion (*Zalophus californianus*)

seals are killed annually, but the population of fur seals there remains a healthy one—as does the population of white sharks.

There is also a New Zealand fur seal (*Arctocephalus fosteri*), which may provide occasional sustenance for white sharks in kiwi waters.

The South American fur seal, *A. australis*, is found all along both coasts of southern South America, from southern Peru, down the Chilean coast and around Cape Horn, and up the Argentine coast to Uruguay. White sharks feed on them in the warmer parts of their range, and indeed the presence of large white sharks off the northern Chilean coast (see pp. 171–73) could well be attributable to the fur seal breeding colonies there. Most recent estimates put the total population at around 400,000 animals.

Just as in Australia, in South America a sea lion shares the coastline with the fur seal, across pretty much the same range. *Otaria flavescens*, the South American sea lion, seems to favor sandy beaches for breeding, while the fur seals prefer more rocky places, but the two species appear to coexist without much conflict.

*Zalophus californianus californianus*, the sea lion of the California coast, is one of the preferred prey items of the white shark. This popular animal—these are the performing "seals" that balance a ball on their noses and clap their flippers together in zoos and circuses—is found from Vancouver to Baja California. According to a study conducted by David Ainley and his colleagues, white sharks prefer younger animals to adults—perhaps because a full-grown bull *Zalophus* is an agile, powerful animal that can weigh 600 pounds—but even the juveniles may be too quick for the shark. (For a discussion of the "sneak attack" tactics sometimes employed by the sharks, see p. 110.) Whatever Ainley's findings indicate, the examination of the stomach contents of captured white sharks and the visible shark-bite scars on surviving sea lions indicate that the sharks often press home their attacks on sea lions, and sometimes consume them.

Occupying the same region along the California coast are the gigantic northern elephant seals, evidently even more desirable prey items for the white shark. In size, *Mirounga angustirostris* is second only to the southern elephant seal, *M. leonina*, among the pinnipeds. (The southern elephant seal occurs too far south to be susceptible to significant white shark predation.) An adult bull of the northern variety can measure 15 feet from proboscis to hind flippers, and weigh upwards of 3 tons. (Southern bulls reach 17 feet and can weigh a ton more.) Elephant seals (sometimes known as sea elephants) acquired their common name from two characteristics they share with terrestrial pachyderms: great size and an elongated proboscis. The great bulls battle fiercely for dominance, hurling themselves at one another in bloody clashes, using their weight and their formidable teeth, until one or the other is driven off and the victor can mate with the females in his particular sector of beach. The cows, which lack the proboscis, are doe-eyed, placid creatures, rarely reaching a ton in weight. During the pupping season (usually in January), northern elephant seals give birth on the beach to 4-foot, 80-pound pups that nurse for three weeks, and which, during that period, may triple or quadruple their weight. After weaning, the mothers abandon them, leaving them in the

On Año Nuevo Island, California, Richard Ellis examines a sea lion that has succumbed to a huge shark bite.

Northern elephant seal (*Mirounga angustirostris*)

This 15.5-foot white shark was discovered near Año Nuevo Island, on the coast of California, with 500 pounds of elephant seal in its stomach.

rookeries for another several weeks. By mid-March they are ready to enter the water, where, in some areas, the white sharks are waiting for them.

Great whites are not particularly partial to young seal meat, however, and in many instances they have attacked adults. We know this from the observations of fresh shark-bite scars on adults, and also from the incontrovertible evidence (quoted in Le Boeuf, Riedman, and Keys, 1982) of a moribund, 15.5-foot shark that washed ashore on Año Nuevo Island in 1977 with one-third (approximately 500 pounds) of a 4- to 5-year-old elephant seal in its stomach, including the whole head, severed cleanly at the neck. On the same island (south of San Francisco, and less than a mile offshore) a year later, a 7-year-old male seal dragged itself out of the water and died on the beach of massive shark bites.

The Farallon Islands, 26 miles west of the Golden Gate, have provided researchers with a platform of opportunity for the study of white shark/pinniped interactions, including actual observations of attacks (Ainley, Henderson, Huber, Boekelheide, Allen, and McElroy jointly authored the 1985 paper on the subject). On four occasions, the researchers saw a white shark attack an elephant seal, and in every instance the attack took place from behind: "The victim was apparently disabled or in a state of shock, because though alive, it did not swim away. From one to five minutes later, the shark bit again, this time to actually consume the victim." Attacking any animal from behind has obvious advantages, but the sharks' choice of elephant seals may derive from another, less obvious, advantage: like all earless seals, elephant seals scull along with their hindflippers, and a single attack on the engine is likely to seriously disable the animal. Another factor encouraging attacks on seals and elephant seals is their habit of swimming alone, unlike sea lions, which congregate in herds. If one sea lion spots a shark, they are all alerted, whereas the solitary habits of the elephant seal render it more vulnerable to attack.

In addition to the sea lions and elephant seals, the Farallones support one of the largest populations of harbor seals, *Phoca vitulina*, on the Pacific

A white shark attacking an elephant seal off the Farallon Islands of California. Rarely are such events photographed.

At Año Nuevo Island, a bull elephant seal rests with its mate in the shallows after an attack by a white shark.

Harbor seal (*Phoca vitulina*)

West Coast, and these little phocids, which rarely attain 6 feet in length, are also fair game for hungry sharks. Elsewhere, harbor seals are found on Año Nuevo Island, in San Francisco Bay, in Monterey Bay, and, sporadically, all along the Southern California coasts and islands, as far south as Baja California. When Sea World of San Diego, hoping to capitalize on the excitement created by Peter Benchley's novel *Jaws*, took five great whites in Southern California waters, two of them were found to have portions of harbor seals in their stomachs.

The harbor seal has the largest distribution of any pinniped. It is found throughout the inshore waters of the North Pacific, from Japan across the Aleutians and Alaska to California; and on both sides of the North Atlantic, from Massachusetts north into Arctic Canada, in Greenland and Iceland, and in the waters of all the European countries that front the North Atlantic. Throughout this vast range, the seals cross paths with the white shark in many locations, such as in eastern Canada, where, according to Judith King, "sharks are said to be the most important predators." There are also records of white sharks preying on grey seals (*Halichoerus grypus*) in both European and Canadian waters, but interestingly, very few white sharks have been sighted on the Atlantic Coast of Europe.

It is curious that numerous carcasses of the northern sea otter (*Enhydra lutris*) found along the central California coastline show evidence of having been attacked but (obviously) not eaten by the white shark. A study by Jack Ames, of the California Department of Fish and Game, and Victor Morejohn, of the Moss Landing Marine Laboratory, suggested that white sharks are responsible for numerous attacks that had previously been described as boat-propellor wounds. Why is it that although sharks account for at least 15 percent of sea otter mortality, no sea otters have been found in a white shark's stomach? It has been suggested that the sea otter, a seagoing member of the weasel family (Mustelidae) and not related to the pinnipeds, has an odor or taste that is repellent to the white shark, but a more likely explanation is that there have not been statistically significant numbers of examinations of white shark stomachs from the narrow geographic range of the sea otter. The jury is still out.

Attacks by white sharks on whales are nothing new; paleontologists have found cetacean bones laid down in Pleistocene deposits as much as 10,000 years ago with scratches that suggest white shark predation. Whether the now extinct *Carcharodon sulcidens*, the likeliest species, was actually preying upon baleen whales or simply scavenging them remains a mystery. But contemporary white sharks are known to feed on living whales, as evidenced by the observations of Theodore Walker, who watched four whites feeding on a baby gray whale in San Ignacio Lagoon, Baja California.

They also feed on whale carcasses. Here is Frank Mundus's eyewitness account of white sharks feeding on a blue whale carcass off Block Island (east of Long Island) in 1960:

It was a fantastic spectacle. Most of the choicer parts of the mammal on the underside had been torn away, and now the sharks were forced to work on the body's sides. To do it they had to come part way out of the water, an awesome sight, clamp down on the flesh, shake their heads to dislodge a chunk, then slide back. They were having quite a dinner party.

A dead whale smells awful (Eskimos refer to bowheads that have died under the ice and then floated to the surface as "stinkers"), and it doesn't require a particularly sensitive sense of smell to locate one—especially in the ocean, where the odor can be carried for miles by tides and currents. Although all of its senses are acute, the white shark's olfactory sense is probably the most effective for long-range detection; even the chum slicks set out by shark fishermen can attract sharks from miles away.

One of the most unusual recorded observations of white shark feeding was recorded by Dr. Peter Best of the South Africa Museum, Cape Town. A pygmy right whale (*Caperea marginata*) had washed ashore at Smitswinkel Bay (an arm of False Bay) in October 1987, and Best had gone to work up the carcass. As he discarded the unwanted portions into the bay, sharks began to congregate, presumably attracted by the blood. There were as many as seven white sharks visible at one time. When Best had completed his work, he had the carcass shoved into the sea. Rather than feed on it in the shallow water of the surf zone, the sharks, *apparently working in concert*, shoved the carcass into deeper water to facilitate feeding. Although there have been many instances where several white sharks have been observed feeding on a dead whale, this is the only recorded instance where the sharks appear to have worked together. * (In his *Fifty Years of Game Fishing*, the Australian angler Ernest Palmer writes that he had seen "two large sharks approach a bull sea lion from opposite sides so that when it turned to avoid one it was taken by the other from the rear.")

Whales that die of natural causes may be difficult to locate in the open ocean, but where there is an industry dedicated to the production of whale carcasses, it is more than likely that white sharks will be found in its

* Best did not actually witness these events firsthand, but was told about them after the fact. The sharks' activities were described to Richard Ellis by Best during a visit to South Africa in 1988.

vicinity. From about 1870 to 1930 a most interesting humpback whale fishery operated at Twofold Bay, south of Sydney. As the story goes, the whalers were assisted in their efforts by a group of wild killer whales that herded the hapless humpies toward the whalers' waiting harpoons. (Killer whales, however, are not the subject of this discussion; killer sharks are.) According to the detailed discussion of this fishery in Tom Mead's 1961 *Killers of Eden*, giant sharks were often dispatched in Twofold Bay. Mead does not identify the species, but to judge from the size—one was "17 feet 8 inches long and 12 feet 'round the girth" and another "seemed to stretch for most of the whaleboat's 30-foot length"—the identification is obvious (a photograph of the 17-footer in René Davidson's *Whalemen of Twofold Bay* confirms it).

Two of the last operating whaling stations in the world were at Durban, South Africa, and Albany, Western Australia. The Durban facility shut down for good in 1975; the Albany whaling station, in 1977. Not surprisingly, some of the largest white sharks on record have been caught in the waters surrounding these stations, and more intriguingly, even when a station has been shut down for years and there is no longer blood and offal to attract them, the sharks seem to persist in hanging around.

That fish are so prevalent in the diets of smaller white sharks may mean that they are unable to deliver a knockout punch to a larger animal. Pinnipeds in particular are protected by fur, thick skin, and a layer of fat, and a successful pinniped kill requires an extremely destructive, immobilizing first strike (see p. 78), leaving the shark with a stricken prey rather than an aroused battler. An adult elephant seal, for example, can weigh 3 tons or more (double the weight of a very large great white), and has great strength and a formidable set of teeth of its own; an attacker had better be serious of purpose. (To close this circle, elephant seals are known to feed on smaller sharks, though not on young whites.)

The teeth of young white sharks (those about 10 feet in length or less) in fact differ from those of their parents. Whereas the teeth of juveniles are relatively long and narrow and designed for grasping slippery, scaly fishes, the teeth of the adults become dramatically broader at the base, which, along with their sharpness and edge serrations, enables them to cut through the tough hide of a seal or to take a chunk from a whale. As the shark grows, its agility decreases, and in time it becomes an ungainly monster that is incapable of catching fishes and other mobile prey items and must accordingly turn to the stealthy mugging of larger, slower prey. For prospective human victims, this shift in adaptation has great significance: a small shark will usually not attack an object as large as a person, and most recorded white shark attacks on people have been perpetrated by the big ones.

To date, there is scant information about the amount of food required to sustain a white shark. Observations in South Australia indicate that the appetite of an adult white shark is enormous, suggesting that they probably do not eat very often. Physiologists have long wondered about the

white shark's efficiency: how many miles per seal? If we knew that, we might be able to predict the time between incidences of what the biologist calls "feeding events," or what the lay person calls attacks. In 1979, Francis Carey of Woods Hole had a unique opportunity to study this problem when fishermen told him of five white sharks feeding on a fin whale carcass off Montauk Point, at the east end of Long Island, New York. Carey and his crew harpooned one of the sharks with an acoustic transmitter while it was occupied at the dinner table. The transmitter then relayed the depth and temperature of the water, as well as the temperature of the shark's musculature, for 83 hours, until the boat broke down. During that three-and-a-half-day period, the shark swam at an average of 2 miles per hour, covering in all 168 miles (including zigzagging), and moved 118 miles from Montauk to the Hudson River submarine canyon off New York City. In a paper published in 1982, Carey and his colleagues crudely calculated the efficiency of an adult *Carcharodon*, and concluded that the white shark has a lower basal metabolism rate than do the smaller shark species. They predicted that the 15-foot shark they had tracked could survive for perhaps 45 days on 66 pounds of whale blubber. Some authors have in fact suggested that dead whales may be a primary food source for white sharks in the western North Atlantic, but it seems unlikely that a pelagic, predatory species would depend on random carcasses—unless there are more whale carcasses out there than we think there are.

During the humpback whaling at Twofold Bay, New South Wales, white sharks were often attracted to the whale carcasses. This 17-footer was one of two harpooned by the Davidson family around 1880.

# The Bite-and-Spit Hypothesis

California surfers still talk about the "shark that bit through the surfer and the board in the same bite." Lewis Boren's story has taken on heroic proportions, but in fact he had simply made the mistake of looking like a large seal when a very large shark happened by. The incident caused me to think more seriously about the increasing number of attacks on surfers, and about the "maneaters vs. manbiters" enigma. Why hadn't Boren been eaten? Why was he bitten only once and then abandoned? What I learned from examining his surfboard and hypothesizing his behavior before the attack (see p. 168) encouraged me in my resolve to explain the white shark's behavioral paradox.

White shark attacks on humans have occurred nearly annually in central California and South Africa, and quite often enough in South Australia and off the Pacific coast of South America. We know that pinnipeds and therefore white sharks frequent these waters. But why does the shark also attack people? And then so seldom eat them? Is it simply driven by hunger, but then finds us too distasteful? Is it warning off intruders?

A decade ago the explanations one would hear for the shark's attack behavior were most unsatisfying. You would not have wanted to entrust your life to them. I decided to investigate (as well as I could, given the rather dangerous nature of the investigation) both the "intentions" of the shark—prior to and during an attack—and the prey's response. I watched white sharks from California to Australia; I studied seal and sea lion behavior, interviewed human survivors, and absorbed all available information about attacks in California and elsewhere. A curious pattern began to emerge, which I named the "bite-and-spit paradox" and later resolved into the bite-and-spit hypothesis.

In a paper I had written in 1981 I discussed elephant seals and sea lions that had survived white shark attacks. I also puzzled about the frequency with which humans survived such attacks. There was obviously something in the shark's behavior that we were missing: why had so many pinnipeds and people lived to tell about their experiences? I recall discussing the problem with Harriet Huber, a biologist associated with the Point Reyes Bird Observatory on the Farallones, and she too was stumped.

To begin with, we know that it is more efficacious for a shark to attack a smaller elephant seal than to take on one of the 4-ton adult males. The big ones—as powerful as a very large great white and a lot wilier—pose too great a risk. The vulnerability of the younger pinnipeds is perhaps also a function of experience: naive youngsters pay the ultimate price for their carelessness. We know that the white shark's only vulnerable area is its eyes, and I hypothesized that the seal's best defensive gambit if attacked is to claw at the shark's eyes. (I recalled a white shark in Australia with what appeared to be healed claw marks across its face, the legacy perhaps of a desperate pinniped.)

The white shark has good reason

to prefer the smaller pinnipeds, good reason to wait before following up its initial attack. Because its eyes are particularly sensitive, it must protect them from the sharp, quick claws of the sea lion. Unlike many other species of sharks, the white does not have a nictitating membrane to protect its eyes, but it *can* rotate them in their sockets, thus keeping them, for the most part, away from sharp, dangerous objects. And a young sea lion weak from loss of blood is not the threat to the shark's eyes that a healthy adult would be.

During the course of the 1936 attack on a swimmer in Buzzard's Bay, Massachusetts, the shark (later identified as a white) at-

tacked the swimmer, and was then seen "standing off and on in the blood-reddened water but a few yards away, seemingly ready to make another attack—and why it did not is inexplicable." If the theory about attacking and then waiting for the victim to weaken is valid, then this behavior is not only explicable, it is normal.

When Chris Pugliesi's dog was attacked by a white shark off Point Reyes, California, in 1986, the same thing may have happened. Lucky, a well-named 3-year-old Chesapeake Bay retriever, had gone swimming while Pugliesi and a friend were fishing from a boat about 30 feet offshore. According to Martha Joseph's account in the

In a welter of foam and spray, a white shark attacks a floating mannequin.

*West County Times*, a 12- to 15-foot great white came up and dragged the dog under. Some 20 seconds later the dog surfaced, and the frantic Pugliesi pulled him into the boat. Lucky had huge gashes in his leg and abdomen, and was bleeding profusely. The fishermen were able to get the dog to the Point Reyes Coast Guard Station, where a doctor (who had been expecting a human victim) was waiting. Lucky was sewn up and lived to swim again, probably because the shark had hit him and waited for him to weaken. Disappearing into a boat is not characteristic of the behavior of the shark's normal prey.

To try to understand the pattern, I had to overcome my terrestrial bias and think like a shark. Try with me to transcend your own point of view and assume that of a white shark perhaps 17 feet long and weighing approximately a ton and a half. You are swimming 30 feet from the rocky bottom, and another 20 feet from the shimmering surface of the sea. It is midmorning and the sun is high in an overcast sky. You haven't eaten for almost a week. Giant kelp, stretching from seafloor to surface, undulates with the ocean's swell. The water is cold, but you are cold-blooded and you do not mind. You sense the odor of a mammal colony, from perhaps just a few molecules of urine in the water.

You turn toward the source of the odor, swinging your head from side to side to detect the strength and direction of the chemical attractant. You swim slowly up the odor trail with measured strokes of your thick, quarter-moon tail. Even in weak light and poor visibility, you see a shadow silhouetted against the sunlit surface of the sea. You feel the pressure waves produced by the animal's swimming; you sense its heartbeat and its breathing. From all of this, you conclude that the animal at the surface is a meal-sized mammal. You alter your approach with a twist of your torso and an almost imperceptible modification of the angle of your winglike pectoral fins. Then,

with a few rapid tail thrusts, you accelerate to 5, 10, 15 miles per hour, and with an upward rush you close in on your prey. Your mouth is now agape, your eyes are rolled tailward, and 100 teeth are exposed. You clamp down, taking a massive bite of the flesh of the unsuspecting prey. The force of the attack carries you and your victim 3 feet into the air. While you both fall back into the water, you continue incapacitating the injured and terrified mammal by biting right through it. But after that single bite you move off, waiting for the victim to weaken and die. You make no further attempt to consume the prey until it flutters weakly and dies, probably from shock and loss of blood. You then proceed to take huge bites from the carcass, shaking your massive head to tear off great chunks of the warm, bleeding meat.

If the shark's victim had been a seal or a sea lion, the action would have been called a feeding event, just another episode in the neverending story of life in the sea. All animals must eat. But if the mammalian victim had been a human, the attack would be front-page news, with headlines screaming "SHARK ATTACK AT LOCAL BEACH!" followed by hysterical accounts of the grisly event: "Killer shark spits out local diver, courageous buddy rescues body, diver dies of blood loss. . . ."

The frequency of attacks in central California has earned the region the regrettable title of White

Shark Attack Capital of the World, though many people believe that unfortunate epithet is better applied to Australia. Take an abundant marine mammal population, add a healthy number of great white sharks, and stir in nearly 8 million people within a 200-mile coastal span, and you have more than a volatile mixture; you have a recipe for disasters waiting to happen. But curiously, of the 50-odd California attacks on humans attributed to *Carcharodon*, only six have been fatal. Can the great white shark be such an ineffectual predator that nine out of ten of its victims escape to tell about it? No, not possible, or its kind would have perished long ago. So why, then, does it only *bite* people, allowing them to die from massive blood loss rather than sustained attack?

Until I had the opportunity to examine the data in detail, the fact that so many white shark victims were not consumed had been a great mystery. It had become part of the popular mythology that the white shark was a man*biter*, not a man*eater*, despite the diverse diet of the species. Others have suggested that our species is distasteful, perhaps because of the sun lotion or neoprene wet suits we occasionally cover ourselves with.

Like so many discoveries, what had been nonsense became sense in an instant. In this case I was at sea, returning to San Francisco on a bumpy boat ride from the Farallon Islands. Perhaps it was the combination of the bumpy ride and the near nausea of a 26-mile voyage, but when I reached the shore, I realized as if with a whack to the side of my head that it all made

sense. Why *should* a shark consume its prey before it has died? A blind or vision-impaired shark would be checkmated, unable to find its next meal. The white shark, I realized, has developed a prudent strategy of bite, spit, and wait—and only then return to consume the prey. In attacks on humans, this provided a much better explanation than any previously advanced theories. But like all hypotheses, it would require testing, and the idea of using human subjects had no appeal.

My first opportunity to watch the Australian white pointers in action had come in 1980, a year before the Boren attack. I was with underwater cinematographer Al Giddings, fish behaviorist Tim Tricas, then a graduate student at the University of Hawaii, and Rodney Fox, the celebrated survivor of a nearly fatal white shark attack. We saw Australian fur seals (*Arctocephalus doriferus*) that had obviously been bitten by sharks, but had survived. We also saw a 1-ton white shark attack a horse flank that had been hung over the side of our dive boat. The shark had rushed at the hunk of horsemeat, lifted its snout, rolled its eyes back at the moment of impact, and gouged out a huge bite. I thought about what I had seen. If the species had developed that eye-roll to protect its delicate organs from the flippernails of a sea lion that was fighting for its life, then it was possible that the "charging lion" attack strategy was not applicable to the white shark at all. Perhaps *Carcharodon* had developed a cautious, stealthy approach, like a seagoing mugger.

Jared Diamond, a Professor of Physiology at the UCLA Medical School, wrote an article in 1986 in

Alive and well on Año Nuevo Island, an adult male California sea lion exhibits the results of an unsuccessful white shark attack.

which he compared the attack strategy of great white sharks (as explained by Tricas and McCosker) to that of the sabre-toothed cats. He proposed that the extinct cats *Smilodon* and *Homotherium* faced similar circumstances when attempting to engage a mammoth, because, like the sharks, the cats were attempting to dispatch prey animals that were often much larger and heavier than themselves. The cat's facial musculature and the angle of its massive upper jaw canines suggest that it would ambush a baby mammoth that had strayed from its mother, open its jaws wide, stab the pachyderm in the abdomen with its fangs, then desert the field of battle until the baby had hemorrhaged and died. The full title of this discussion is "How Great White Sharks, Sabre-toothed Cats and Soldiers Kill," and Diamond concludes with this anthropocentric observation:

Yet one more predator has independently evolved a similar solution to the problem posed by a formidable victim. The most dangerous prey of all is an armed man, routinely hunted by other armed men. Inexperienced soldiers aim for the head or heart, but these small targets are easily missed. "Always aim for the stomach when you shoot" was the advice of an experienced African bush fighter. "It is just

as good, because no man can live long after his intestines have been shot away." Nor could an elephant seal or a baby mammoth.

Now the seemingly contradictory California survivor statistics began to make sense. In the United States, where divers are rigorously trained to employ the buddy system and thus never to dive alone, the attack victim stands a good chance of survival if his companion has the courage to pull his body to the safety of the boat or the shore. Consider the case of Albert Kogler, discussed on p. 160. Although bitten repeatedly, he died of *multiple lacerations and loss of blood*. In all that bleeding and thrashing (circumstances that previously had been assumed to drive sharks into a "feeding frenzy"), the shark never pressed its advantage, and although Kogler died, there was no significant loss of flesh.

By contrast, in my studies with Dr. Alfredo Cea Egaña, a Chilean physician and scuba diver in 1984, I discovered that three of the four Chilean white shark victims were partially or entirely consumed. Of the four, the only survivor was the swimmer who had a buddy, an exception in Chilean waters, where solo diving is the norm. Can any-

thing safely be concluded from these differences in the behavior of Chilean divers and white sharks? Not really. Four incidents cannot confirm or refute a hypothesis. But the numbers are certainly suggestive.

Through the research I had compiled, I *was* able to verify the long-standing hypothesis that other shark experts and I had proposed: that the great white shark typically takes a huge, massively destructive bite to immobilize its prey, then retreats before moving in for the kill. If the bite-and-spit hypothesis is valid, it accounts for the numerous cases of sea lions with healed shark-bite scars: the sea lion, rather than fluttering helplessly in a bath of its own blood, escapes to land—a venue denied the shark—and lives to swim another day. (Not all sea lions escape, of course; if they did, the sharks would starve to death.)

Tim Tricas and I introduced the "bite-and-spit" hypothesis to the scrutiny of science in a 1984 paper entitled "Predatory Behavior of the White Shark, with Notes on Its Biology." (In case you are wondering how order of authorship of a scientific paper is decided, this publication included the following postscript in its acknowledgments: "Senior authorship of this paper was determined by the outcome of a pinball match played at Port Lincoln, South Australia, in January 1980.") I later refined my hypothesis in a 1985 paper called "White Shark Attack Behavior: Observations and Speculations about Predator and Prey Strategies."

*John McCosker*

*carcharias*? The great spatial separation of the adults and juveniles, not to mention the presumed speed and agility of the juveniles, precludes significant intraspecific cannibalism, at least after birth. And in a manner not unlike that of the giant octopuses, pregnant *Carcharodon* and those having just birthed appear to be hormonally driven to fast so as to avoid consumption of their own. The fact that no pregnant female has been captured using baited lines or traps supports this hypothesis. And the young, 4 feet long and 50 pounds at birth, and growing fast, presumably have little to fear from anything in the sea. Apparently nothing eats white sharks, except for the scavengers that feed upon their carcasses. (Our own species, though it cannot be said to "feed" on white sharks, occasionally makes a meal of one.)*

Like all large fishes, sharks have internal and external parasites.

* In his 1919 *Copeia* discussion of the large sharks off North Carolina, Russell J. Coles described the taste of the white shark as "the very finest shark, or, in fact, fish of any kind that I have ever eaten, its flavor being quite similar to a big, fat, white shad." In 1959, when the collecting crew of Marineland of Florida found an 8.5-foot, 390-pound white shark dead on one of their lines, they brought it back to the lab, where it was weighed and measured, and its jaws preserved. Curator F. G. Wood then initiated what he described as a scientific inquiry: first he removed two steaks, resembling those from a swordfish. Then, "the steaks were skinned, washed well in seawater and placed in the refrigerator. The following day about noon they were sprinkled with lemon juice, salt and pepper, dotted with butter, and placed in a laboratory apparatus known as a broiler until lightly browned on both sides. The results exceeded all expectations. Fellow scientists who participated in the experiment agreed that they had never eaten better fish."

White sharks have been found to be the unwilling hosts of various leeches, trematodes (flatworms), and copepods (sometimes known as fish lice). These parasitic creatures probably annoy the sharks, and if the infestation is massive enough, may even kill them, but they "feed" on white sharks only in the way that ticks or mosquitoes feed on people: they may take minute amounts of flesh or blood, and under unusual circumstances may be responsible for the death of the host, but they do not feed on the animal as a *predator*.

The remoras (family Echeneidae), also known as shark suckers, have been observed accompanying (or attached to) other species of sharks, presumably to feed on the scraps of the sharks' meals. This particular symbiotic relationship is described as *commensal*, which means simply "dining at the same table." Although remoras might attach themselves to white sharks (by means of a sucking disk on top of the head), and hitchhike along on the shark's travels, they run a risk in doing so. As Lineweaver and Backus wrote, "Sharks are imperfect symbionts. Sometimes they eat remoras."

Colinvaux ends his discussion by observing that an

evolutionary principle tells us that the existence of these animals creates a theoretical possibility for other animals to evolve to eat them, but the food calories to be won from the careers or niches of hunting great white sharks and tigers are too few to support a minimum population of animals as large and horribly ferocious as these would have to be. Such animals, therefore, have never evolved. Great white sharks and tigers represent the largest predators that the laws of physics allow the contemporary earth to support."

Contemporary, yes, but the remains of Megalodon allow us images of a bigger, fiercer animal, residing at the apex of an extraordinary prehistoric food chain.

*John McCosker*

OPPOSITE: A male great white cruises above the eelgrass off South Australia's Neptune Islands.

# 7 Distribution of the Great White Shark

**W**hite sharks are found throughout the temperate marine waters of the world, but they appear to prefer those regions where there are now, or have been in the past, substantial populations of seals, sea lions, or fur seals. There are seal and sea lion populations off the South African, New Zealand, South Australian, central Californian, and central Chilean coasts, and the pinnipeds there often exhibit scars from shark bites. The mere presence of pinnipeds, however, does not automatically generate populations of white sharks. Southern Argentina and southern Chile are known for their congregations of southern sea lions, and yet the offshore waters do not seem to be occupied by white sharks. The same is true of Alaska and the Aleutian and Pribilof Islands groups, where hordes of fur seals aggregate, and of course, of the Antarctic, which supports more pinnipeds than any other region on earth. It would appear, then, that only the right combination of pinnipeds and water temperature will be propitious for white sharks.

White sharks seem to have a particular preference for northern elephant seals, and they are well-documented off the Farallon Islands, 26 miles outside California's Golden Gate, and at Isla del Guadalupe, off Baja California, both localities known breeding grounds of these enormous pinnipeds. The even larger southern elephant seal, found in Patagonia and various sub-Antarctic island groups, where the waters are quite cold, seems not to be as bothered by *Carcharodon*.

When Peter Gimbel set out in 1969 to hunt for and film the great white, he went to South Africa, Sri Lanka, and, eventually, South Australia, where at last he found his quarry. *Carcharodon carcharias* can generally be found off South Africa and southern Australia, but it has never been reported from Sri Lanka. It is also found off both coasts of North America, and it has been reported as abundant—but far from plentiful—off New Jersey and New York in the east (evidently sustained there in part by whales and whale carcasses, rather than by pinnipeds), and off central California in the west. On the U.S. East Coast, in fact, there is a "monster fishery,"

Divers haul a dead great white out of the water in Western Australia.

where white sharks are hunted for sport and trophies. Even though the white shark does not often leap clear of the water in the style of a marlin or a mako, its great size makes it one of the premier trophies for big-game fishermen.

The same sort of sport fishery exists in South Australia and South Africa, but in all three fisheries, the number of white sharks taken has declined noticeably in recent years, suggesting that even a fairly substantial population cannot withstand an intensive, directed, long-term onslaught. South Australia has been, and remains, the white shark fishery of choice. The largest fish ever caught on rod and reel, a female white shark that weighed 2,664 pounds, was hauled in there by Alf Dean in 1959. The great white occurs generally along the entire southern Australian coast, from as far north as central Western Australia, thence south and east across South Australia and Victoria, and for hundreds of miles up the east coast beyond New South Wales.

The sport fishery in South Africa has also produced some enormous specimens, and it was the suggestion of 19-footers caught off Durban that brought Peter Gimbel and his crew there in their search for the great white shark. His "Blue Water" expedition filmed oceanic whitetips and bull sharks off Durban, but found no white sharks there. On another occasion, it might have. Although no 19-footers have been caught, some very big "blue pointers" have been caught off Durban (they once fished for them from piers there) and elsewhere along the Natal coast.

During the whaling days out of Durban, which ended in 1975, white sharks were very likely attracted to the shore station, where blood was hosed into the sea. (In the early days of the whaling operations the townspeople objected strenuously to the smell and to the shark-attracting offal in the water, and the station was moved from inside the harbor, around a promontory known as The Bluff, to the ocean side of the harbor away from the bathing beaches.) Most of the actual whaling—that is, the killing of whales—took place some distance from shore, and if there were

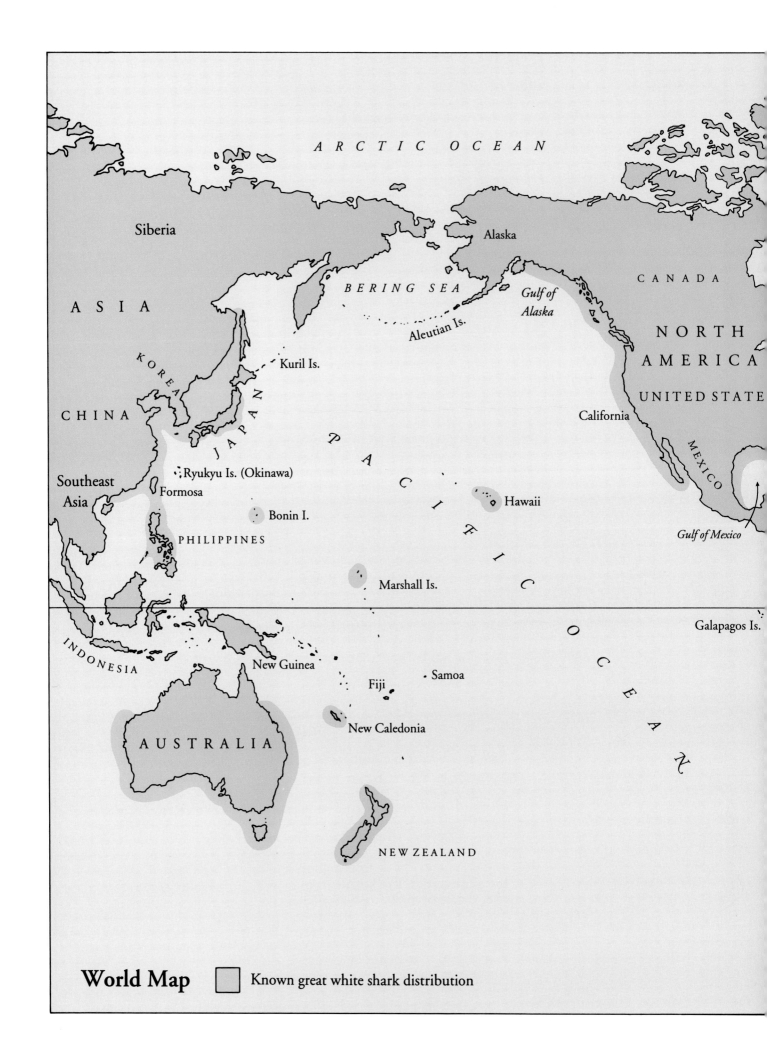

Siberia

ARCTIC OCEAN

Alaska

ASIA

BERING SEA

Gulf of
Alaska

CANADA

KOREA

Kuril Is.

Aleutian Is.

NORTH
AMERICA

CHINA

JAPAN

California

UNITED STATE

Southeast
Asia

Ryukyu Is. (Okinawa)

Formosa

PACIFIC

MEXICO

Hawaii

Bonin I.

PHILIPPINES

Gulf of Mexico

Marshall Is.

OCEAN

Galapagos Is.

INDONESIA

New Guinea

Fiji

Samoa

AUSTRALIA

New Caledonia

NEW ZEALAND

**World Map**  Known great white shark distribution

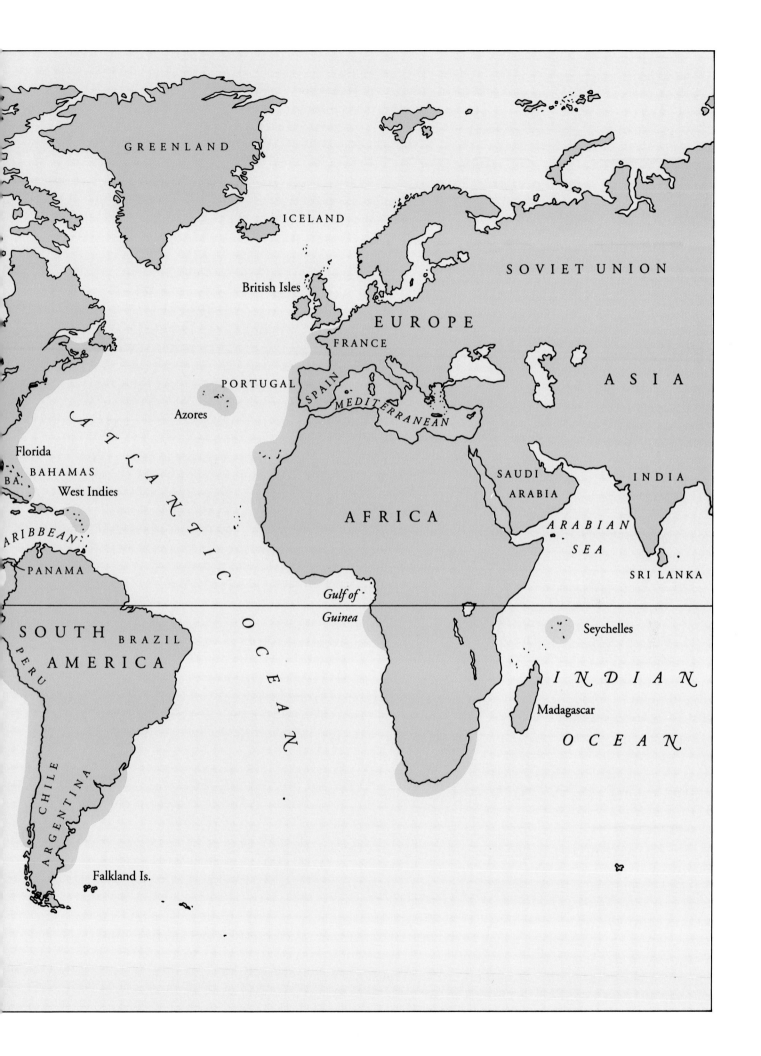

GREENLAND

ICELAND

British Isles

SOVIET UNION

EUROPE

FRANCE

PORTUGAL

Azores

SPAIN

MEDITERRANEAN

ASIA

*ATLANTIC*

Florida

BAHAMAS

BA

West Indies

CARIBBEAN

PANAMA

AFRICA

SAUDI
ARABIA

INDIA

*ARABIAN
SEA*

SRI LANKA

*Gulf of
Guinea*

*OCEAN*

SOUTH

BRAZIL

AMERICA

PERU

Seychelles

*INDIAN*

Madagascar

*OCEAN*

CHILE

ARGENTINA

Falkland Is.

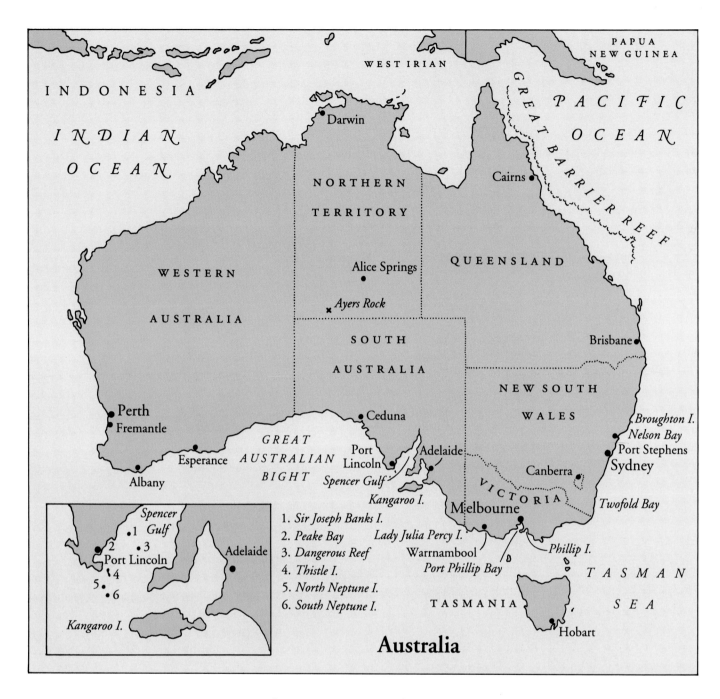

**Australia**

1. *Sir Joseph Banks I.*
2. *Peake Bay*
3. *Dangerous Reef*
4. *Thistle I.*
5. *North Neptune I.*
6. *South Neptune I.*

to be whites, they would probably be found in deeper, offshore waters. Gimbel, along with Ron and Valerie Taylor and Stan Waterman, accordingly went down in cages some 90 miles off Durban, filming the sharks that were feeding on the carcass of a harpooned sperm whale, but they saw only bull sharks, blue sharks, oceanic whitetips, and a single 14-foot tiger shark. Valerie Taylor, quoted in Peter Matthiessen's *Blue Meridian*, believed there were no large whites around Durban, and if the crew were to go to South Australia instead of hanging around South Africa, they would find the sharks they were looking for. In her journal, she wrote, "The water is too warm here for whites, and there are no sea creatures suitably large and abundant for a shark as big and hungry as a white to feed upon."

Valerie was wrong about Durban; in the years immediately preceding the arrival of the "Blue Water" film team, a veritable white shark derby was being conducted off the South Pier. And indeed, at the time the "Blue

Water" film crew was filming off Durban, there certainly were "sea creatures suitably large and abundant" for white sharks to feed on: the whaling station at The Bluff was bringing in dead whales almost every day. Moreover, the entire Natal coast from the Tugela River to Margate was meshed with shark nets, and in the years 1966 to 1972, 143 white sharks had been caught in the nets. (From 1978 to 1987, another 389 white sharks were caught in the nets. The average for those seventeen years is 32 white sharks per year.)

The largest white shark known from Durban was a 16.5-footer harpooned by a whaling captain named Arvid Nordengen in 1962. The "Blue Water" expedition was essentially a fishing trip, and as is said of all such exercises, "They should have been there yesterday." Even though they were on the very grounds where Nordengen had shot his 16.5-footer, and even though they were using the best possible bait—a sperm whale carcass—they did not find a single white shark.

If they had rounded the southern tip of Africa and dropped anchor somewhere in Table Bay, off Cape Town, they might have saved a lot of time and fuel. Probably having to do with the abundance of fur seals on the Cape coast, that area sustains probably the greatest population density of white sharks in the world. A comprehensive study of the sharks of southern Africa (Bass, D'Aubrey, and Kistnasamy, 1975), published by the Oceanographic Research Institute of Durban, reported that "Although we have few definite records, small *C. carcharias* appear to be fairly common in southern and southwestern Cape waters."

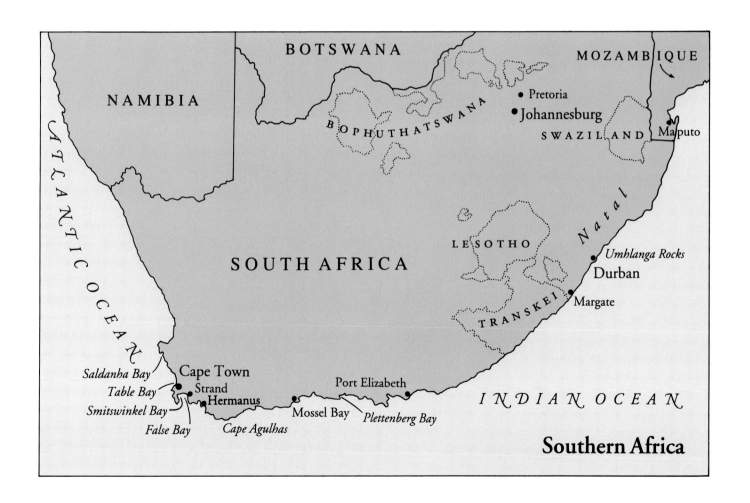

Southern Africa

In his book on South African shark attacks, Tim Wallett, who at the time was employed by the Natal Sharks Board in Durban, wrote that "the great white shark is common in the seas off the Cape coast. During the summer, the species comes inshore, particularly in False Bay, at Hermanus and Mossel Bay. They are often seen and caught near the beach. These specimens are rarely shorter than 3.0 metres [10 feet] in length." In the same 1983 book, Wallett wrote, "During the summer months Macassar Beach [in Table Bay, off Cape Town] is one of the most heavily populated great white shark areas in the world." This quote appears under a photograph of shark fisherman Danie Schoeman, who has caught no fewer than *eighteen* great whites in Table Bay. (More about Schoeman—and other South African fishermen—when we discuss fishing for the great white.)

At the New Zealand whaling stations of the Perano family in Tory Channel, white pointers were regular visitors. In *The Perano Whalers of Cook Strait,* author Don Grady recounts some of the whalemen's stories. We are told that they usually dispatched the invading sharks with the weapons ordinarily reserved for 40-ton whales. As with many whaler's tales, some of these stories might be a little exaggerated, such as the one that had them removing the jaws from a shark that would have measured close to 28 feet if its spine had not been deformed, and claimed that when they cut the jaws out, "both Joe Perano and Harry Heberley were able to stand up side by side in the huge jaws." In May 1950, near a station known as Fishing Bay, Mrs. E. Huntley was fishing when she spotted a huge shark. Her screams attracted the attention of Gil Perano, who rushed to her rescue in a whale-chaser: "Cairo Huntley instinctively picked up a bomb-lance and thrust it into the water on top of the big shark. Its insides were blown to pieces with four sticks of gelignite." When they measured what was left after the detonation, the shark was 21 feet long.

Most people do not spend their lives searching for giant sharks. On the other hand, giant sharks *do* spend their lives looking for things to eat, and occasionally they encounter a swimmer or diver. That is not to say that white sharks are dedicated maneaters—they are not—and in fact if their existence were not so often documented by their violent contacts with men and women, they might go almost unnoticed. This is especially true along the coast north and south of San Francisco, where there have been more recorded white shark attacks than anywhere else in the world (a statistic nurtured in part by there being so many people in the water). The dubious distinction of being the second-worst area for swimmers belongs to South Australia; in the area of Spencer Gulf, south of Adelaide, there have been many attacks on swimmers and skin divers, several of them fatal.

Attacks have also been recorded in Massachusetts, New Jersey, Oregon, New Zealand, Chile, Panama, Argentina, Mexico, Italy, and of course South Africa (see the table on pp. 140–42). A particularly gruesome series of attacks, four of them fatal, occurred off the coast of New Jersey in the summer of 1916, and although it was assumed—from the flimsiest of evidence—that a white shark had been the perpetrator, subsequent analysis has suggested that the killer was one or more bull sharks.

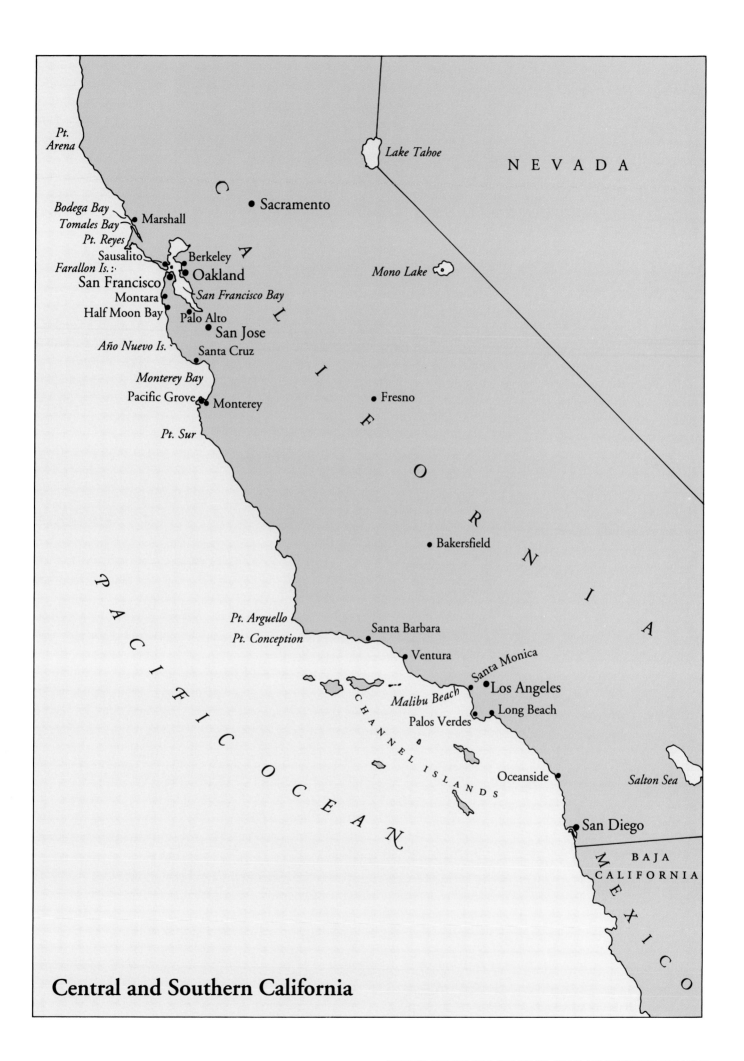

Pt.
Arena

Lake Tahoe

NEVADA

Bodega Bay
Tomales Bay ● Marshall
Pt. Reyes
Sausalito
Farallon Is. ∴
Berkeley
San Francisco ● Oakland
Montara
Half Moon Bay
San Francisco Bay
Palo Alto
● San Jose
Año Nuevo Is.
Santa Cruz

● Sacramento

C A L I F O R N I A

Mono Lake

Monterey Bay
Pacific Grove
● Monterey

Pt. Sur

● Fresno

● Bakersfield

P A C I F I C   O C E A N

Pt. Arguello
Pt. Conception
● Santa Barbara
● Ventura
Santa Monica
Malibu Beach
● Los Angeles
Palos Verdes
● Long Beach

C H A N N E L   I S L A N D S

● Oceanside

Salton Sea

● San Diego

BAJA
CALIFORNIA

M E X I C O

**Central and Southern California**

A young white shark—possibly feeding—leaves the water in San Ignacio Lagoon, Baja California.

The distribution of white sharks—or of any other sharks, for that matter—is difficult to document. Sharks are fishes, after all, and as such spend most of their lives underwater, out of sight of people. Where there is not a directed local fishery for a given species, distribution analyses must be little more than guesswork. Occasionally, however, luck lends a hand. In a 1968 *National Geographic* article by Nathaniel Kenney, there appeared a photograph with this caption: "Pursuing an elusive meal, a young shark—possibly a great white—broaches in San Ignacio Lagoon, Baja California." From the photograph it is obvious that the shark is indeed a great white, and aside from the astonishing good fortune that the photographer was on hand when the fish unexpectedly leaped from the water, two other benefits accrue: first we see a white shark in what we assume is a natural feeding activity (not one provoked by handouts), and second, we have documentation of the occurrence of the great white shark in the lagoons of Baja California. The photographer, Ted Walker, has since added (in a letter to Richard Ellis), that "From time to time white sharks are seen in the lagoon, and their presence made evident by their breaching. I watched from the air four medium-sized sharks biting a baby gray whale that appeared near death. The sharks hung on like bulldogs." Other species of whales and pinnipeds are also found in the Sea of Cortez (Gulf of California), and in 1965, Kato reported *Carcharodon carcharias* from the waters of Mazatlán, east of Cabo San Lucas, near the mainland across from the southernmost tip of the Baja peninsula.

Underwater photographer Howard Hall observed whites off Isla del Guadalupe (Baja California), and subsequent attacks upon humans there confirmed their presence, but Walker's is probably the first photograph ever taken of a white shark in the inshore lagoons. It is interesting to note that the caption-writer could say "possibly a great white," for there is no question about the identity of the shark; so little was known about this species—"Blue Water, White Death" had not yet been released—that no one was prepared to risk a positive identification. (Even more revealing of our changing attitudes toward sharks in general are the titles of two *National Geographic* articles that appeared thirteen years apart: the 1968 piece by Kenney was entitled "Sharks: Wolves of the Sea," and Eugenie Clark's comprehensive shark article in 1981 was called "Sharks: Magnificent and Misunderstood.")

In the inshore waters of the western North Atlantic, there is a situation that offers almost a controlled population study. Shark tournaments have been held for more than twenty years off Long Island and New Jersey, and scientists from the Narragansett (Rhode Island) laboratory of the National Marine Fisheries Service have carefully monitored the results. Since Jack Casey, H. L. ("Wes") Pratt, and Chuck Stillwell have been counting, 26 out of a total of 5,465 sharks caught in these tournaments have been whites, a ratio of 1:210. Most of these have been juveniles, but there have also been some large whites caught in the Mid-Atlantic Bight. Fishermen have hooked or harpooned some very large specimens in this region, in such circumstances as to suggest that adult white sharks feed on whales as a regular item.*

Before the passage of the 1972 Marine Mammal Protection Act, which made it illegal to kill whales, dolphins, or porpoises in U.S. waters, shark fishermen would harpoon pilot whales and use their flesh to attract sharks. (This practice used to occur in Australia and South Africa, as well, before those countries also put a stop to whaling.) Most of the large white

* During these tournaments, sharks not only are caught, they are tagged as well. Messrs. Casey, Pratt, and Stillwell have been providing tags for fishermen throughout the northeast, and encouraging the release of smaller specimens, in the hope that some may be recaptured later, perhaps far away. The recapture statistics have provided invaluable data on the movement, abundance, and migratory habits of various shark species of the North Atlantic. By far the most abundant shark in these waters is the blue, but fishermen and scientists tag and release some 5,000 sharks annually, including sandbars, duskies, tigers, blacktips, makos, hammerheads, and assorted other species in lesser numbers. White sharks are not abundant in this region, and although most fishermen would rather keep one than release it, they are occasionally tagged and released, and sometimes even recovered. In the 1990 "Shark Tagger Summary," it was reported that a white shark that had been tagged off the coast of Virginia was recaptured 14 months later off Massachusetts, some 384 miles from the site of the original tagging.

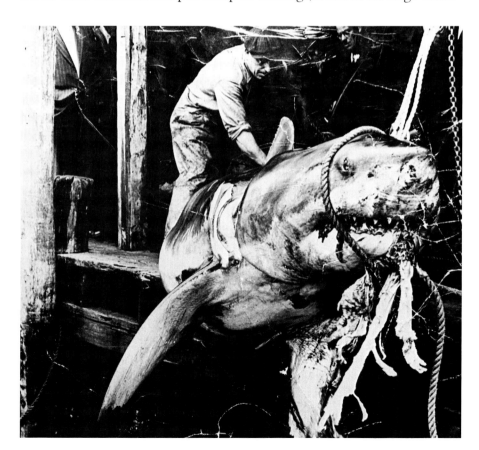

Around 1928, this huge shark was caught in a mackerel net 15 miles off Cape May, New Jersey, by fisherman Torvaldt Feldt.

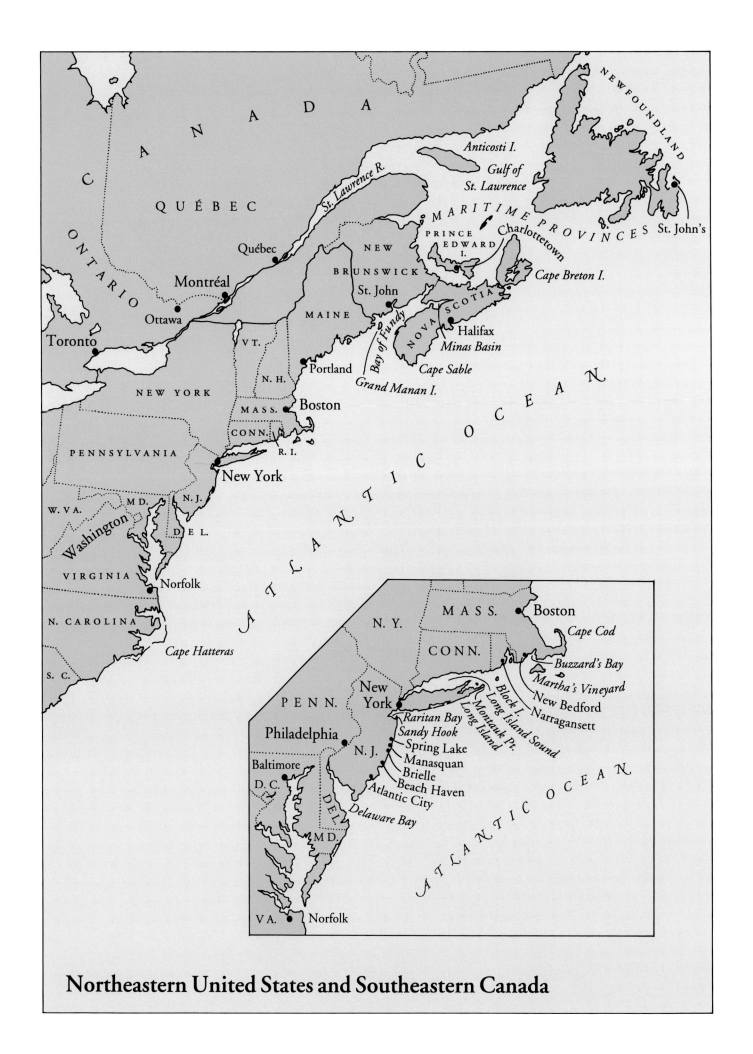

sharks recorded from the Mid-Atlantic Bight (south of Long Island) have been encountered feeding on the carcasses of whales, and in the days of whaling, Azorean and Western Australian whalers, as well as South African, reported white sharks congregating around the carcasses of their dead whales. Jack Casey and his colleagues have plotted the distribution of white sharks in the Mid-Atlantic Bight, and they conclude that "white sharks are likely to occur singly or as scattered, unassociated individuals over several square kilometers." White sharks seem to be loners, and do not often associate in schools, or even pairs, as far as we know—until word of a whale carcass or shower of tuna chunks goes out.

As might be expected, however, there are anomalies in the records. Off Sandy Hook, New Jersey, for example, in August 1964, Casey and colleagues caught no fewer than *ten* juvenile white sharks on a single 32-hook longline. A possible explanation for this aggregation, according to the authors, was a sport fishery for bluefish, which resulted in the discarding of fish heads and entrails in the area. (Because Sandy Hook is a popular swimming area, the presence of these sharks was not publicized at the time, "in the interest of public relations.") In several recorded instances, as many as five or six individuals have been attracted to the same chum slick or the same dead whale, which suggests that the species is at least not averse to group feeding.

Of course great whites have to pair off every once in a while. Otherwise there would be no baby white sharks. In a 1985 study of the distribution of white sharks off the California coast, biologist Peter Klimley has hypothesized a "life history pattern" that includes suggestions of mating and birthing behavior: "Large females move southward to give birth to pups during late summer and early fall. As the pups grow larger they move north . . . where they live both inshore and offshore." Klimley does not account for the movement of the males, but he does indicate that equal numbers of males and females were taken in his study area.

Jack Casey (left) and Wes Pratt of the Narragansett laboratory of the National Marine Fisheries Service examine a 2,075-pound male white shark harpooned off Center Moriches, Long Island, in June 1979.

RIGHT: Curious Brazilians examine a 14-foot *tubarão branco* harpooned by fishermen off Angra dos Reis in 1968.

BELOW: Off Sandy Hook, New Jersey, in 1964, fisheries biologists hauled in ten juvenile white sharks on a single longline.

ABOVE: Alfred Cutajar, known locally as the "Son of God" for his sharkfishing skills, with the 23-footer he caught off Malta, in the Mediterranean. He was alone in a small boat, a mile from shore, when he encountered the shark.

LEFT: Off Prince Edward Island, Canada, this gigantic white shark, 17 feet 8 inches long, was caught in a fishing net during the summer of 1983.

Elsewhere, we know that the species occurs in the Azores; there are records of whites taken in the harbors of the various islands, and a 15-footer hangs in the museum at Ponta Delgada. A very large white shark was recorded at Cojimar, Cuba, in 1948, although its 21-foot length and remarkably precise weight of 7,302 pounds have been questioned (see pp. 51–54). Another very large white shark was taken in Brazil. Central Chile probably has a healthy population of white sharks, to judge from the number of fatal attacks on divers there in recent years. White sharks have been trapped in fishermen's nets in Prince Edward Island, Nova Scotia, and Rhode Island, and there are documented eyewitness accounts of the species in Massachusetts, Florida, and North Carolina waters. (The person who recorded white sharks in North Carolina was Russell Coles, who evidently made a practice of jumping into the water to engage the sharks in combat; see pp. 227–28.)

The shark that Steno dissected in Florence in 1666 had to have come from the Mediterranean, and although the occurrence of the species has been sporadic over time, they can still be found there. Though the details are now lost, Norman and Fraser describe a female that was "caught at Agamy, near Alexandria in the Mediterranean, in the summer of 1934." (This shark, which was described as being 14 feet long and weighing 2.5 tons, was the one that was supposed to have had nine young, "each two feet long and weighing 108 lbs.")

The island of Malta, located south of Sicily in the Mediterranean, has in recent years been the scene of several spectacular captures, including the huge fish caught in 1987 by fisherman Alfred Cutajar and reported (very doubtfully) as being 23 feet long. In a letter to John McCosker, John Abela, a Maltese with a true dedication to sharks—he bought the head of Cutajar's monster for $450.00 and refused to part with it when someone offered him twice that amount—described the 1987 shark and recounted stories of Cutajar's earlier triumphs, including a 20-footer caught in 1973.

There is historical and recent evidence of white sharks being found in Hawaiian waters, and several specimens have been captured alive or harpooned off Okinawa. They are mentioned in Marshall's book about the fishes of the Great Barrier Reef, along northeastern Australia, but it was not until recently that one was captured in the Coral Sea of northeastern Australia. Although they are not common in south Florida, there are a couple of records of whites there, including a 455-pounder caught by a fisherman in the Florida Keys in 1988, and shark biologist Don Nelson's chilling story of swimming (unintentionally) with a 12-footer in Florida waters (see pp. 137–38).

But should you be searching for white sharks, do not bother with Florida or Hawaii—though they certainly occur there, it is most unlikely that you would find them. Your prospects would be better if you went to Dangerous Reef, South Australia.* Peter Gimbel learned that after an expedition that lasted almost two years, and was marked by failures off South Africa, Sri Lanka, and elsewhere. Many divers and big-game anglers who seek "the ultimate thrill" have journeyed to Port Lincoln, South Australia, to dive with the maneaters (people in cages, sharks outside).

How then, do white sharks end up in Hawaii? Probably by swim-

* In Gimbel's day, you could easily find white sharks off Dangerous Reef, and a decade later they were still plentiful. By 1990, however, the population seems to have been nearly fished out by trophy-hunters, and recent diving expeditions off South Australia have often come up completely empty.

Now that it is out of the water (and dead), this Montauk 2,390-pounder can be approached with a degree of nervous confidence.

ming from some North Pacific coast, whether in Asia or North America. Northern elephant seals have wandered as far as Midway Island, at the northwestern end of the Hawaiian chain, and we can be confident of their Mexican or Californian origin. A stray white shark in Hawaii has probably made the same trip, although the surface-current patterns are slightly more favorable from the Asiatic side. But once there, does it migrate? Does it stay, as a permanent resident? Too few studies of tagged individuals have been performed to afford us an answer, and the world's museums hold too few of these large specimens, particularly from different oceans, to allow us to examine them side-by-side for possible morphological variations between geographic regions. As with so many other aspects of its biology, the lifetime, seasonal, and daily movements of *Carcharodon carcharias* remain to be discovered.

© RICHARD ELLIS-1975

# The White Shark Attacks

Much can be learned about shark behavior from eyewitness accounts of their attacks, but in most shark attacks, the identity of the attacking shark is not known. In his 1974 analysis of the Shark Attack File,* David Baldridge wrote "more often than not, identifications were made on the weakest of evidence and were evidently at times no more than snap judgments by casual observers." In his summary of the attacks where the species of shark was identified—however erroneously—Baldridge found just 12 percent of the total (32 out of 267) assignable to white sharks. Clearly, not even a substantial minority of the recorded attacks by sharks on people are perpetrated by this species, but since the appearance of "Jaws," the book and the movie, white sharks have been blamed for more than their share.[†] (Of course an attack by a great white is more likely to do serious damage than is an attack by a shark of another species.)

There are obviously instances where people have been in the water with white sharks and were *not* attacked. In some of these cases, the people were not aware of the sharks at all, since swimmers with their heads out of the water, or even those with their faces *in* the water, cannot see very much of what is going on around them. There is one instance, however, when a lone diver was confronted repeatedly by a large shark, and there appears to have been no question of its identity. Don Nelson, then a graduate student at the University of Miami (and now a research biologist at California State University at Long Beach), was spearfishing off Grassy Key, in Florida, on New Year's Day, 1960, when he glanced over his shoulder and noticed a large shark swimming slowly toward him. "I

---

* Because of an apparent increase in worldwide shark attacks in the 1950's, the American Institute of Biological Sciences convened the "Shark Research Panel" in New Orleans in June 1958. One out-

† The discrepancy between Baldridge's figures and ours is a function of time and reportage. Baldridge was analyzing only the data in the Shark Attack File as of 1974, whereas we have had access to an-

* growth of this meeting was the establish-
ment of the Shark Attack File, supported
by the U.S. Office of Naval Research, the
National Science Foundation, and the
Smithsonian Institution. Records were
kept of every shark attack (often relying
on clipping services and voluntary sub-
missions), and data were assembled on
time of day of each attack, water temperature, age and sex of victim, and, if
known, the species of shark. Maintained
at the Smithsonian, the Shark Attack File
was microfilmed for security, and eventually transferred to the Mote Marine
Laboratory at Sarasota, Florida. After Baldridge's 1974 analysis of the data in the
file, funding was discontinued, since the
ONR believed that the necessary data base
had been accumulated, and that continu-
ing to record every attack would therefore
serve no useful purpose.

† other 16 years of material. It is also possible that there has been an actual increase
in white shark attacks in recent years, a
subject that will be discussed at some
length.

realized," he wrote, "that it could only be a white shark or possibly an extremely large mako." The shark swam directly at him:

I was thankful for the speargun I held but decided against firing my one spear except as a last resort. The shark came so close that I had to withdraw the gun for fear of touching its snout and possibly inciting it. Finally, with the shark at arm's length, I shouted and shook the gun in its face. The shark turned—not much— but enough to avoid hitting me and slowly passed me by on my left side about a meter and a half away. For a very long minute or so the shark and I swam parallel, eye to eye, until it moved away and circled in the distance. The shark approached me head-on three more times; each time I had to repeat the shouting and gun-waving.

Nelson—who has since dived with many other kinds of sharks—was aware that he was in the water with the fabled maneater. "Unlike all other sharks I have encountered on the reef," he continued, "this one seemed interested in me alone, even in the absence of struggling sounds or fresh odors. I had the distinct impression that he was visually examining me as a possible meal."

*Carcharodon carcharias* is known with confidence to have committed only a small percentage of all documented shark attacks on humans—it is estimated that of about 100 shark attacks on humans annually, world-wide, about 30 are fatal—and we will discuss only those few cases where there is evidence that the shark is known or suspected to have been a great white. Sometimes the identification is easy, as in the instance when the attacking shark was dragged onto the beach attached to a boy's leg. When the person telling the story is an experienced diver, it is easier to believe that he or she knew what species they had confronted. If, on the other hand, the person has had little experience with sharks (except perhaps through a viewing of "Jaws"), there is no reason to assume that he or she could distinguish a white shark from a blue shark or a bull shark. There are, in fact, cases where subsequent analysis has indicated that a shark believed to have been a white was not. Unless the attacking shark is *known* to have been a white, either from reliable observation, analysis of bite marks, a tooth left behind, or some other fairly conclusive evidence, it has not been included in this discussion. In the accompanying table, only those attacks known with a fair degree of certainty to have been committed by white sharks have been included.

**THE FAR SIDE**    By GARY LARSON

Bathing Scene, Asbury Park, N. J.

Mrs. O. D. Tucker,
Ludlow,
Massachusetts.
R. D.

During July 1916, sharks killed four people and injured another along the New Jersey shore. This postcard was sent from Asbury Park during that month.

Probably the most celebrated shark attacks in American history took place in the summer of 1916, and although a white shark was then believed to have been the culprit, a closer examination of the evidence seems to implicate one or more bull sharks.* Still, these attacks, and their aftermath, seemed to set the tone for both press reportage and public response in later years, and they serve as an apt prelude to those attacks that are known to have been committed by white sharks.

During a twelve-day period in July 1916, no less than five men were attacked by sharks in New Jersey, four of them fatally. On July 1, 23-year-old Charles Vansant, playing in the surf some 15 yards from shore at Beach Haven, was bitten on the left thigh. Although companions dragged him ashore and quickly applied a tourniquet to his leg, he had suffered a massive loss of blood, and he died less than two hours after the attack.

On July 6, at the beach resort of Spring Lake, some 45 miles north of Beach Haven, Charles Bruder was attacked while swimming 400 feet from shore, and both his feet were bitten off. Although a lifeboat was launched immediately when he began to scream, and he was taken quickly to shore, he died within minutes.

Six days passed before another attack. At Matawan, 30 miles north of Spring Lake, an 11-year-old boy named Lester Stillwell was swimming with friends when he was pulled under. (Although a "large dark gray shark" had been spotted earlier in Matawan Creek, nobody actually saw the shark that attacked Stillwell.) Would-be rescuers dived into the creek searching for Stillwell's body, and one of them, a 24-year-old tailor named Stanley Fisher, was savagely bitten on the right thigh. A great chunk of his thigh was removed, and even though he was rushed to a hospital, there was no way to reverse the massive tissue and blood loss and he died on the operating table.

By this time, the news of the Matawan Creek attacks had spread, and even as a group of boys were climbing out of the water some 400 yards from the site of the Stillwell-Fisher attacks, 12-year-old Joseph Dunn was

* Not all agree. In 1987, R. G. Fernicola, an amateur shark researcher, published an exhaustive study of the "Jersey Man-eater," in which he tentatively concludes that a white shark *was* responsible.

## Documented Attacks by the Great White Shark Worldwide, 1926–1990

| Date | Victim | Location | Fatal? |
|---|---|---|---|
| 7.08.26 | Norman Peixotto | San Leandro Bay, Cal. | no (1) |
| 7.25.36 | Joseph Troy | Buzzard's Bay, Mass. | yes (2) |
| 11.01.42 | W. S. Bergh | Clifton, South Africa | yes (6) |
| 9.23.43 | Sailor | Gulf of Panama | yes (3) |
| 10.08.50 | R. Campbell | Imperial Beach, Cal. | no (1) |
| 12.07.52 | Barry Wilson | Point Aulone, Cal. | yes (1) |
| 1.22.54 | Alfredo Aubone | Buenos Aires, Argentina | no (1) |
| 2.06.55 | Peter Jacobs | Pacific Grove, Cal. | no (1) |
| 8.14.56 | Douglas Clarke | Pismo Beach, Cal. | no (1) |
| 10.27.56 | Graham Smith | False Bay, South Africa | no (6) |
| 4.28.57 | Peter Savino | Morro Bay, Cal. | yes (1) |
| 5.07.59 | Albert Kogler | Baker's Beach, Cal. | yes (4) |
| 5.30.59 | Tony Dicks | Port Elizabeth, South Africa | no (1) |
| 10.04.59 | James Hay | Bodega Bay, Cal. | no (4) |
| 4.24.60 | Frank Gilbert | Tomales Point, Cal. | no (4) |
| 5.19.60 | Suzanne Theriot | Santa Cruz, Cal. | no (4) |
| 3.12.61 | Brian Rodger | Aldinga Beach, S. Australia | no |
| ?.?.61 | Manfred Gregor | Ricchione, Italy | no (1) |
| 5.21.61 | Rodney Orr | Tomales Point, Cal. | no (4) |
| 8.20.61 | David Vogesen | Bodega Bay, Cal. | no (4) |
| 1.14.62 | Floyd Pair, Jr. | Farallon Islands, Cal. | no (1) |
| 11.11.62 | Leroy French | Farallon Islands, Cal. | no (4) |
| 12.09.62 | Geoff Corner | Caracalinga Head, S. Australia | yes |
| 8.12.63 | Rodney Fox | Aldinga Beach, S. Australia | no |
| 9.29.63 | Crisologo Urizar | El Panul, Chile | yes (5) |
| 1.11.64 | Jack Rochette | Farallon Islands, Cal. | no |
| 2.05.64 | Leslie Jordan | Dunedin, New Zealand | yes |
| 2.08.64 | Alan Saffrey | False Bay, South Africa | no (6) |
| 11.29.64 | Henri Bsource | Victoria, Australia | no |
| 12.13.64 | John Harding | Wooli, New South Wales | no |
| 1.23.65 | Ronald Bowes | Durban, South Africa | no (6) |
| 1.22.66 | D. Barthman | Cypress Point, Cal. | no |
| 2.26.66 | Raymond Short | Coledale Beach, New South Wales | no |
| 3.09.67 | William Black | Dunedin, New Zealand | yes |
| 3.19.67 | Len Jones | Paradise Reef, South Africa | no |
| 8.19.67 | Bob Bartle | Jurien Bay, W. Australia | yes |
| 7.27.68 | Frank Logan | Tomales Point, Cal. | no (4) |
| 12.09.68 | Dick O'Brien | Thistle Island, S. Australia | no |
| 7.20.69 | R. Colby | Pigeon Point, Cal. | no |
| 9.06.69 | Donald Joslin | Tomales Point, Cal. | no (4) |
| 4.11.71 | Theo Klein | Buffalo Bay, South Africa | yes (6) |
| 6.30.71 | Gideon Scheltema | Mossel Bay, South Africa | no (6) |
| 8.17.71 | David Robertson | Cape St. Francis, South Africa | no (6) |
| 10.02.71 | Calvin Ward | Sea Ranch, Cal. | no |
| 5.28.72 | Helmuth Himmrich | Tomales Point, Cal. | no (4) |
| 7.19.72 | Kenny Gray | Santa Barbara, Cal. | no (4) |
| 9.09.72 | Hans Kretschmer | Point Sur, Cal. | no (4) |
| 9.09.73 | Albert Schneppershoff | Isla del Guadalupe, Mexico | yes |
| 1.09.74 | Terry Manuel | Streaky Bay, S. Australia | yes |
| 5.26.74 | Leroy Hancock | Tomales Point, Cal. | no (4) |
| 7.26.74 | Robert Kehl | Albion, Cal. | no (4) |
| 8.05.74 | R. Sanders | San Gregorio, Cal. | no |

| Date | Victim | Location | Fatal? |
|---|---|---|---|
| 9.02.74 | Dale Webster | Franklin Point, Cal. | no (4) |
| 9.02.74 | Jack Greenlaw | Franklin Point, Cal. | no (4) |
| 9.14.74 | Jon Holcomb | Farallon Islands, Cal. | no (4) |
| 9.28.74 | Kirk Johnston | Point Sur, Cal. | no (4) |
| 7.19.75 | Gary Johnson | Point Conception, Cal. | no (4) |
| 7.23.75 | Robert Rebstock | Point Conception, Cal. | no (4) |
| 8.17.75 | D. Robertson | Cape St. Francis, South Africa | no (6) |
| 9.09.75 | Gilbert Brown | Usal Creek, Cal. | no (4) |
| 12.06.75 | Robin Buckley | Farallon Islands, Cal. | no (4) |
| 9.24.76 | M. Shook | Coos Bay, Oregon | no (4) |
| 10.06.76 | Marshall Flanagan | Seal Point, South Africa | no (6) |
| 10.18.76 | William Kennedy | Moonstone Beach, Cal. | no (4) |
| 11.27.76 | Geoffrey Spence | Clifton, South Africa | no (6) |
| 12.18.76 | J. Worrell | San Miguel Island, Cal. | no (4) |
| 9.14.77 | Glen Friedman | Tomales Point, Cal. | no |
| 11.30.77 | Andre Hartman | Partridge Point, South Africa | no (7) |
| 9.27.78 | Eric Lombard | Miller's Point, South Africa | no (7) |
| 12.12.78 | Flip Steenkamp | Sodwana, South Africa | yes (6) |
| 3.11.79 | Calvin Sloan | Año Nuevo Island, Cal. | no (4) |
| 11.26.79 | Kenneth Doudt | Cannon Beach, Oregon | no (4) |
| 1.03.80 | Shaun Wright | Ballito, South Africa | no (7) |
| 1.05.80 | José Larenas Miranda | Los Vilos, Chile | yes (5) |
| 10.17.80 | Curt Vikan | Moonstone Beach, Cal. | no |
| 10.27.80 | Chris Cowen | Douglas Co., Oregon | no |
| 3.04.81 | Carlos Vergara | Coquimbo, Chile | no (5) |
| 12.19.81 | Lewis Boren | Monterey, Cal. | yes |
| 2.07.82 | Harvey Smith | Stillwater Cove, Cal. | no |
| 6.29.82 | Alex Macun | Ntlonyana, South Africa | yes (6) |
| 7.24.82 | Casimir Pulaski | Point Buchon, Cal. | no |
| 8.29.82 | John Buchanon | Morro Bay, Cal. | no |
| 9.19.82 | Michael Herder | Bear Harbor, Cal. | no |
| 8.20.83 | Randy Weldon | Tillamook Co., Oregon | no |
| 9.20.83 | Attie Louw | False Bay, South Africa | no (7) |
| 12.24.83 | Neil Williams | South Neptune I., S. Australia | no |
| 9.11.84 | H. Ingram | I. del Guadalupe, Mexico | no |
| 9.15.84 | Omar Conger | Pigeon Point, Cal. | yes |
| 9.30.84 | Robert Rice | Tillamook Co., Oregon | no |
| 9.30.84 | Paul Parsons | Tomales Bay, Cal. | no |
| 1.04.85 | Donald James | False Bay, South Africa | no (7) |
| 1.17.85 | Bruce Eldridge | Natal, South Africa | no (7) |
| 3.05.85 | Shirley Ann Durdin | Peake Bay, S. Australia | yes |
| 10.24.85 | Patrick Gee | East London, South Africa | no (7) |
| 9.03.86 | Philip de Bruyn | Dyer Island, South Africa | no (7) |
| 12.06.86 | Frank Gallo | Carmel, Cal. | no |
| 12.22.86 | Richard Olls | SAOU Beach, South Africa | yes (7) |
| 1.28.87 | Tommy Botha | Cape Province, South Africa | no (7) |
| 8.15.87 | Craig Rogers | Tunis Beach, Cal. | no |
| 9.13.87 | Peter McCallum | Cape Province, South Africa | no (7) |
| 10.12.87 | Dawid Smit | Cape Town, South Africa | no (7) |
| 4.24.88 | Mark Rudy | Morro Bay, Cal. | no |
| 8.11.88 | Carl Lafazio | Crescent City, Cal. | no |
| 12.15.88 | Juan Avalos | Valparaiso, Chile | yes |
| 1.26.89 | Tamara McCallister | Malibu, Cal. | yes |

(*table continued*)

| Date | Victim | Location | Fatal? |
|---|---|---|---|
| 1.26.89 | Roy J. Stoddard | Malibu, Cal. | yes |
| 9.9.89 | Mark Tisserand | Farallon Islands, Cal. | no |
| 9.17.89 | Gerjo van Niekerk | Smitswinkel Bay, South Africa | no (7) |
| 10.23.89 | Wyndham Kapan | Cannon Beach, Oregon | no |
| 11.26.89 | Gerjo van Niekerk | Smitswinkel Bay, South Africa | yes (7) |
| 1.12.90 | Sean Sullivan | Montara, Cal. | no |
| 6.24.90 | Monique Price | Mossel Bay, South Africa | no (7) |
| 8.9.90 | Rodney Orr | Jenner, Cal. | no |
| 8.28.90* | Rodney Swan | Trinidad Head, Cal. | no |

(1) Shultz and Malin, 1963     (5) Egaña and McCosker, 1984
(2) Gudger, 1950               (6) Wallett, 1983
(3) Kean, 1944                 (7) Levine, 1988
(4) Miller and Collier, 1981

TOTALS: California, 56; South Africa, 31; Australia, 11; Oregon, 6; Chile, 4; New Zealand, 2; Argentina, 1; Italy, 1; Massachusetts, 1; Mexico, 2; Panama, 1.

NOTES: Except for the fatal attack on Terry Manuel, "events" involving Australian abalone divers have been omitted from this list. The divers are in a line of work in which they almost expect to be attacked; to have included their experiences would have been like including racing-car accidents in a list of highway automobile accidents.

Attacks in the vicinity of Bodega Bay, California, are recorded as such here, for simplicity. They did not occur within the Bay.

*On July 1, 1991, while this book was in press, Eric Larsen, a 32-year-old California surfer, was attacked by a white shark near Año Nuevo Island. Nearly ten hours of surgery and more than 400 stitches were required to close the wounds to his left leg and arms. The scenario was typical of the recent California attacks: the shark delivered a massive bite that did not kill the surfer, and rapid medical attention saved his life.

bitten on the lower left leg. But although he was severely lacerated, no bones were crushed and no arteries were severed, and Dunn made a full recovery.

Using dynamite, guns, harpoons, spears, and nets, the residents of Matawan assaulted the waterways, hoping to capture or kill all of the sharks in the vicinity. Although many sharks were thus dispatched, it was never proved that any of them was responsible for the attacks in Matawan Creek. (Conceivably, the earlier attacks at Beach Haven and Spring Lake were the work of a single shark, but even that seems unlikely.) For two days, the newspapers were full of shark reports and stories of "monsters" caught in the region. Then, on July 14, a 7.5- to 8.5-foot white shark was trapped in a drift net in Raritan Bay—just 4 miles northeast of the mouth of Matawan Creek—and bludgeoned to death by a man named Michael Schleisser. When this shark was cut open, it was found to contain 15 pounds of flesh and assorted bone fragments, which may or may not have been human. (One of those who "positively" identified the remains as human was Dr. Frederick A. Lucas, director of the American Museum of Natural History in New York, who only a few days earlier was quoted in the newspapers as saying that sharks could not possibly inflict the kind of damage that was done to Bruder.)

On the front page of *The Home News* ("For the People of Harlem and the Heights") for July 19, 1916, is a photograph of Michael Schleisser and the white shark. The headline of the accompanying story reads, "Harlem Man in Tiny Boat Kills a 7 1/2-Foot Man-Eating Shark," and the subhead read, "Beats it to Death with Broken Oar, Directly off Matawan Creek,

Where Two Brothers Were Attacked and Killed by Sea-Tiger Last Week. Examination By Director of Museum of Natural History Shows Human Bones in Shark's Stomach."

Schleisser and his friend John Murphy had gone fishing from South Amboy (New Jersey), setting a small drag net that then snagged the monster. The shark towed their 8-foot motorboat on a wild, stern-first ride, but Schleisser finally killed it by repeatedly bashing it on the head with a broken oar. The 350-pound carcass was taken to the offices of the newspaper at 125th Street, where "the yawning jaws and vicious teeth" were viewed—according to an article the following Sunday—by "at least 30,000 men, women, and children."

Sharks—especially those that were suspected of being maneaters—were an unusual sight in New York City. One woman called it "cute," and a man maintained that the fish in the window was not a shark at all, because the mouth of a shark was on the side, not on the front, and he identified the fish as a porpoise.

Even though the great white shark had not then achieved any particular notoriety, the "evidence" of the human flesh and bones satisfied various experts that the "Jersey Man-eater" had been caught. Secondary, or circumstantial, evidence came to light in 1950, when E. W. Gudger, also of the American Museum of Natural History, published a paper on a fatal shark attack in Buzzard's Bay, Massachusetts, that had taken place in 1936. The details of this attack will follow, but relating the Buzzard's Bay attack to other attacks, Gudger said that he remembered seeing in a fish shop a set of jaws labeled "The Jaws of the New Jersey Man-Eater." He wrote: "I examined these jaws and noted the characteristic broadly triangular saw-edged teeth, which showed that these teeth came from a *Carcharodon carcharias*—and presumably from the New Jersey shark of

VICIOUS LOOKING HEAD of a blue-nose shark caught yesterday off Belford, New Jersey. The body measured 9¼ feet long. Belford is less than ten miles from the mouth of Matawan Creek, in which a man and a boy were killed and another boy seriously mangled by a man-eating shark. It is possible that this picture shows the head of the monster that has been terrorizing the New Jersey shore for ten days past.

On July 15, 1916, shark hunters caught this "blue-nose shark" (probably a bull shark) off Belford, New Jersey, during the frenzied hunt for the Jersey maneater.

Michael Schleisser poses with the 7.5-foot white shark he and a friend killed in Raritan Bay, New Jersey, in July 1916. Because the attacks ceased, many people believed that this shark had been the culprit.

1916." The shark caught by Michael Schleisser in Raritan Bay probably was a white, but only the flesh and bones in its stomach tie it to the New Jersey attacks, and none too conclusively.

White sharks are known to inhabit the Mid-Atlantic Bight (Raritan Bay is an arm of the Bight), but there is no evidence that they have ever demonstrated an inclination to enter fresh water, there or anywhere else in the world. That particular propensity is characteristic—and even diagnostic—of only one species of large shark, the bull shark. The earlier attacks at Beach Haven and Spring Lake were probably the work of one or another species of carcharhinid sharks, but despite the contrary "evidence," the Matawan attacks were probably committed by a single shark—very likely a bull shark, to judge from the nature and freshwater site of the attacks. Since whatever evidence there was is long gone, we are free to imagine—as Richard Fernicola does—a single white shark, finding itself in Matawan Creek and in a panic, swimming back and forth biting people, then escaping to Raritan Bay, where it is caught and killed by Michael Schleisser.

The aforementioned study by Gudger details a single attack on a 16-year-old boy named Joseph Troy, who was swimming about 150 yards offshore at Mattapoisett, Buzzard's Bay, Massachusetts, in 1936. Troy's left leg was seized and he was dragged under the water. His companion pulled the bleeding boy to shore, and he was taken to New Bedford Hospital, some 11 miles away. Five hours after the attack, he died from shock and loss of blood.

Relying on the report of Dr. Hugh M. Smith, a fisheries biologist at Woods Hole, Massachusetts, Gudger discusses at some length the identity of the attacking shark, and from the description of its color ("an unusual amount of white on the sides") and the shape of its tail, concludes that "it clearly appears that the offending shark was a man-eater (*Carcharodon carcharias*) estimated to be 10 or 12 feet long." Furthermore, Gudger lists twenty "definite records of *Carcharodon* in and near Buzzard's Bay from

1871 to 1927," and details the years in which they were sighted, and by whom. (A man named Vinal Edwards, who was "particularly on the lookout for sharks," seems to have sighted most of them.) Since there had been no recorded shark attacks—by any species—along the Massachusetts coast for the 65 years in question, this one was completely unexpected. Although white sharks seem to be not uncommon in Buzzard's Bay today, Gudger wrote that "it may truly be said that the chance of being bitten by a shark in these waters is about on all fours with the chance of being struck by lightning in these same regions." And indeed, since the 1936 incident, there has not been a documented white shark attack in Northeastern waters, even though great white sharks have clearly been present.

In an article in *Military Surgeon* in 1929, Colonel J. M. Phalen wrote, "Here in Panama, it was not uncommon to hear the opinion expressed that the shark did not attack man." The people who expressed that opinion were wrong. In 1928, 17-year-old Abraham Moreno had been attacked by a carcharhinid shark in Panama Bay and killed. Some 15 years later, a sailor was swimming off Rey Island in the Gulf of Panama (both Panama Bay and the Gulf of Panama are on the Pacific side of Panama) when he was attacked by a shark in full view of his shipmates. His left leg was badly lacerated, and although a tourniquet was applied and he was rushed to the nearby naval hospital, he died of loss of blood within three hours. Tooth fragments removed from the man's leg were sent to John T. Nichols, curator of fishes at the American Museum of Natural History in New York, and according to Dr. B. H. Kean, who wrote up the incident for the *Journal of the American Medical Association* in 1944, they were identified as "tips of the teeth of a small so-called man-eater shark, *Carcharodon carcharias*, and from a small individual of this species, probably not more than 7 or so feet long."

The waters of southeastern Australia, particularly around the popular beaches of Sydney, have long been reputed to be shark-infested. In 1938, according to Gilbert Whitley, there were 557 sharks "of varieties considered dangerous" caught along the surfing beaches of Sydney: hammerheads, whalers (a group including the bull shark), tiger sharks, grey nurses, and unspecified "pointers." Today, many of Sydney's beaches are "meshed": steel nets are hung from poles and cables offshore expressly to keep the sharks and the bathers separated. The Shark Menace Advisory Committee, established by the government of New South Wales, devised the scheme in 1934, and the Sydney system was adapted in the 1960's to the beaches of Durban and the Natal coast, in South Africa, in response to a grisly series of shark attacks there. In both South Africa and New South Wales the system is still in use. (The nets do have their dark side: a great many fishes and marine mammals become trapped in them and die.)

Dr. Victor Coppleson, a Sydney surgeon with an interest in the medical aspects of the interactions of sharks and people, had by 1958 accumulated enough data to publish *Shark Attack*, a summary of his findings

# The Bull Shark

Curiously, the great white shark may not top the list of identified perpetrators of attacks on humans. This honor may go to the bull shark, which, under many different names and in many parts of the world, has probably attacked more people than any other species of shark. Because data from tropical regions of the world are difficult to collect and verify, we cannot make that charge with assurance, but in his comprehensive *Sharks of the World*, Leonard Compagno writes, "It would not surprise the writer if this species turned out to be the most dangerous living shark because of its large size, massive jaws and proportionately very large teeth, abundance in the tropics, . . . indiscriminate appetite and propensity to take largish prey, and *close proximity to human activities in both fresh and salt water*." Italics have been added to emphasize the inshore habitat of this species, since "proximity to human activities" is obviously a major contributing factor in attacks on swimmers and divers.

Before zoological science "synonymized" them into the single, nearly pantropical species we now recognize as *Carcharhinus leucas*, many different names were accorded the bull shark. In Central America it was known as *Carcharhinus nicaraguensis*, the Lake Nicaragua shark. In East Africa, it was *C. zambezensis*, the Zambezi shark. In South Africa, it was *C. vanrooyeni*, Van Rooyen's shark. In India it was *C. gangeticus*, the Ganges River shark. And in Australasia, it was *C. amboinensis*. (If this is not confusing enough, *C. amboinensis* is now the name of the Java shark, a separate species.)

Whatever its name, however, the bull shark is far more common than the white shark, and therefore just as dangerous to humans. It just doesn't *look* as ferocious, and although it cannot chomp with the authority of a large great white, its bite has often been fatal (see in particular the South African histories beginning on p. 174). It is a typical carcharhinid shark, grayish in color, with a rounded snout and small eyes. It reaches a maximum length of 10 feet, and at that size it will weigh about 400 pounds. The white shark can be double the length and nearly ten times the maximum weight of a bull shark, and it has acquired a reputation that is commensurate with its size and fearsomeness, if not its numbers. Whereas the white shark is a fairly rare species, the bull shark is common throughout the warm-temperate and tropical waters of the world, and it displays a marked inclination to enter shallow and even fresh water. (One was found as far up the Mississippi as Alton, Illinois, 1,750 miles from the sea!)

It was this inclination to enter fresh water, unique among the big sharks, that resulted in the classification of the "Lake Nicaragua Shark" as a separate species. It was thought to be strictly a resident of the lake until the 1960's, when Dr. Thomas Thorson and his students decided to go to Nicaragua and see for themselves. They tagged bull sharks in the Caribbean and later recovered them in the lake, thus demonstrating that the sharks could and did ascend the river, and dispelling the notion that the species was a "landlocked version" of the bull shark.

*Richard Ellis*

OPPOSITE: The bull shark, *Carcharhinus leucas*, shown eating a South African fish known as the white steenbras (*Lithognathus lithognathus*). Very common in the tropical seas of the world, the bull shark may be responsible for more attacks on people than is the white shark, though less often fatally.

and opinions. Although many of Coppleson's conclusions have now been discounted—for instance, he supported the "rogue shark" theory, which argues that a given shark, having tasted human flesh, continues to haunt a particular area in search of more—he did assemble an extensive list of known or suspected attacks in Australian waters and elsewhere. In only a few cases does he identify the attacker, but he did write that the white shark is the "most ferocious," and that it "moves swiftly through the water . . . and usually follows ships, trailing them for long distances."

In southeastern Australia, most of the attacks have been committed by the various carcharhinids that Australians know as "whalers," including the bronze whaler, *Carcharhinus brachyurus*, and the bull shark, *Carcharhinus leucas*. It is therefore interesting to compare Coppleson's records with the 1916 New Jersey attacks, since the conditions around Sydney are quite similar to those of the Jersey shore, and the resident shark species, especially the bull, are known attackers. In a 1987 review of Australian shark attacks, Roland Hughes wrote of the bull shark, "It frequents shallow water near beaches, and is a versatile and opportunistic feeder that will attack without provocation."

According to a report published in the Sydney newspaper *The Sun* for February 16, 1930, 18-year-old Norman Clark "was seized by a monster shark while bathing off Middle Brighton Pier . . . and was terribly mauled and dragged into the bay. His body has not been recovered." In a subsequent review of the incident by Lewis Radcliffe of the U.S. Bureau of Fisheries, the shark was described as having been "between 15 and 20 feet long." Radcliffe tentatively identified the species as *Carcharhinus arenarius*, a grey nurse, but this species (now known as *Eugomphodus taurus*) rarely reaches a length of 10 feet. The whalers, the other possible suspects, also do not reach 15 feet, so if the size estimate is correct (under the circumstances, the observers could easily have got it wrong), the only possible culprit would have to have been a white pointer.

This "photograph" appeared in the tabloid *National Examiner* for August 21, 1990. It is reproduced here without permission (requests went unanswered) and without comment.

Years later in South Australia, four divers were attacked by white sharks over a four-year period, and there was no question whatsoever about the species of attacker. In March 1961, Brian Rodger was spearfishing off Aldinga Beach, some 55 miles south of Adelaide. As he was about to dive after a pair of kingfish, a shark grabbed his left leg. Rodger twisted himself in the shark's grip and tried to poke it in the eye. But in pain and panic, he managed only to jam his hand down the shark's throat, ripping his arm on the finely serrated teeth. The shark in any case released its grip momentarily, and as it came back toward him, Rodger shot it in the head with his speargun. The shark swam off—perhaps not accustomed to such a powerful and determined defense—and Rodger swam toward shore. He was picked up by a rescue boat and rushed to the Royal Adelaide Hospital. Although he had lost a great deal of blood and was verging on shock, he was saved. More than 200 stitches were required to sew him up. Brian Rodger, a knowledgeable diver, was in a position to see the shark perfectly, and he knows it was a white pointer (as the Aussies call them), about 12 feet long.

Brian Rodger was attacked by a white pointer in 1961, off Aldinga Beach, South Australia, while taking part in a spearfishing competition. His leg still shows the massive scars left by the shark's teeth.

The next year, while 16-year-old Geoff Corner was participating in a spearfishing contest in about 25 feet of water off Caracalinga Head, South Australia, he was attacked by a large white shark. His companion, Allen Phillips, banged the shark on the head with the paddles from the surf ski they had been using, and the shark released its grip and lay below the surf ski, waiting. (A surf ski is a large surfboard that the rider sits on and paddles like a kayak.) When Phillips then tried to pull Corner onto the ski, he found that he was already dead. The shark followed them into shore, but never attacked again. Phillips recognized the species by its pointed snout and black eye, and in retrospect the shark seems to have exhibited the "bite-and-wait" tactic that seems to characterize the attack behavior of the great white shark.

Then in 1963, in what is perhaps the best-known of all shark attacks, Rodney Fox was savagely mauled by a white pointer. He too was in a contest off Aldinga Beach, where Brian Rodger had been attacked. Perhaps it is a reflection of the Australian character—or foolhardiness—that these intrepid divers kept holding these contests in the same waters year after year, despite what had become annual attacks. Aware by now of the terrible risks, the contest organizers had at least changed the rules so that the divers no longer competed with strings of bleeding fish attached to their belts. Now they were required to hand over each catch to partners in the nearby boats.

Fox was diving after a large dusky morwong (a bottom fish of the kelp beds) when he felt a blow on his right side as violent as if he had been struck by a moving car. He found himself in the mouth of a white shark, and the shark was squeezing his midsection with its powerful jaws. Like Rodger, Fox tried to poke the shark in the eye, but like Rodger he succeeded only in jamming his hand into the shark's mouth. For whatever reason, the shark released him and he swam toward the surface. But this shark did not stand off and wait; it closed again with the badly injured diver. Fox managed to wrap his arms around it—to prevent it from biting him again—and this time it took him toward the bottom. Because he was running out of air—and out of blood, though he would not know that until later—he let go of the shark and struggled back to the surface through water that was rust-red with his own blood. The shark followed him up, and just when Fox was prepared to meet his maker, the shark veered off, took the fish line that hung from Fox's waist, and dragged him down again. Evidently, the teeth of the shark severed the line, for Fox was suddenly free of the pressure that had seemed to be pulling him to his death. (He later commented that "It seemed ridiculous to drown after all I'd been through.") When he was pulled into a boat that had responded to his cries, it was seen that his ribcage, lungs, and upper abdomen had been punctured, his ribs were crushed, and he had obviously lost a lot of blood. The arm that he had poked into the shark's mouth was bare to the bone. He was held together by his wetsuit.

A near-miraculous series of events saved Fox's life. The boat had been on the scene and had got him quickly ashore. There was an ambulance on the beach, and it rushed him to hospital in less than an hour. On duty in the emergency room of the Royal Adelaide Hospital was a surgeon who had returned from England that very day from a specialized course in chest surgery. Operating immediately, he took 462 stitches to sew Fox together again.

Just three months after his near-fatal attack, Rodney was back in the water, and the following year the South Australian Team Championships were won by Brian Rodger, Bruce Farley, and Rodney Fox. He became a professional abalone diver, working the same dangerous waters, and he also began a legendary career of diving in shark cages with visiting photographers and scientists. In the course of things he has become one of the world's foremost authorities on the natural behavior of the great white shark.

Several years ago, Fox gave up abalone diving, because it was "too bloody dangerous." Ab divers risk not only shark attacks, but also the bends, air embolisms, bone necrosis, and even brain damage from remaining under water for six to seven hours at a time. "I only have one body," said Fox, "and I nearly lost it once already." Although he now restricts his professional diving to the shark cages, he still loves to dive recreationally, and he is probably one of the best all-around divers in the world.

Although there were no more attacks off South Australia (the *state,* that is) from 1963 to 1974, the white pointers continued to seek seals elsewhere in southern Australian waters. In 1964, Henri Bource was diving off Lady Julia Percy Island, south of Port Fairy, Victoria, the source of the British Museum's mis-measured Port Fairy jaws. Bource, a cinematographer, wanted to film the sea lions that hauled out on the island. (His story is told in Hugh Edwards's 1975 *Sharks and Shipwrecks.*)

Alone with the sea lions, Bource suddenly noticed a strange and eerie silence, and the pinnipeds seemed to vanish. He dived to the bottom, then surfaced to look around. At that moment he was smashed by what he later described as "a tremendous force." His mask and snorkel were ripped off during the attack, and in excruciating pain he too tried to poke the shark in the eye. (That these Australians would all try to poke the shark in the eye suggests that they knew—old wives' tales or not—about the

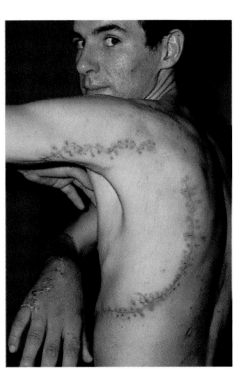

Rodney Fox shows some of the 462 stitches that were required to sew him up after the 1963 attack at Aldinga Beach, South Australia.

Henri Bource of Victoria, Australia, prepares to dive again. He lost his left leg to a white shark off Lady Julia Percy Island in 1964.

sensitivity of white sharks' eyes.) When Bource bobbed to the surface he realized to his horror that his left leg was gone below the knee. He was hauled aboard a boat that took him to shore at Port Fairy, where an ambulance was waiting. At Warranambool Hospital the flow of blood was stanched, and he survived to dive again.

Rarely does the attacking shark find itself on shore, but that is what happened at a beach north of Sydney, on the southeast coast of Australia, in February 1966. Thirteen-year-old Raymond Short was swimming at Coledale when something grabbed his right leg. He began to scream, and the lifesavers ran into the waist-deep water to rescue him. As they pulled him to shore, they saw that there was a shark hanging onto his leg. Because they couldn't pry the shark's jaws open, Raymond and the shark were dragged onto the beach together. One man repeatedly bashed the shark on the head with a surfboard, eventually causing it to relax its grip. Raymond was rushed to a hospital, and after a two-hour operation his leg was saved. The shark was identified as a young female white pointer, some 7 feet long and weighing about 300 pounds.

As their victimage suggests, there is probably no group of people in the world who have had as much firsthand experience with free-swimming great white sharks as the abalone divers of South Australia. The abalone "industry" took shape in 1964, when young Neil Williams decided he could make a living collecting "earfish" and selling the meat for two shillings and sixpence a pound to the South Australian Fisheries Collective, who would sell it abroad. (Even today, Australians do not consume much

Diving for abalones off South Australia has been a good deal safer since the introduction of the self-propelled cage.

of the abalone caught in their waters, and most of the firm, white meat is exported to Japan, Taipei, Bangkok, and Korea.) At first, Williams barely eked out a living, but as abalone prices rose, more divers joined him. It is a cold, wet, dangerous life, and in addition to the risks regularly attendant upon diving, ab divers constantly face the most serious threat of all: the white pointer.

The South Australian *Port Lincoln Times* is replete with stories of the narrow escapes of the ab divers. When Dick O'Brien encountered a white pointer in 1968, the shark actually attacked him, but he fended it off with his ab iron, a chisel-like bar used for prying the mollusks from the rocks. In November 1970, Graham McCallum took refuge in an underwater cave 60 feet down for over half an hour while a white pointer circled slowly overhead. Trevor Garnaut described his experience with a 12-footer that swam up to him in the waters off Thistle Island and circled him as he clung to the bottom: "My heart climbed into my mouth. The shark stopped 6 feet away and stared at me. It looked monstrous. . . . Finally it swam away, only to return. It did this four or five times, disappearing for a few minutes, only to swim back from another direction. I was not going to move." In November 1972, diver Colin Andrews was confronted by a white pointer "which swam right up to him and pushed at him with her nose." According to the newspaper account, "It was the first time in which an abalone diver has actually been touched by a white pointer."

Neil Williams, who started the whole business of diving for abalone, has had his own share of encounters with white pointers. Describing one that took place in 1972, he is quoted in the *Port Lincoln Times* as saying, "Many things went through my mind as the shark circled. Was I going to be the first abalone diver to be taken by a shark? After only brushing Colin, would it attack me? It opened and closed its mouth as it went by and I could see its teeth clearly."

As it turned out, it was not Williams but another abalone diver who became the first to be taken by a shark. On January 9, 1974, Terry Manuel was diving for abs near Streaky Bay, in the Great Australian Bight, that defines most of Australia's long southern coastline. The diver works the bottom, while in the boat his "sheller" waits for him to bring up a net bag of abalone. This time, Manuel surfaced some 150 yards from his boat screaming "Shark!" Sheller John Talbot gunned the boat toward Manuel, and as he tried to pull him into the boat, he saw that the diver's right leg was severed below the hip. A white shark, which he estimated to be about 10 feet long, continued to dispute Talbot for possession of the body in the blood-reddened water. "I could feel it pulling on him," said Talbot. When he finally got Manuel aboard, the diver was dead.

Less than two months after Terry Manuel was killed, divers were back in the waters of South Australia again. They were looking for great white sharks, not to kill them but to film them. The second unit of the film crew for "Jaws" had arrived in Port Lincoln to shoot the footage of real sharks that would be intercut with the shots of the model sharks that were being built in Hollywood. Ron and Valerie Taylor were the principal underwater camerapersons, and Rodney Fox was the principal advisor.

The abalone divers protested strongly that riling up the sharks would endanger their lives, and mounted several fishing expeditions to catch what they described as "educated" sharks in order to get them out of the water. Neil Williams was quoted in the *Port Lincoln Times* as saying, "The crews are stirring up normally docile sharks to attack cages. What happens to divers like us who do not have the protection of a cage? We appreciate that white pointers are potentially dangerous at any time, but this is markedly increasing the threat." Curiously, neither Williams nor the *Times* mentioned the death of Terry Manuel.

In December 1983, nine years later, Williams once again almost became a statistic. He had been diving off South Neptune Island when he found himself face to face with a 12-foot white pointer. "The shark opened its mouth as if it wanted to eat me, so I shoved the half-full bag of abs right into its mouth. . . . It was bloody lucky," explained Williams, "that the bag was half full. What if I'd just begun to fill it?" The shark chomped down on the mesh bag, lacerating Williams' fingers badly. Evidently finding a bag of rock-hard shells not to its liking, the shark turned and swam away, leaving Williams crouched on the bottom, holding his bleeding hand and trying to figure out how to keep the blood from attracting the shark again. As he watched the shark circle around him, he

Neil Williams, the man who invented the lucrative business of abalone diving in South Australia and retired in one piece years later, after several close encounters with white sharks.

held the bleeding hand tightly with the other. His main fear—other than that the shark would eat him—was that it could bite through his air hose. When he saw—or rather *hoped*—that the shark was not coming back, he swam to the surface and tumbled into the boat. Having got to the age of 48, perhaps Neil Williams has now had enough of abs and white pointers.

Williams had begun diving for abalone with a primitive scuba tank and home-made face-mask in 1964, but he and the other divers soon switched over to an on-board compressor that pumped air down to them through a hose as they scrabbled along the bottom. By monitoring the diver's bubbles the sheller could position the boat over the area where the diver was working. This procedure enabled the divers to stay below much longer, but of course some of them flagrantly abused this privilege, sometimes staying under for seven or eight hours at a time. A bubble-blowing, rock-knocking diver who stayed below for several hours was almost certain to attract the attention of South Australia's *other* great underwater predator.

More recently, a South Australian abalone diver named Jim Ellis invented a device whereby the odds, which had heretofore significantly favored the shark, have been brought to parity. Ellis developed a one-man shark cage that encloses the diver in a grid of steel mesh. Hydraulic controls allow him to direct the cage this way and that. All, of course, for protection from the great white.

But it was not only the ab divers who were at risk. On March 4, 1985, a great white shark proved once again that whatever else might be said about the species, the term "predictable" does not apply. Shirley Ann Durdin, a 33-year-old mother of four, was snorkeling in water about 7 feet deep in Peake Bay, just north of Port Lincoln. With her husband and another man, she had been diving in this shallow bay for scallops. The threesome was on its way to shore when Mrs. Durdin was savagely attacked, and in a spray of blood and froth, she was bitten in half by a white shark that was described by eyewitnesses as being 20 feet long. Fishermen on shore tried to get to her, but by the time they got their boats in the water, all they could see was the headless torso of the victim. And while they watched, the shark came back and made off with the rest of her body. It was the first fatal white shark attack in South Australian waters since the death of Terry Manuel in 1974, and the first time ever that an Australian victim was known to be eaten.

The west coast of Australia, some 3,000 miles from Sydney, is also home to white sharks, and where there are white sharks and swimmers, there is going to be some sort of collision. Bob Bartle and Lee Warner were diving at Jurien Bay, about 150 miles north of Perth in August 1967. Both men were spearfishing in the cold, wintry waters of the eastern Indian Ocean when a huge black shape hurtled beneath Warner and hit Bartle amidships. As the shark shook Bartle violently from side to side, Warner put his speargun on top of the shark's head where he reckoned the brain to be, and fired. It had no effect. The shark bit Bartle in half, and swam around with the man's legs protruding from its mouth. Warner tried again to shoot the shark, but from almost point-blank range, he missed. In Hugh Edwards' *Sharks and Shipwrecks*, Lee Warner is quoted as saying,

Abalone diver Jim Ellis, the inventor of the one-man self-propelled cage, showing one of the reasons he retired from the trade.

I saw Bob's gun, which was still loaded and floating just below the surface. I grabbed it gratefully, and swinging it around, tried to belt the spear into the shark's eye. But the eye was set close to the top of its head and somehow the spear just whistled harmlessly over the top of its head. It was the worst shot of my life. I don't know how I could have missed, and I've cursed myself a thousand times since.

Warner made it to shore and commandeered a boat to search for his friend's remains. They found Bartle's severed torso, and saw the shark slowly swimming away, close to the bottom. There is some doubt about the species of shark that killed Bob Bartle, since Warner has said that its jaw was "much wider than its body," a description that fits the tiger shark much better than it does the white. The method of attack, however, and the shaking of the body are characteristic of the white, and most authorities are prepared to chalk up another fatal attack to *Carcharodon*.

Two more Australian incidents, neither of them attacks, are worth noting. In one, a man saved a white shark from drowning, and in the other a man found himself in the nightmarish position of being in the water with feeding white sharks *in the dark*—and was not attacked. In both cases the man was Ron Taylor. In 1972, Ron, Valerie, and Rodney Fox were working with the Italian filmmaker Bruno Valatti off Dangerous Reef. On January 17, a 12-foot male became entangled in the steel trace that kept the cage suspended from the film boat *Temptation*. The shark plunged and bucked, yanking the cage below the surface with Ron and Valerie in it. The flotation tanks prevented the cage from being dragged far under, but they also put more and more strain on the cable as the shark writhed in its steel trap. Finally exhausted, the shark hung head-down alongside the cage. The crew towed it into shallow water and Ron removed the trace that had been strangling it. When the shark was free, Ron gave it a shove and it swam off.*

Near midnight *on the next day*, Ron and Rodney were working to tether the cages to Rodney's 20-foot abalone boat when Ron slipped on the

* A year later, another shark, this one a female, was trapped in the same way, and released in the same fashion.

With his "sheller" and his one-man cage, Port Lincoln abalone diver John Kroezen races to the site where he will dive for the valuable gastropods.

deck of the boat and fell into the dark water where three big sharks were feeding on half a horse. "I knew that Ron would not survive," wrote Valerie. "He would die, torn to pieces in the cold black southern ocean." The currents pulled Ron and the boat farther apart, but he managed to swim to the boat in the dark, with the sharks gnashing and gurgling around him. Rodney hauled him out of the water just as one of the sharks passed beneath his legs, illuminated by the eerie overhead lights of the film boat. If Ron Taylor had not believed the story of Androcles and the lion before these incidents, he probably subscribed to it afterwards.

South Australia is famous for its white sharks and infamous for its white shark attacks, and it is where great whites are most easily studied, but it is not where the greatest number of white shark attacks occur. That distinction belongs to California. The coastline between Monterey Bay and Tomales Point, centering on San Francisco and the Farallon Islands, has been called the Red Triangle, as well as the White Shark Attack Capital of the World. Of all the documented white shark attacks throughout the world, just over half have occurred along this 120-mile stretch of water.

Daniel Miller, of the California Department of Fish and Game, and Ralph Collier, an amateur shark attack analyst, prepared a comprehensive study of white shark attacks in California and Oregon. For this 1981 report, they tracked down and analyzed 47 unprovoked attacks, and interviewed most of the survivors of the attacks. Although they were looking for attacks by any species, they concluded "that the principal attacking species from Point Conception and San Miguel Island northwards was the white shark." And although all of California and Oregon were studied, "the frequency of shark attacks in the 100-mile area between Año Nuevo Island and Bodega Bay [the heart of the Red Triangle] is ten times greater than the frequency of attacks over the remainder of the California coastline."

Before leaping to the conclusion that this region is teeming with maneating sharks (which it is, comparatively speaking), it is important to realize that there are more people keeping track of the attacks here than anywhere else, and we therefore risk having a very biased sample. Moreover, there are probably more shark researchers in California than anywhere else, among them Robert Lea, David Ainley, W. I. Follett, Greg Cailliet, Ralph Collier, Peter Klimley, Daniel Miller, and the junior author of this book, to name only the more prominent. With all these folks swapping information, it is likely that every bump and scratch will be recorded—within hours. (While there are white sharks aplenty in South Africa and Australia, the experts are concentrated in California.)

When did the California attacks begin? One might assume that early coastal Indians held the great white shark in respect. Anthropologists can recreate the marine fare of these Indians on the basis of midden studies. These prehistoric garbage dumps, often of considerable size, were replete with fish bones, sea otter parts, and the shells of clams and abalones. In order to capture such prey, the Indians would have had to enter the do-

An abalone diver in South Australia waters in the one-man, self-propelled shark cage. Ab divers encounter white pointers as a regular part of their work, but before the introduction of the mobile cage, free-swimming divers encountering free-swimming sharks were at grave risk.

main of the shark, and it is therefore likely that off some fog-shrouded subtidal beach, an indigenous Californian met an indigenous *Carcharodon*. The rest is forgotten oral history.

It was not until 1926 that a modern Californian, Indian or otherwise, was attacked by a shark, but even that attack cannot be blamed on *Carcharodon* with any degree of assurance. Young Norman Peixotto was swimming with his dog on July 8, 1926, at San Leandro Bay, a southeastern arm of San Francisco Bay. Newspapers reported that they had not been in the water long when a "5-foot-long shark" hurled itself at the dog. As the injured animal swam for shore, the shark turned on the boy. Twice he was pulled beneath the surface before he was saved by an oncoming boat. Peixotto and the dog suffered serious cuts, but both survived.

The reported length of the shark would appear too small for an attacking *Carcharodon* (the small ones seem never to attack large prey), and the circumstances surrounding the Peixotto incident allow considerable margin for error. Still, we include the account here because a small white shark is the most likely culprit. (Since then, there has not been another record of *Carcharodon* within the Bay, a happy circumstance probably best explained by the many significant changes in Bay ecology, the increase in boat traffic, and a substantial reduction in the pinniped populations on which white sharks normally feed.)

The first confirmed California white shark attack occurred December 7, 1952. Seventeen-year-old Barry Wilson was swimming off Pacific Grove in Monterey Bay, about 25 yards offshore, in rough, murky water about 30 feet deep. Observed by an onlooker on a nearby hillside some 30 yards away, a white shark, estimated to have been 12 to 13 feet in length, grabbed Wilson from beneath. In his book *Shark Attack*, David Baldridge recounted the viewer's experience:

OPPOSITE: In 1972, a white shark became entangled in the mooring lines from a cage off Australia and nearly drowned. Here, Ron and Valerie Taylor dive to free it.

LEFT: After freeing the shark and dragging it to shore, the Taylors took its temperature and released it.

He saw Wilson suddenly jerk himself around in the water and peer in all directions. A look of terror appeared on the swimmer's face as the shark showed itself, deliberately approaching the youth on the surface. It struck from the front, heaving the boy out of the water to the level of his thighs. Wilson fell back into the water and was immediately pulled under, with both hands on the shark's back and pushing at arm's length trying to free himself. He reappeared in the center of the bloodied water and screamed for help while frantically striking at the water with his hands. The shark was then seen to make two close passes before disappearing momentarily from view. The man up on the rocks shouted to the second swimmer who, completely ignoring the great danger to himself, went immediately to the aid of his friend and began towing him ashore. Soon he was joined by four members of a skindiving club who had been swimming about 150–200 yards from Wilson. While these men were attempting to pass an inflated rubber tube around the inert victim, Wilson's body gave a lunge as if someone had pushed him from behind. . . . Swirls of water could be felt on the legs of the swimmers as the fish passed very near to them. It seemed that the shark would come closer whenever the swimmers stopped kicking their feet while attempting to rearrange Wilson's body on the tube. Yet at no time did it appear to try to bite any of the rescuers.

Wilson was dead when they brought him ashore, having succumbed to exsanguination from a severed femoral artery and massive flesh excision. The event would be repeated time and again in subsequent decades.

Over the next seven years, four more Northern California swimmers were attacked and two died. Perhaps the most frightening attack occurred at the entrance to San Francisco's Golden Gate on May 7, 1959, an experience still vividly remembered by residents because of the heroic efforts of a teenage girl to save the victim. Albert Kogler was enjoying a late afternoon swim with Shirley O'Neill at Baker's Beach. As David Baldridge writes in his book *Shark Attack* (basing his story on contemporaneous newspaper accounts), the two were treading water about 50 yards from shore, casually chatting and looking around. As the girl turned away from her companion, she heard him scream. She looked and saw an enormous shark at the surface between them. He screamed "It's a shark—get out of here!" She recalled,

It was just blood all over—I knew I couldn't leave him—he just kept screaming and screaming. I could tell the fish was chewing him up. It was a horrible scream. He was shouting 'Help me, help me!' I grabbed for his hand, but when I pulled, I could see that his arm was just hanging on by a thread. So I grabbed him around his back, but it was all bloody and I could see the insides.

Demonstrating incredible fortitude, she swam with him to shore. Kogler was given last rites on the shore, where he died, just after sunset, from shock and massive hemorrhage.

The eleven attacks by white sharks along California in the 1960's were mostly upon abalone divers. The popularity of the sport and the delicacy of the gastropod had brought neoprene-suited snorkelers to the coast in droves, often to the Farallon Islands. The Farallones are small, rocky outposts, 26 miles off San Francisco, that are a haven for seabirds, sea lions, and white sharks. (A long-term study of the vast seabird rookeries on the Islands is reported in a study by Ainley and Boekelheide.) Scuba-diving classes and dive clubs often visited the islands, and the 1962 attack on Leroy French (Al Giddings' partner in the Bamboo Reef diving school) was not good for business.

Giddings and French had taken a class out to the islands on a mid-November day. As Giddings counted heads before raising the anchor, he realized that French was not on board. He scanned the water and was horrified to see French in the jaws of a white shark. Without thinking, Giddings leapt overboard and swam to French's assistance.

Upon returning to the site (with McCosker, years later), Giddings recalled the moment, forever embedded in his memory:

I saw a great tail come up over Leroy's head, behind him. He couldn't see it, but he could see reflected in my eyes the terror and total amazement and could hear the rush of water behind him. And of course he had already been hit once, so he knew it was coming again. Before my unbelieving eyes, the tail went up, then went down alongside him. [Leroy] disappeared and was gone. I continued to the spot where he had disappeared, and as I was looking around frantically, he popped up next to me, clawing, spitting, and screaming in a way that I would not have thought humanly possible. Somehow I swam behind him, turned him on his back, and took off with him. We got to the boat and lifted him out of the water, blood all over, all over me. We got him on deck and applied a tourniquet. A helicopter took him out. Two years and 450 stitches later, he was walking again.

There would be 33 more attacks by white sharks along the central California coast during the 1970's and 80's, but during this period only one swimmer was attacked; the remainder of the victim list consisted of eleven surface snorkelers and abalone divers, ten surfers, four scuba divers, five hookah divers, a kayaker (or perhaps two), and a paddleboarder. The increase in total attacks, with a concurrent reduction in the number of attacks on swimmers, can be attributed to changing patterns in people's marine behavior. Our species learns—slowly and sometimes painfully—to avoid certain life-threatening situations. For the most part, Californians stopped swimming in shark-infested waters, but they did not anticipate the sharks' new preference for snorkelers and surfers, which, as we shall explain elsewhere, is probably a case of mistaken identity.

Surfers fasten their boards to their ankles with a "leash" made of elastic shock cord, so that if and when they fall off, they will remain attached to the board and will not have to chase it in to shore as it surfs itself away from them. This device, though it makes retrieving a lost board easier, has a downside: if attacked, the surfer cannot maneuver away from a shark. When Curt Vikan was surfing at Moonstone Beach in northern California's Humboldt County in October 1980, his board was ripped out from under him with tremendous force, and he watched in horror as a white shark estimated at 12 feet in length held the board out of the water and bit a chunk out of the end. Vikan himself was uninjured, and when the shark released the board, Vikan caught a wave and headed for shore. (Some four years later, another surfer, William Kennedy, was also attacked at Moonstone Beach.)

The fatal and much-publicized attack that took place during the week before Christmas in 1981 clearly exemplifies the disproportionate fear that surrounds all shark attacks. Disproportionate, you will ask? Lewis Boren died, after all. Both his body and his surfboard were penetrated in a single closure of the giant fish's jaws. But the newspapers for the day he

# Of Seals and Surfboards

The first recorded white shark attack on a surfer occurred in Hawaii in 1969. Since 1972, there have been at least 20 attacks on surfers in California and Oregon, and many near-misses. But surfers were paddling around in the same "shark-infested" waters long before that. What explains the dramatic increase in attacks? I believe it is the introduction of the short surfboard.

The early Hawaiians rode the waves (usually straight in to shore) on 18-foot, 100-pound planks of koa wood. Gradually, smaller and smaller boards came into use, but it was not until the late 1950's that styrofoam and fiberglass began to be used in the manufacture of surfboards. Even then, the surfboard remained a great heavy plank, and the surfers were primarily concerned with riding the larger waves and avoiding "wipeouts" in the crashing surf. But the emphasis shifted from simply surviving a wave-born ride to performing acrobatic feats on the face of a smaller wave, and accordingly the boards evolved further, becoming steadily smaller and more maneuverable. By the early 1970's the boards had become so small that a surfer lying on one found his or her legs trailing behind him, well off the board (the shorter board had no effect on the arms, which had *always* been used for paddling). It is not difficult to imagine that, silhouetted from below, a surfer on a 5-foot surfboard, with arms *and* legs gyrating, closely resembles a seal. And if the surfer, from beneath, looks like a seal to a human observer, with the ability to make sophisticated distinctions, imagine what it must look like to a shark, for whom anything that looks like a seal probably *is* a seal.

To test my theories, I went back to South Australia with Al Giddings and Rodney Fox in 1985. I was planning to present the sharks with "humans" in various attack situations: the surface diver, the surfer on a short board, the scuba diver on the bottom. Instead of sacrificing our own bodies in the interests of science, however, we used mannequins. We dressed the dummies in brand-new O'Neill wetsuits, and prepared for some pretty indelicate experiments. The sharks, which had been attracted by Rodney's odoriferous chum slick, attacked the surfboard riders and surface divers—shaking them so vigorously that had they been real divers, they would surely have been killed—but they ignored the dummy on the bottom.

We now knew that the sharks would attack anything that even moderately resembled a seal on the surface, but we weren't so sure about the wet-suited dummies that had been weighted to sit or stand on the bottom. Adult white sharks, particularly in Australian waters where their primary food is sea lions, probably prefer to attack moving prey. I felt that we hadn't proved anything by leaving a stiff, vaguely anthropoid object on the bottom. Something more was required to convince my companions, and even myself, that adult white sharks will attack only at the surface, but the idea of using humans as experimental attack victims seemed to go beyond good sense.

A shark's-eye view of a surfer on a small surfboard. It may be that sharks mistake this silhouette for that of a seal.

So I went down in one cage with Al and a mannequin, and Rodney and Chuck Nicklin (another photographer) went down in the other. The dummy was the least nervous of us all, unaware that it risked grievous harm. Three 12- to 14-foot sharks soon appeared. Giddings attached a line and a weight to the mannequin, so that it could be tethered to the bottom. And as we timed the movement of the sharks, he opened the cage door and went out. The moment of truth had arrived, and the dictum "publish or perish" took on a whole new meaning.

Al dragged the dummy along the sandy bottom, struggling with its weight. Rather than try to swim, he had overweighted himself with an additional 20 pounds and had deliberately left his fins behind. He looked as if he were lumbering along in dream time as he hauled the dummy well away from the cage, so that our influence on the sharks' behavior would be minimized. But through the foggy faceplate, I could see the fear in Al's eyes as he slowly made his way back to the cage with the three maneaters returning to the scene. To the best of our knowledge, Al had done what no one had attempted before: he had ventured out among adult white sharks and returned to the cage.

Once again safe in the cage, Al and I watched the sharks as they swam alongside us and alongside the mannequin. But they did nothing. And we waited. At 60 feet, the standard dive tables suggest that we were approaching a 60-minute limit, and this was not our first

OPPOSITE: With the mannequin posed seductively to his right, Al Giddings tests his "shark intimidation theory." The shark is not amused.

BELOW; A white shark attacks a floating dummy in a wet suit during a series of experiments off South Australia.

dive of the day. Because we were running out of time, I decided to make the inanimate dummy a little more attractive to the sharks, so I tied a short line to a ten-pound tuna (we had brought baits down with us in the cage), and followed Al out of the cage. We attached the tuna to the mannequin to imitate the heedless practice of some spearfishermen, and returned it to the bottom. Just as we regained the safety of the cage, one of the sharks began to take notice of the mannequin, and after several passes it couldn't resist. It gobbled up the tuna and gnawed the midsection of the dummy.

Because we were running out of

air and concerned about the nitrogen accumulating in our blood, we retrieved the mangled remains of our mannequin and floated the cages to the surface. In the safety (but hardly the comfort) of the galley of the *Nenad* we discussed what had happened. We all agreed that it is safer to be on the bottom than at the surface in the presence of white sharks (see the story of Neil Williams, p. 153), but since the diver ultimately must come up for air and the shark need not, this defense leaves something to be desired. We also concluded that only mad dogs, Englishmen, and dedicated scientists should wander around on the bottom of the ocean

On the bottom, a young male goes for the mannequin—now that a large chunk of tuna has been added to its accessories.

in the presence of adult white sharks.

The following year, in the same place—and probably with some of the same sharks—a group of adventurous scientists and filmmakers left the cages, and indeed wandered around on the bottom in the presence of adult white sharks. Bob Johnson, Marty Snyderman, and Howard Hall, having filmed an episode for "Wild Kingdom," took a walk on the bottom. There were no fewer than six sharks swimming around them, and, according to Johnson, "They didn't even seem interested in us." The divers brushed against the sharks, grabbed their pectorals, and even went for a short ride on the back of one of them. If anything, this behavior supports my hypothesis that white sharks are more interested in surface prey than in seafloor prey. And the shark that had attacked our mannequin the year before was no exception—it was interested only in the tuna we'd introduced to the situation.

*John McCosker*

**THE FAR SIDE**        By GARY LARSON

"What is this? ... Some kind of cruel hoax?"

was killed reported numerous highway deaths, Libyan assassination squads at work, leftists in Guatemala killing five policemen at random, and Poland preparing for strikes and forceful resistance to its oppressive military regime. The attack on Boren outdrew all these events for headlines.

By some strange coincidence, both of us were in Monterey on December 19th, the very Saturday that the Boren attack occurred. We were there to visit with Dave Powell, the Director of Husbandry at the then-under-construction Monterey Bay Aquarium. One of us (Richard) had come out from New York, and the other (John) drove down from San Francisco. We had lunch in a restaurant overlooking the Bay and we couldn't help noticing the threatening sea. A late morning blow had come up and the gray overcast skies were turning to rain. The sea was breaking at 8 to 10 feet, providing the kind of thrill that would attract only serious surfers. As we later learned, Boren had gone out late in the morning with friends, had come in for lunch, and had returned alone later in the afternoon, to catch the larger waves. He was riding a 5-foot 4-inch fiberglass board at Spanish Bay, near Asilomar, just south of Monterey. The following morning, surfers Christian Kai and David Murphy found the board with a large chunk missing from the left side. Farther up the beach they found the missing, jagged-edged piece. Boren's body was not discovered until Thursday, when it was found floating in a small cove almost one-half mile north of the bay.

McCosker joined Dan Miller, then a senior marine biologist with the California Department of Fish and Game, and Paul Crossman of the Monterey Coroner's Office, in attempting to explain what had happened to the surfer. An examination of the corpse and the board indicated that a very large shark had bitten through both as Boren was lying prone, obviously unaware of the shark's approach. His arms were evidently outstretched at the time of the attack, for the jaws had cut cleanly through the left ribs

Lewis Boren's surfboard. When Boren's body was recovered, it bore similar bite marks.

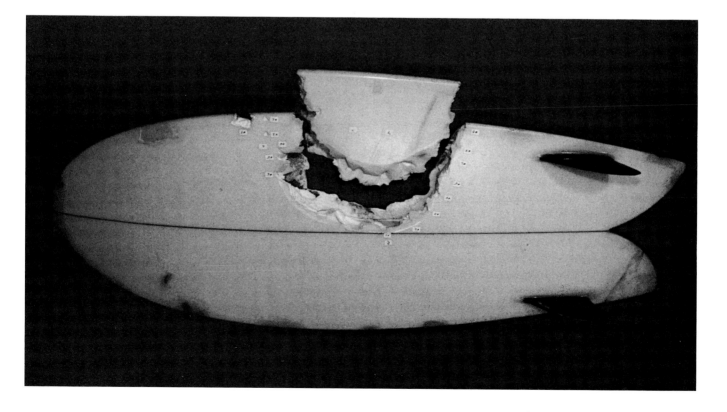

and chest. He probably died instantly. Bloodstains on the board proved not to be Boren's, but in fact were from the shark's gums.

The size of the jaw impressions on the board and on the body made it possible to estimate the size of the shark. Since the radius and circumference of the bite are affected by the extent of protrusion of the jaws, McCosker used the distance between puncture marks as an indicator of the shark's size. The shark had taken a bite that was 15.7 inches wide and 10.2 inches into the board, yet a count of the teeth indicated that the shark did not have the board all the way into its mouth. The distance between the second and third teeth on either side of the center of the jaw indicated that the shark was at least 18 feet in length, and perhaps as long as 20. It is not difficult to imagine the reaction of the press to such information.

A wake was held on a cold, windy night in Asilomar. Boren's fellow surfers built a large bonfire and sacrificed a few broken boards to the surf and shark gods. The surfing lanes were much less crowded in the months that followed. In May 1982, *Surfer* magazine published a full-page epitaph entitled "A Warning Dressed in White," in which the following appeared: "Neither Lewis nor the white menace will be forgotten. The big question that remains now is what's in store for people surfing in the Monterey area now that this killer has raised its ugly head?" A self-proclaimed shark-hunter soon headed for Monterey from San Francisco with the intention of killing the shark in the water, but he was arrested en route for carrying a concealed weapon, and was later hospitalized and placed under observation. The shark was neither captured nor seen again, and another five years would pass before a white shark would attack a human being in Monterey County.

Careful investigation of the events surrounding shark attacks have been conducted by H. David Baldridge of the U.S. Navy, Perry Gilbert of the Mote Marine Laboratory in Florida, David Davies of Durban, South Africa, and many other researchers. The Shark Attack File was maintained by the American Institute for Biological Sciences from 1959 until its defunding in 1973. In 1981 (as mentioned above), Daniel Miller, of the California Department of Fish and Game, and Ralph Collier, of the privately funded Shark Research Committee, Inc., published an exhaustive analysis of California and Oregon attacks from 1926 to 1979. Finally, Robert Lea, also of California Fish and Game, joined Miller in a 1985 update of attacks from 1980 to 1984. The combined data from all these studies have produced some very interesting information about white shark attacks. They show that in the northeastern Pacific, *Carcharodon* attacks occurred mostly north of Point Conception, California (and twice at Isla del Guadalupe, Baja California); that most attacks occurred in clear water at less than 60 degrees Fahrenheit; that shark attacks usually did not occur in kelp beds; that they occurred only during the day (which may say more about the behavior of people than about that of white sharks); that prior to the mid-1970's most of the attacks were on free-swimming skindivers, but that in later years surfers became the most common victims; that in nearly all cases, the victim was at the surface when the attack took place; and that he or she was "mugged" and spat out.*

* Attacks by sharks upon surfboards have caused some confusion in the record-keeping. Whereas some students of shark attacks consider any attack by a large shark to be life-threatening (even one on a fiberglass surfboard with no ensuing harm to the surfer), purists adhere to the view that in order to qualify as a legitimate attack, an incident has to affect a person. Nearly half of the recent attacks upon surfboards have left dental fragments and dents in the fiberglass but not in the surfer. We have excluded those attacks from this discussion.

### Confirmed, Unprovoked White Shark Attacks along Oregon, California, and Mexico, 1926–1990

| Coastline | Swimmer | Snorkeler | Surfer | Hookah | Scuba | Kayaker | Totals |
|---|---|---|---|---|---|---|---|
| Oregon | 1 | — | 6 | — | — | — | 7 |
| Central and Northern California | 8 | 23 | 14 | 5 | 4 | — | 54 |
| Southern California | — | — | — | — | — | 2 | 2 |
| Isla del Guadalupe, Mexico | — | 2 | — | — | — | — | 2 |
| Totals | 9 | 25 | 20 | 5 | 4 | 2 | 65 |
| Fatalities | 3 | 2 | 1 | — | — | 2 | 8 |

SOURCES: Miller and Collier (1981), Lea and Miller (1985), Cook (unpublished manuscript), and McCosker (unpublished data).

NOTE: Not included are the attacks on R. Campbell, October 8, 1950, and R. Pamperin, June 14, 1959, and several incidents in central California in which the surfer and/or the surfboard were/was not damaged. Attacks on scuba divers are listed only if the diver was submerged; scuba divers attacked at the surface are listed as "snorkelers." "Southern California" is defined as south of Point Conception.

Since Lea and Miller's report in 1985, at least eleven more attacks have occurred in Baja California, California, and Oregon waters, bringing the known total to 65 since 1926. In only eight of the 54 California incidents did the victim die. In almost every one of these cases, the cause of death was exsanguination, not consumption by shark.

The general absence of attacks by white sharks south of Point Conception in central California was puzzling at first, but one of us (McCosker) had grown up in southern California, and thereby knew about abalone diving. In the south the ab divers are permitted to use scuba gear to find the shellfish, whereas the northern divers must hold their breath while diving for the valuable mollusks. This curious quirk in the law treats the southern half of the state more favorably, clearly placing the abalone at a disadvantage there, and at the same time turning northern divers into sharkbait. As experiments with mannequins have demonstrated (see p. 162), scuba diving is a much safer pursuit than free diving, except when the diver is near the surface. The white shark is accustomed to looking upward in search of its next victim. Breath-holding divers, up and down again too often, are much more vulnerable to attack; scuba divers, by contrast, spend too little time at the surface to be at significant risk. The sharks are accustomed to attacking large mammals at the surface, and skin divers—like sea lions—have to come up to breathe.

Not surprisingly, a white shark in southern California recently decided to refute our learned hypotheses. As this book was nearing completion, an attack south of Point Conception seemed to contradict our contention that white sharks for the most part attack people in the cooler northern California waters where there are more potential victims at or near the surface. On January 26, 1989, Tamara McCallister, 24, and her companion Roy Jeffrey Stoddard, also 24, left Malibu Beach in their ocean kayaks, intending to paddle about a mile and a half to the north. (Malibu, perhaps best known for the beachfront houses of the Hollywood glitterati, is 25 miles west of downtown Los Angeles and about 100 miles southeast of Point Conception.) Nearly 24 hours later, the two kayaks were found lashed together more than 50 miles up the coast, probably having drifted with the prevailing current, thus in a westerly direction. In the underside of one of the kayaks were major abrasions and three large holes, suggesting the impact of a biting white shark. Two and a half days later, Tamara's body was found floating at the surface, about 5 miles from shore at Ventura, 45 miles northwest of Malibu. She bore the unmistakable wounds of a massive white shark bite, including a 13-inch gouge taken from her left thigh. Warren Lovell, the county coroner, concluded that she had sustained other bites, and had bruises on her hands, but her lungs contained no water. That last condition suggests that she had not drowned before she was bitten, and the damage to her hands would indicate that she had fought with her attacker. Tamara McCallister is therefore listed as the 50th verified white shark victim in California, and her companion, whose body was never found, is presumably the 51st.

As with the Boren attack in Monterey, McCosker was asked to explain why this attack had not fit the normal pattern. Why a kayaker? Why so far south of Point Conception? Why was Tamara not eaten after being bitten? And is it now unsafe to swim or kayak in southern California waters? Since nobody had seen the attack, all we can do is speculate on what actually happened. Kayakers often lash their kayaks together when they rest or swim. The clothing Tamara was wearing suggested that they were not stopping to swim but rather to rest. Since white sharks have been known to attack boats, surfboards, and logs,* an attack on a lashed pair of kayaks is not altogether surprising. Two kayaks with their paddlers disturbing the water would certainly attract and tempt a hungry shark. Why south of Point Conception? Why not? White sharks live all along the Pacific coast of North America, from Alaska to Mexico, and are occasionally caught by commercial fishermen off southern California. But why was Tamara's body not consumed? We cannot answer that with assurance, but we can imagine a scenario wherein her boyfriend, in his last heroic act, was himself consumed as he tried to protect her. After eating a grown man, the shark may have been sated. (Admittedly a shaky proposition, for would a shark that regularly feeds on elephant seals be satisfied with a 150-pound human meal?) In any event, we have the evidence of a particularly grisly attack (or perhaps a pair of attacks), and *Carcharodon* was responsible. Once again, the white shark seems to defy whatever parameters we try to identify for its conduct.

* Logs rarely report shark attacks, but there are logs in the collection of the California Academy of Sciences with white shark teeth embedded in them. The massive, unexpected jolts experienced by the attackers can only be imagined, and follow-up attacks on logs seem unlikely.

The coast of Chile is much like that of California and Oregon. It is more than 2,600 miles long, reaching from subtropical waters in the north to sub-Antarctic waters at Cape Horn, at the tip of South America. (The coast of California, by comparision, is just 840 miles long.) The Chilean coast has its kelp beds, but instead of abalone (*Haliotis*), it supports large edible mollusks called *locos* by the divers and *Concholepas concholepas* by the scientists. Locos have been heavily collected in the shallower inshore seas, and deeper diving is now necessary. Spearfishing has also become increasingly popular here, for recreation and for profit. Divers wear full rubber wetsuits in the chilly Chilean waters, and often dive with the aid of a hookah (a tube that supplies them with compressed air from a compressor on board a boat). The Chilean divers differ principally from the California divers in diving alone. The buddy system, so important in America, is not practiced in Chile, and the results with regard to white shark attacks are grimly predictable:

Crisologo Urizar was spearfishing at the surface at Bahía el Panul, some 7 miles south of the town of Coquimbo, and a locality known for sea lions and an occasional shark. On September 29, 1963, he was attacked and eaten by a shark, with only fragments of his wet suit and fins left behind as evidence.

José Larenas Miranda was attacked at Punta Negra, just north of Valparaiso, on January 5, 1980, while hookah-diving for locos; his boatman watched him descend and then saw the bubbles stop. A white shark surfaced with Miranda's torso in its mouth—the head, left arm, and shoulder were gone. The boatman rammed the shark, which then disgorged the remains.

On March 4, 1981, Carlos Vergara was attacked at Bahía Totoralillo (another fishing village, north of Coquimbo) while spearfishing in the vicinity of a sea lion haulout area. Some three hours before the attack, fishermen had been dynamiting for fish, which attracts sharks. Vergara was bitten on the leg as he began a vertical dive, but he kicked the shark in the head and swam to shore. After extensive surgery at a nearby hospital, he survived.

Juan Luís Tapia Avalos was diving for locos off Valparaiso on December 15, 1988 (the austral mid-summer is in December), when he was attacked by a 16-foot *tiburón blanco*. He died instantly, and his diving partners brought his body to shore.

These Chilean stories were related to McCosker by Dr. Alfredo Cea Egaña, of the Universidad del Norte in Coquimbo. Dr. Egaña investigated each attack, interviewed eyewitnesses, examined the corpses, and forwarded the information to California. McCosker and Egaña then jointly published the accounts of the first three of the attacks listed above. An account of the fourth attack, which occurred after the publication of the 1984 paper, was sent to us by Dr. Eduardo Reyes of the Universidad Técnica Santa María in Valparaiso. All four attacks occurred in central (thus temperate) Chile; the entire coast, from the Peruvian border all the way around the Horn, is populated by South American sea lions and fur seals, which are known as *lobos marinos* to chilenos, and *Otaria flavescens* and *Arctocephalus australis*, respectively, to scientists.

The nature of the risk of attack in Chile is quite comparable to that in California: diving for locos is much like diving for abalone; where there are sea lions in temperate waters, there will be white sharks; and where locos (or abalone) and great whites and divers share the same waters, there will be attacks. That the Chilean casualty list is so much shorter than the central California list is simply a function of the numbers of active divers; there are almost as many people between Monterey and San Francisco as there are in all of Chile. Three out of the four Chilean divers who died were swimming alone, whereas California divers are usually in a position to be rescued—or at least pulled from the water—by a diving companion or by the crew of a boat dispatched to the scene.

Great white sharks are relatively common off the coasts of South Africa (which are washed by the Indian Ocean on the east and by the South Atlantic on the west), and fishermen, swimmers, and surfers are common too. Wherever conditions are propitious for encounters between people and white sharks—and they certainly are in southern Africa—attacks are likely. The history of shark attacks in South African waters has been as bloody and ill-recorded as that for any other location, and the historians have attributed the attacks variously to raggedtooths (known locally as "raggies"), bull sharks (known locally as Zambezi sharks or even "Zambies"), and (of course) white sharks, sometimes known in South Africa as "blue pointers."

Durban is the principal city and seaport in Natal Province, on South Africa's east coast, and early in the twentieth century it became the center of a thriving whaling industry. By 1912, no fewer than five companies had factories on The Bluff. At first, the whales were processed right in the harbor, but the stench of dead whales was so overpowering that the locals lobbied to have the factories moved around to the seaward side of the promontory. Eventually, the various whaling companies were consolidated into the Union Whaling Company, and until 1975, various species of whales were processed close to the beaches of Durban. In the early days of Durban whaling, the primary object was baleen whales, particularly humpbacks and blues, but when their numbers decreased (as a result of massive overfishing) the whalers turned to sperm whales. The catcher boats towing bloody carcasses of whales would often steam close to shore on their way to the whaling station (where the carcasses would then be transported by train to the processing plant), inevitably attracting hungry sharks. There were reports of huge tiger sharks and, not surprisingly, blue pointers as well.

Although the records are scanty, it is believed that many of the attacks in Durban waters in the 1940's were the work of white sharks. During the glory days of Durban whaling, an intensive sport fishery for sharks was conducted from the South Pier of Durban's harbor, and although other species were caught, white sharks were what all hoped to land. The South Pier angling will be discussed at length, on pp. 195–98, but we mention it here to suggest that processing whales in close proximity to bathing beaches is as good a definition of "looking for trouble" as it is possible to find. According to Marie Levine's study of South African attack statistics, more than half of the shark attacks that took place between 1940 and 1975 (the year whaling ended) took place off the Natal coast, but when the whaling ceased, the larger proportion of white shark attacks shifted to the waters of Cape Province, to the southwest.

In the early history of South African attacks, the records often did not identify the species, but it had become obvious to everyone that there was a shark problem. Prior to the arrival of the whaling industry, as early as 1907 in fact, the Durban City Council had erected a net barrier off the beaches, and although it was successful—there were no attacks off Durban during the 21 years of its existence—it was allowed to deteriorate and was not replaced. We have no records for the 1930's, but between 1943 and 1951, 21 attacks were recorded, and the city council, mindful of the offshore nets that had been set up off Sydney, Australia, decided to employ them. (Offshore netting is based not on the barricade principle, but rather on the idea that the sharks will become trapped in the nets and drown, thus reducing their numbers, and, in turn, the frequency of the attacks. The 1907 arrangements had been simply corrals set into the sand, in which the bathers frolicked while the sharks remained outside.) Where the nets were in place, off Durban's popular Indian Ocean beaches, the number of attacks dropped to near zero. But north and south of the city, where there were no nets, the attacks continued.

On the 18th of December 1957—the month would come to be known as "Black December"—Robert Wherley was bodysurfing at the seaside resort of Karidene when he was attacked by a shark and had his left leg bitten off at the knee. Two days later, at Uvongo, farther down the coast, 15-year-old Allan Green was standing on a sandbank when a shark pulled him under and took massive bites from his chest and stomach, killing him. Then on the 23rd, as Margate holidaymakers watched in horror, Vernon Berry was attacked by a large shark and died on the beach shortly after he was pulled from the water. In the panic that ensued, fishermen went out after the killer sharks, and spotter planes buzzed overhead hoping to locate them, but to no avail: 14-year-old Julia Painting was attacked at Margate minutes after a plane had passed over her. She was pulled from the shark's jaws by Paul Brokenshaw, and from the bloody water by her uncle. She survived. The Mayor of Margate quickly decreed a ban on all bathing in the sea while a South African Navy minesweeper dropped depth charges and hand grenades into the water. Not only did this fail to remedy the problem, it exacerbated it by attracting sharks to the fishes that had been killed or stunned by the explosions. Just two weeks later, on January 9th, Deryck Prinsloo, standing in waist-deep water at Scottburgh, was attacked and mauled by a shark. Rushed to a hospital, he was dead on arrival.

Shark enclosures, looking not unlike the marine corrals of 1907, were hastily erected at Margate, Ramsgate, and Port Edward, but they proved to be expensive, and almost impossible to maintain in the heavy surf. While swimming outside one of these enclosures on April 3, Nicholas Badenhorst was torn apart by a shark. Both arms and his right leg were ripped off and a massive bite was taken from his abdomen. The hotels of the Natal beaches emptied as quickly as if plague had been reported. Among the remaining visitors was Fay Bester, a 28-year-old mother of four. On April 5th, at Uvongo, as she was watching the repair of the steel nets, a shark rushed her and bit her nearly in half. From December 1957 to April 1958 there had been six shark attacks in Natal waters, four of them fatal.*

In 1958 David Davies was appointed the first Director of the South African Association for Marine Biological Research, with responsibilities that included directing both the Durban Aquarium and the Oceanographic Research Institute. Because of his personal and professional interest in the shark attacks that had plagued Natal waters, Davies began to publish an individual "Investigational Report" on each subsequent attack. No. 1 was devoted to an attack on a fishing boat; No. 2 (written with Jeannette D'Aubrey) was entitled "Shark Attack off the East Coast of South Africa, 24 December 1960, with Notes on the Species of Shark Responsible for the Attack." (Davies had just published an account of an April 1960 attack on Michael Hely in the ichthyological journal *Copeia*, and concluded—incorrectly, as it turned out—that the attacking shark had been a raggedtooth.) The species responsible for the December 24th attack—in which Petrus Sithole lost both legs to a shark and died immediately—was identified from tooth fragments as a carcharhinid, probably a bull shark, *Carcharhinus leucas*. Two weeks later, Michael Land, 13, was attacked at Winkelspruit, 22 miles south of Durban. Although his right foot was bitten off, he survived. Again, the attacking shark was thought

*J. L. B. Smith, the man who described the coelacanth, examined the available evidence in the 1957–58 attacks, and "after considerable investigation," concluded "that a heavy-bodied, wide-mouthed species of *Carcharhinus*, not previously reported from Natal, was present in unusual numbers, and from bites on victims it was clearly the culprit in at least some cases." He named this culprit *Carcharhinus vanrooyeni*, a name that has not survived, and if indeed the attacking shark was a carcharhinid, it was probably the bull shark, *C. leucas*.

David Davies, then Director of the Oceanographic Research Institute in Durban (left), with Jeannette D'Aubrey and J. A. F. Garrick. The little fellow is a rockhopper penguin, a potential prey item of the great white along the South African coast.

to have been a bull shark (though the name was given as the Zambezi shark, *C. zambezensis*, which at that time was believed to be a separate species).

In Investigational Report No. 4 ("Shark Attack off the East Coast of South Africa, 22 January 1961"), Davies acknowledged that "At the present rate of incidence on humans, this section of the east coast of South Africa is one of the most seriously affected areas in the world." While swimming in 6 feet of water perhaps 30 feet from shore, Michael Murphy was bitten on the left leg. He was rushed to Addington Hospital in Durban, but despite arterial grafts, his leg had to be amputated.

Then on February 1, 1961, while swimming at Nahoon Beach, East London, 14-year-old Michael Zimmerman was attacked and killed by a carcharhinid shark.

In 1961, Davies, who quite unexpectedly found himself at the very epicenter of the shark problem, was invited to join the Shark Research Panel of the American Institute of Biological Sciences. He continued to study the problem first-hand, generating elaborate studies of the factors he believed were associated with the attacks (turbidity, water temperature, salinity, depth, distance from shore, etc.), and in 1964 he published his findings in a comprehensive book entitled *About Sharks and Shark Attacks*. (His career was cut short at the age of 43 by injuries he sustained in an automobile accident in November 1965.)

Although there had been nets of one sort or another off the Natal coast since 1952, it was not until 1964 that the Natal Anti-Shark Measures Board was established. The NASMB was empowered to set out nets, patrol them, and close those beaches where they believed there was danger, either from sharks not yet in the nets or, rarely, when the nets could not be cleared because of bad weather. Workers set out some 385 nets at 46 beaches, to trap and drown various species of sharks.

The first director of the Sharks Board was Beulah deVilliers Davis. Starting in a shed with a Land Rover, two cameras, and a life jacket, Davis has turned the Sharks Board into a huge organization, with an annual budget of hundreds of thousands of Rands and a headquarters building at Umhlanga Rocks that looks not unlike the sprawling offices of a multinational corporation. (Beulah Davis served as director for 24 years and retired in July 1990; she was succeeded by her long-time deputy, Graeme Charter.) In addition to offices and meeting rooms, there are sheds and machine shops for the ski-boats, garages for the various land vehicles, and laboratories for the examination of the carcasses of the sharks that are brought in.

The predominant species caught between 1966 and 1974 were two similar species of blackfins (*Carcharhinus brevipinna* and *C. limbatus*, 2,126 total), duskies (*Carcharhinus obscurus*, 1,789), scalloped hammerheads (*Sphyrna lewini*, 1,520), and ragged-tooths (*Eugomphodus taurus*, 1,152). (These figures are taken from an unpublished 1975 paper by Beulah Davis and Tim Wallett of the NASMB. The totals are for the years 1966–72, and it is assumed that the numbers of the various shark species have not changed appreciably in recent years.)

In the shark nets set by the Natal Sharks Board, great white sharks are occasionally trapped and drowned.

It should be clear by now that the nets were especially effective in catching sharks that posed no particular threat to swimmers. In Wallett's 1978 study of South African shark attacks, he lists "those shark species caught in Natal's nearshore waters which have been implicated in shark attacks," and (in order of the number of attacks known for each species), they were the great white, the tiger, and the Zambezi (or bull). In other words, although the nets very effectively reduced the *absolute* numbers of sharks off the Natal beaches, they did relatively little to keep down the number of potential maneaters. This discrepancy may of course be a function of the relative abundance of the various species, since you cannot capture many sharks of a particular species if they do not exist in large numbers, but it might also be argued that large numbers of dead or dying sharks in the nets *attract* the larger species—the whites, the tigers, and the bulls—that feed on the smaller ones.

And the numbers of these three species caught in the nets, though in no way comparable to the figures for blackfins and duskies, are still sufficient to make a swimmer pause before plunging into the surf at Amanzimtoti or Umhlanga. According to statistics assembled by the Natal Anti-Shark Measures Board (now known simply as the Natal Sharks Board), during the years 1978 to 1989, 536 tiger sharks were caught in the nets, an average of 45 per year; 730 Zambezi (bull) sharks (61 per year); and 490 great whites (41 per year). These numbers reflect only relative abundance, and that not very well, since there might be a "net avoidance" factor that we have no way of calculating: some species might avoid or escape (or be deterred by) the nets better than others. Every year, then, 40-odd white sharks are caught in the nets off the Natal beaches. But how many are not caught?

An inclination to attribute most Natal attacks to the bull or Zambezi shark (set in motion by David Davies) has resulted in the obscuring of attacks in these waters by white sharks. Recent re-examinations of the tooth fragments, the method of attack, and the photographs of the bite wounds have caused researchers to reconsider the shark species in three of the attacks previously attributed to *C. leucas,* and it is now believed that Deryck Prinsloo, Michael Hely, and Michael Land were attacked by white sharks.

In recent years, the Sharks Board has come under fire for the random effect of the nets, for they kill not only sharks, but also hundreds of dolphins and turtles and thousands of gamefishes, skates, rays, and sawfishes. The question has been raised whether the protection of swimmers is sufficient justification for the destruction of hundreds of "innocent" creatures, and further, whether the shark nets work at all. At root, the rationale for retaining the nets might be simply their public relations value: tourists at the Natal beaches, believing that the nets are protecting them, continue to patronize the hotels and resorts, even though the number of dangerous sharks along the beaches has not been significantly reduced. In other parts of the world where shark attacks are a serious problem—California and Florida, for example—no cumbersome (and expensive) bureaucracy has been established to protect people from shark attacks. In California, the problem of attacks is well-known, and people understand that they swim, dive, and surf at their own risk.* In Florida the problem is less publicized,

* Not surprisingly, the new San Jose entry in the National Hockey League will be known as the Sharks, and the shark on the logo is clearly a great white.

but it exists nonetheless: in 1981, for example, there were fourteen attacks along the Florida coasts, two of them fatal. Several Sydney beaches are meshed, but Australians permit swimming and diving anywhere at all—including the area around Dangerous Reef—and the people who go in the water understand the risk.

To upset an entire ecosystem for the protection of bathers seems excessively anthropocentric. Leonard Compagno, a dedicated defender of the sharks who was trained in California but now pursues his research at the Shark Research Center at Cape Town, has written,

> A more radical alternative for Natal than shark management would be to eliminate the anti-shark measures entirely, and to try to educate the public to accept the occasional shark attack as an inevitable result of entering the sea. This may seem utopian at present, but many land predators that are now protected were hunted as vermin not so long ago.*

The question of shark repellents concerns us only peripherally, since most people who seek intimate involvement with white sharks, e.g. fishermen and divers, want to get *closer* to the sharks rather than keep them away, and for them, therefore, the emphasis has been primarily on *attractants*. For other species, however, there have been any number of proposals, ranging from bubble curtains (introduced under the erroneous impression that sharks would not cross a barrier of bubbles) to the "Shark Chaser" of World War II, which was based on the equally erroneous notion that sharks are inhibited from feeding by the presence of copper acetate (a component of decaying shark meat) in the water. (In an excellent study, "Shark Attack: Feeding or Fighting?", David Baldridge essentially dismissed the enduring—but incorrect—notion that all sharks that attack humans do so simply because they are hungry.) There have also been special life jackets that protected a downed pilot from inquisitive sharks by encasing him in an envelope of water, something like a giant, floating condom.† Studies of a Red Sea flatfish known as the Moses sole (*Pardachirus marmoratus*) indicated that the little fish secretes a milky fluid that severely inhibits shark attacks, but the application of this secretion—a very complex substance that chemists found prohibitively expensive to duplicate in useful amounts in the laboratory—proved to be monumentally impractical for divers (its active ingredient was later found to be common in detergents). Other researchers tried other substances, ranging from dishwashing liquid to shampoo, but in almost all instances, even when the substance inhibited the shark's biting mechanisms, the concentration required to be effective was far too great to be practical.

In a 1990 summary of the history of shark repellents, Baldridge wrote, "Many decades of research by numerous investigators have clearly shown that extremely rapid repellency in terms of a radical change in behavior will require far more than just a minimal assault on the chemical senses of an aggressive shark." This paper, entitled "Shark Repellent: Not Yet, Maybe Never," concludes by suggesting that the only way to develop an effective repellent is to isolate a semiochemical or pheromone that, for reasons associated with its own survival, somehow signals the shark not to attack. As we have seen, however, the attack scenario of the white shark is a complicated procedure, and it seems unlikely—at least in the immediate

*In April 1991 the South African Environment Ministry proposed legislation that would declare the white shark protected in South African waters, and with the retirement of Beulah Davis as director of the Natal Sharks Board, the meshing of the beaches has also come under review. Even the Sharks Board, heretofore a completely autonomous institution, will have to obtain permits, "pending the introduction of alternative methods of beach protection apart from the anti-shark gillnets now in use."

† When Ron and Valerie Taylor tested a steel-mesh "shark suit" against blue sharks off San Diego in 1980, Valerie was wearing only a mesh jacket and was bitten on the leg. Later that year, in the Coral Sea, a gray reef shark attacked her head, and although the steel mesh protected her, she sustained minor tooth punctures on her chin. A year later, the Taylors decided to perform a similar "white shark experiment" off South Australia, wisely using a seaweed-stuffed dummy instead of a live diver. The white shark that appeared at Dangerous Reef was "by far the most aggressive" animal they had ever worked with, and although the mesh-suited dummy survived the attack, they speculated (in a 1981 publication) that the shark's agitation might have been "due to an electro-chemical field generated between the steel suit and the boat." It would appear, at the least, that deterrents against white shark attacks are still in the development stage. A really solid bite by a good-sized white shark would of course crush whatever was inside the mesh, whether the mesh itself survived or not.

future—that a chemical will be discovered that can convince an attacking white pointer that a seal or a salmon is detrimental to its evolutionary well-being.

In his 1963 study of South African shark attacks, J. L. B. Smith wrote that, around the Cape Peninsula, "so far, only 3 species of dangerous large sharks have been found, *Carcharhinus obscurus* [the dusky shark], *Prionace glauca* [the blue shark], and, very rarely, *Carcharodon carcharias*." He was wrong on virtually all counts. The dusky and the blue shark are not usually considered dangerous to humans (the Sharks Board reports one attack in Natal by a dusky during 1966–74, and none at all for the blue), and although the white shark is not common in Cape waters—it is not *common* anywhere—it is unquestionably responsible for more genuine attacks there than any other. Tim Wallett has written, "It is not surprising that the majority of Cape attacks, where the attacking shark could be identified, were by great white sharks."

In April 1971, Theo Klein, a 53-year-old visitor from Germany, was swimming in Buffels Bay near the town of Knysna when he was attacked by a large white shark. The shark tore his stomach out, killing him instantly, and then came back repeatedly to bite large pieces from the floating carcass. In December of the same year, Sheryl Teague, 16, was swimming with her sister in Fish Hoek Bay, an arm of False Bay. Pulling through on the backstroke, she unknowingly stuck her right arm into the mouth of a shark. She screamed and pulled her arm out, suffering severe lacerations when the arm raked across the shark's teeth. A lifesaver on a surfboard came out to rescue her, and when his board capsized, he swam her to shore. The shark, seen by several people after the "attack" and clearly identified as a blue pointer, was probably as startled as Sheryl.

Twenty-year-old Marshall Flanagan, an Australian coming to South Africa to surf, probably thought the waves would be better and the sharks fewer. He was wrong, at least about the sharks. While Flanagan was paddling out to catch a wave, his companion spotted a fin slicing toward him and shouted "Shark!" The shark then pushed Flanagan through the water for about 15 feet before releasing him. The tendons of two fingers were severed when Flanagan tried to push the shark away, and he suffered a great gash in his leg when the shark clamped down on him *and* the board. A tooth fragment removed from his leg identified the attacker as a white.

At Fourth Beach, Clifton, on the Atlantic coast of the Cape Peninsula, on November 27, 1976, Geoffrey Spence was swimming some 500 yards from the beach. He was giving his companion Robbie Nel his version of the opening scene of the movie "Jaws" (the scene where the girl is attacked from below and pushed violently through the water) when he, Spence, was attacked from below and pushed violently through the water. Though he was lacerated from shoulder blade to lower rib cage, the shark did not hit him again. Spence was brought ashore in a dinghy and sewn up on the beach, where he described the shark as "black" (as most sharks, whites included, would appear from above) and about 10 feet in length. (In almost exactly the same location in 1942, a shark had attacked W. S. Bergh, had bitten his legs clean off, and had then dragged the rest of his body out to sea.)

Surfing off Ntlonyana Beach in June 1982, Alex Macun was attacked by what a companion described as "a great white about three meters long." The attack knocked him off his board and flung him into the water. He surfaced briefly, but was dragged under again and was never found.

In September 1987, Peter McCallum was attacked at Jongensfontein Bay, and in October, dental student Dawid Smit was spearfishing near Seal Island in False Bay when an "enormous" shark grabbed him and dragged him through the water as his father watched from a boat. Both men survived the attacks.

Probably the most bizarre—and horrifying—episode in the annals of South African attacks involved Gerjo van Niekerk. On September 17, 1989, while he was skindiving in Smitswinkel Bay, his torso was raked by the teeth of a white shark. Interviewed after the attack, he said that he loved diving, and insisted that the experience had not dampened his enthusiasm for the sport. Less than two months later, he was diving for perlemoen (abalone) when he was killed—and probably eaten—by a white shark. According to the Natal *Mercury* for November 27, 1989, a human leg washed up on the beach at Melkbosselstrand, and was positively identified as that of Gerjo van Niekerk by his parents. (This account was provided by Marie Levine, whose exhaustive study of South African shark attacks is in press.)*

Of all the large sharks, only great whites demonstrate an inclination to attack boats. One might think *Carcharodon* should be able to distinguish an inanimate object from a living one or even a carcass, but on several occasions sharks have attacked wooden boats. In one notable instance a shark attacked a fishing boat off Cape Breton Island, in northern Nova Scotia, dumped its two occupants into the water and swam away. Although neither of the two fishermen was attacked, one of them drowned. The other survived to describe their harrowing experience.

In writing of the white pointer in Australian waters, Ernest Palmer has written:

There have been many instances in South Australia where people seated in the stern of a boat have been struck by the nose of an attacking shark and sent sprawling to the deck, and in one case the person suffered a heart attack and died as a result. . . . Unless the shark is seen swimming up the slick, the first intimation of its presence is usually a violent thud upon the rudder, keel or side of the boat and the propeller is frequently mouthed and shaken by the shark, presumably to test whether the object is edible. In one case a shark attacked the propeller of a boat in which I was fishing whilst it was moving. The propeller struck the shark on the head three times but it continued to follow until we anchored and caught the shark with three nasty gashes in the head.

Stewart Springer, in a footnote to his 1971 paper on Steno (Niels Stensen), describes "the only instance of an attack on a shark fishing boat" in the Salerno, Florida, fishery:

A 10-meter commercial shark fishing boat was attacked by a 5.5-meter *Carcharodon* with repeated ramming and tooth-raking, always aimed at the same spot on the boat. According to the two fishermen aboard the attacked boat it was only by constant maneuvering to protect their flanks that they were able to save the

*Gerjo van Niekirk may have supposed he would be safe after that first attack, on the theory that lightning never strikes twice. If so, he was wrong. And in fact Rodney Orr has also been attacked twice, off the coast north of San Francisco in 1961 and again in 1990. He recovered quickly from the second attack, even though at one point his entire head was gripped firmly in the shark's jaws. To our knowledge, no one else has survived *or* endured two white shark attacks.

In South Australia a diver turns away as a very large white shark appears ready to attack the boat.

vessel. . . . The fishermen returned with the shark's liver, its teeth, and a badly scarred boat as evidence.

In his study of shark attacks in southern African waters, Wallett presents an incredible register of attacks by sharks on boats. In some cases, a shark hooked by a fisherman actually leapt into the boat, but in many others, the behavior of the shark had very little to do with its being hooked, and might very well be attributed to frustration or pique.

The first record comes from July 1936, when men aboard the 10-metre long fishing boat *Lucky Jim* were fishing for snoek off Cape Point. One of the fishermen, "Smart" Pepino, was fishing at the stern when a large shark appeared and raced toward the boat. It left the water with a graceful leap, landed on the transom, and slid into the fish well, knocking Pepino overboard. The noise of the shark beating around the fish well's interior attracted the other fishermen's attention. As they rushed towards the stern, somebody shouted, "It's eaten Smart!" Consternation swept through the men until a cry for help sounded from behind the transom. Pepino, who could not swim a stroke, had been saved by the air trapped in his oilskin. The unfortunate fellow had floundered to the boat's side, found he couldn't reach the gunwale and had made his way to the stern. When the fishermen looked overboard, there was Pepino clinging to the rudder. He was finally pulled aboard and the shark was dispatched.

Although the species of this shark was not recorded, there were so many attacks on boats where the white shark *was* implicated that it seems not unreasonable to assume that the shark that dumped "Smart" Pepino into the drink was a white. In 1958, for example, a boat that was trolling in Plettenberg Bay suddenly stopped in the water for no apparent reason. Looking over the transom, Wallett reports, the fishermen saw "a great white shark with the propeller lodged firmly in the remains of its mouth and head. Obviously the shark had been attracted to the propeller and had attacked it."

Again, Wallett reports that

In April 1960 a large shark repeatedly charged a 5-metre ski-boat in Saldanha Bay on the south west Cape Coast. During one of its rushes it leapt from the water and bit the transom, leaving teeth embedded in the wood. It then began ramming the side, each impact almost capsizing the craft. Fortunately, another boat arrived and came to their assistance. Later the shark was identified as a great white from tooth fragments removed from the transom.

In the first of what was to become his series of investigational reports, David Davies discussed an attack on a fishing boat during October 1960. Eight men were fishing from a 24-foot boat, and as one of them pulled in a shad (the fish we know as *Pomatomus saltatrix,* the bluefish), a large shark rushed at the fish but missed it, "hitting the gunwale of the boat with considerable force and then falling back into the sea." He continued:

With all lines in and the boat ready to move off, the shark circled the boat again and suddenly charged at great speed, making a vicious bite in the side of the boat. The boat was damaged to the extent of an 18-inch hole, fortunately above the water mark, and a large fragment of the tooth was later found embedded in the woodwork.

The tooth fragment was from a lower-jaw tooth of a white shark.

In 1974, Danie Schoeman was fishing off Macassar Beach. After

A male white shark in a "tail stand" posture, nosing the zinc anode attached to the rudder of the *Nenad* .

As it prepares to attack the boat's diving platform the shark rolls its eyes back. The sensitive pores on its snout can be clearly seen.

chumming, he leaned over the side to wash his hands. In the dark something smacked him in the face, and as he leapt back, a great white shark landed in his boat. As the shark chewed on one of the seats, Schoeman lanced it in the head. (Schoeman is recorded as having had his boats attacked no less than five times, and he has caught eighteen large white pointers. We will hear more of "The Great White Catcher of False Bay" when we discuss fishing.)

More? In February 1976, E. C. Landells and his crew were about a quarter of a mile off Melkbaai, South Africa, when they stopped to get a closer look at two sharks. One of the sharks accelerated toward the boat and rammed it at speed, smashing a hole in it the size of a man's head.

Clearly, the white shark is a "boat-biter." But why? As we have mentioned elsewhere, white sharks bite floating logs and other large objects, such as dead whales, perhaps to determine whether they are suitable for eating. Moreover, recent underwater observations by Tricas and McCosker in South Australia suggest that the sharks are merely responding to the electrical fields produced by potential prey (see p. 71), but in this case the fields are generated by the electrochemical interaction between the propeller or rudder and the sacrificial zinc or magnesium anodes on the underside of a modern boat.

In 1953, in the cold waters of Cape Breton Island, New Brunswick, Canada, a 12-foot white shark rammed a dory and sank it. The shark did not attack the lobstermen who were pitched into the water, but one of them drowned.

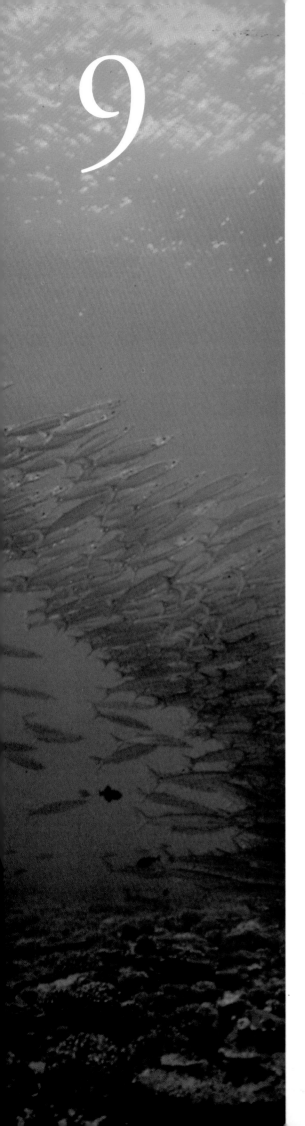

# 9 Fishing for the White Shark

For as long as they have been on the sea, men and women have been fishing. And the chances are that they have been catching white sharks—willingly or not—as long as they have been dropping a bait where whites happen to congregate. Because of the white sharks' omnivorous habits, they are not particularly difficult to hook; they will eat virtually any animal matter that is offered to them, from horsemeat to whalemeat, from dogs to fish. In the not too distant past, however, sharks of all species were "trash fish," and since they were considered neither edible nor noble, fishermen ignored them—if they could. Still, it is hard to ignore a ton of fish that takes your bait or bites a hole in your boat, and eventually the great white took its place alongside the great game fishes of the world—the swordfish, the marlins, the tuna. The white shark is not as furious a fighter as a marlin, or even as great a jumper as a mako, but it gets bigger, a lot bigger, and that—alongside its notoriety—makes it a premier game fish.

When Zane Grey, the famous author of western novels, had made enough money writing, he traveled around the world in pursuit of his obsession, hooking world's-record big-game fishes. Because he was a writer as well as a fisherman, we have a lucid, comprehensive record of his prize catches, but because he was at heart a fisherman, the record he left might be less than purely objective. For example, in describing the results of a 1926 trip to New Zealand, he wrote that "This extraordinary fishing [was] surely never surpassed in the angling history of the world." He hunted not only marlin and swordfish in antipodean waters, but also thresher sharks, makos, tiger sharks, and white sharks. (A New Yorker named Francis Low had caught a 998-pound great white off Manasquan, New Jersey, in 1933, which stood as the record for the largest fish ever caught on rod and reel until 1936, when Grey caught a 1,036-pound tiger shark in Australia. Low's shark was presented to the American Museum of Natural History, and as of this writing, it is displayed in the Hall of the Biology of Fishes.) Grey caught an 800-pound white pointer in Australian waters, and also produced and starred in a film that he made in Australia called "White Death." In a collection of his father's writings, Loren Grey wrote that the film was about a huge white shark that had terrorized the inhabitants of a small village on Australia's east coast and was captured by the hero, who was, not surprisingly, Zane Grey.

In his 1937 *Tigers of the Sea*, Col. Hugh Wise, one of the first writer-anglers to fish intentionally for sharks (as opposed to catching them accidentally), tried to explain his interest in them:

Why fish for sharks? It is a poor way to start this story with the acknowledgment that the quarry sought is not equal, as a game-fish, to some others. I hope this admission may not be interpreted as discrediting the sport of angling with rod and reel for sharks, fishes whose vitality, stubbornness, and power compensate for qualities which they may lack. They really are worthy antagonists in struggles the interest of which is enhanced by the joy of combat with savage monsters.

Of a 9-foot, 300-pound white shark that he caught off Virginia, Wise wrote:

Perhaps I should be satisfied that he was a modest edition of this largest and most ferocious species of our North Atlantic, for the Great White Shark is said to

Zane Grey, celebrated writer of western novels, with the 1,036-pound tiger shark that he caught in the waters off Sydney, Australia, in 1936.

ABOVE, RIGHT: The largest fish ever taken on rod and reel, according to the International Game Fish Association: Alf Dean's world's record, 2,664-pound white shark, caught at Ceduna, South Australia, in April 1959.

ABOVE, LEFT: In 1950, Sir Willoughby Norrie, then Governor of South Australia, caught a white shark that weighed 2,225 pounds. Here he holds the hooks that did the job.

LEFT: Zane Grey with the 800-pound white shark he caught off Australia in 1939, just seven months before his death. An avid big-game fisherman, he has often been credited as the originator of the name "white death" for these sharks.

attain a maximum length of more than forty feet. Such a shark could not be handled on a cable, and one of half that size would make the fight almost hopeless on rod, for it requires a skillful angler with the best of tackle to land a ten-footer.

When asked why he spent so much time in pursuit of sharks, Alf Dean, the world's record holder (who estimated that he had caught more than 50 *tons* of white pointers), said, "I certainly am not obsessed with killing sharks. I don't like them, but I don't hate them."

Port Lincoln, a small fishing community located on Spencer Gulf in South Australia, has been the world center of white shark fishing for almost 50 years, but 50 years before *that*, commercial fishermen occasionally hauled in a white pointer. In 1941 G. R. Cowell hooked and landed a 1,919-pounder off Kangaroo Island, and from that moment onward, fishermen came to Port Lincoln with dreams of 1-ton fishes dancing in their heads. (The British, or "long," ton is the equivalent of 2,240 pounds.)

In 1950, off the Sir Joseph Banks Islands in Spencer Gulf, Sir Willoughby Norrie, the Governor of South Australia, caught a 2,225-pound white shark, only 15 pounds short of the coveted British ton. (Norrie's shark did not qualify for a world's record because someone had adjusted his reel as he was playing the fish, and according to the IGFA rules, the angler must not be assisted in any way by another person.) Two years later, off Streaky Bay, Alf Dean brought in a 2,333-pounder; the magical 1-ton figure was at last reached. Then Bob Dyer caught a 2,345-pounder off Brisbane, and the record was his. In the years that followed, Dean and Dyer continued to catch white sharks, but the contest ended (to date, anyway) when, fishing off Ceduna in 1959 in the Great Australian Bight, Dean hooked the 2,664-pounder that still stands as the record for the largest fish ever caught on rod and reel.* (Dean has fought much larger fish; in 1952 he fought a shark nicknamed "Barnacle Lil" that he estimated at 20 feet and 4,000 pounds for almost two hours before he lost it.) With the exception of the 12-pound-line class, where a 96-pound South African shark is the record, every record white shark caught on rod and reel has been pulled from Australian waters.†

Fishing for white pointers in Australia is a unique kind of fishing. There is none of the trolling or casting with the hope that a fish will rise from the depths to take your bait. (That of course is exactly what they used to do in South Africa, but that is another story.) In Australia, you never catch a fish that you have not seen first. The white pointers are attracted to the boat by a trail of chum (or "berley," as the Aussies call it), which consists of oil, blood, and other delicacies shown by experience to appeal to the white pointer's sense of smell. It may take *days* for the sharks to arrive, and when they do, the crew keeps feeding them, adding chunks of meat or fish to the bloody fluid. Often more than one shark is attracted to the chum and the angler must decide which one he or she wants. (Off Dangerous Reef in 1949, R. G. Cowell reported "seven in sight at one time," and Ernest Palmer has written that he had "on several occasions

* On May 1, 1990, Dion Gilmore, while fishing in Streaky Bay, South Australia, caught a female white pointer that was just over 17 feet long and weighed 3,350 pounds. Although many local newspapers hailed the catch as a new world's record, the data have not been submitted to the IGFA, which suggests that the angler fears the catch would not be recognized. (As was the case in 1976 with Clive Green's 3,388-pounder, the bait used seems to have had more than a little to do with marine mammals. A seal carcass with the head cut off, found under the Streaky Bay jetty, has not only cast doubt on the record, but has prompted the authorities to investigate, since seal killing is illegal in South Australian waters.) It appears as if Alf Dean's world's record white shark caught off Ceduna (just north of Streaky Bay) will retain its title.

† Alf Dean, who was born on July 3, 1904, at Irymple, Victoria, died on February 12, 1991, in Adelaide, South Australia. When British shark fisherman Vic Sampson caught a 1,702-pound female white shark off Kangaroo Island, South Australia, the following month, he was quoted as saying, "When I arrived in Australia, I discovered that the world record holder Alf Dean had just died, and this shark seemed a fitting tribute to him."

BELOW, LEFT: The Simms family of South Australia with a white shark, around the turn of the century.

BELOW, RIGHT: One of the few women to compete in the white shark derby: Dolly Dyer of Australia with her 912-pound women's record catch.

seen as many as twelve individuals in a favoured feeding area.") When the angler feeds a hooked bait to the chosen shark, the battle begins.

And indeed, the hooking of the shark is the easy part. When you are hauling on a fish that weighs as much as a small car, you have to be both strong and careful. Obviously, once you have the shark securely hooked, if the line connecting you to the fish is strong enough, all you have to do is reel it in. But this is not the way big-game fishing works; the idea is to get the largest fish on the flimsiest line—only this shows your skill. You must "play" the fish, sometimes for hours, taking up the slack when the fish approaches the boat, and then letting it out—grudgingly—as the fish once again moves away. (Unlike their cousins the makos, white pointers rarely jump clear of the water. Nevertheless, there are instances—such as Cowell's 1,570-pounder—when they do. According to the *Port Lincoln Times*, "He hooked it and brought it in in 1-1/2 hours, during which the shark jumped clean out of the water twice, making a thrilling sight— 1,500 pounds of fighting fury clearing the sea like a giant porpoise.")

It is tremendously hard work. Here is Colin Thiele's 1979 recount-

ing of Alf Dean's battle with the shark known as "Barnacle Lil," on Good Friday, 1952:

The battle was on now. Alf refused to let up for an instant—winding in, giving ground, winding in, giving ground, winding in. . . . It was really a question of judgment and strength. Before long the perspiration was streaming down his face, but the monster seemed as fresh as the morning.

Barnacle Lil rarely showed herself. She swam below the surface, veering this way and that, slackening the line as she turned, burning it off the reel irresistably when she ran. Alf sensed every move, felt the strain of every heave in the bones and muscles of his back. . . .

Alf was putting as much strain as he dared on his rod and line. When the shark ran he held her back as much as he could; when she eased her run he worked frantically to exploit the split-second chance. No matter how great the resistance he hauled back long and hard like Hercules, then dropped the rod forward in a flash and wound desperately to win a couple of revolutions of his reel. It was as painstaking as it was painful. But slowly, relentlessly—a finger's length, a foot's length, an arm's length—he was drawing the huge fish toward the boat. His reel groaned as he drove it round. The clutch was unbelievably hot from friction, the teeth of the gear wheel literally gnashing as they meshed and turned.

BELOW, LEFT: Alf Dean with one of his smaller prizes: a mere 1,004-pounder taken at Streaky Bay, South Australia, in 1953.

BELOW, RIGHT: Fisherman Ernest W. Palmer of Adelaide poses with the 1,434-pound white pointer he caught off Kangaroo Island.

After 75 minutes of this agony, the reel jammed, the line snapped like a thread, and Barnacle Lil was gone.

In 1965, as if in retribution, no less than three victims of white shark attacks joined Alf Dean and Ron Taylor aboard the *Glenmorry*, a tuna boat out of Port Lincoln. It had been three years since Brian Rodger had been attacked, two years since Rodney Fox had been mauled, and less than a year since Henri Bource had lost his leg. This was to be a fishing expedition, but Fox had built a sharkproof cage, and all three of the attack victims would enter the cage on that memorable expedition. Taylor was also planning to shoot some underwater photographs of white sharks, something that had never been attempted before.

At Memory Cove the cage was lowered into the water and Ron Taylor got some distant shots of the sharks that had been chummed up, but they were too far out of camera range to be of any value. By the third day, they had caught four sharks and the afterdeck of the *Glenmorry* looked like a charnel house. As Bource was fighting a 10-foot male, another, larger shark charged in and chomped onto its hooked relative, taking huge chunks out of its head and gills. The survivors of the shark attacks had exacted a measure of revenge, but the important legacy of this expedition was the introduction of the shark cage, and although the photographs taken from the cage were not particularly good, Taylor later hung over the duckboard and shot what were, at the time, the most spectacular pictures of white sharks ever taken. They made a film of this expedition, which they called "Hunt for the Great White Shark." Peter Gimbel saw the film, and within a couple of years (with an unproductive detour in South Africa), he was in South Australia to film "Blue Water, White Death." One of the photos Ron Taylor took from the *Glenmorry* was used for the poster advertising this sensational film.

At about the same time that Bob Dyer and Alf Dean were hauling in their record-breaking sharks off Australia, the sport was picking up on the other side of the world. In 1951, Frank Mundus, who would later describe himself as "the world's most illustrious and colorful charter boat captain and shark fisherman supreme" was taking up "monster fishing." This enterprise would lead to the capture of a lot of very large white sharks, the death of a lot of pilot whales and porpoises (see p. 194), and, as an ancillary and unexpected result, the inspiration for Captain Quint in the novel *Jaws*.

Frank Mundus began his fishing career in Brielle, New Jersey, but soon moved north to Montauk, Long Island. As he took fishermen out for bluefish, tuna, or striped bass, an occasional shark would be hooked. When other captains hooked sharks—usually blues—they would cut them loose or even shoot them, since sharks were considered an inedible and destructive nuisance. To Mundus, however, they suggested something different, something that would distinguish him from others in the vast navy of charter captains, and by 1958 his "monster fishing" was in full swing.

Before the passage of the Marine Mammal Protection Act in 1972, it

The competition for the largest white shark taken on rod and reel see-sawed between Alf Dean and Bob Dyer, who is shown here with a monster taken off South Australia.

# The White Shark in Captivity

**10**

E ven before "Jaws," the attractive power of the white shark challenged aquarium husbandry experts and tantalized aquarium directors. The rarity of the species, as well as the difficulties of capture and transport, have denied most aquariums the opportunity to display a healthy specimen. All attempts so far have been outright or qualified failures.

The problems involved are as diverse as they are numerous. Our technology and our considerable body of information on the biology of this creature are unavailing; the animal remains unable or unwilling to conform to our needs. Most of the "smaller" specimens have been between 7 and 8 feet in length, which immediately presents a major problem: a small white shark is, by comparison with other species usually exhibited in aquariums, a very big fish indeed.

*Carcharodon carcharias*, like many other sharks, must keep moving in order to breathe. But how do you keep a shark moving while transporting it in a truck? And if you cannot keep it moving, how can you keep it from asphyxiating? We know so very little about the temperament of this animal, but we can assume that an angry or disoriented white shark is going to be more trouble than a calm one. And finally, there is the problem of the press and public sentiment: once captured, such a shark immediately becomes a celebrity of the stature of Joy Adamson's lioness "Elsa." Woe betide the aquarium that lets one die. The white shark nevertheless remains the holy grail of the aquarium business.

Dr. Leighton Taylor, a shark scientist and the past director of the Waikiki Aquarium, in Honolulu, suggests in a 1985 article that the first opportunity for the public to view a captive white shark might not have come from the temperate American coast at all, but from Hawaii. In March 1961 a 13-foot specimen was captured in Honolulu Harbor, and was displayed at Hawaii Marineland for 24 hours before it died. Frank Inoue, a local, remembers that an employee of the Oceanarium rode the nearly dead shark around the aquarium tank for several hours.

In December 1962 an 8-foot male was captured off St. Augustine and brought to Marineland of Florida. According to the press release issued at that time, the "new record for a maneater in captivity" was 35 or 36 hours, which record "exceeded the old one by almost 35 or 36 hours." After showing some signs of recuperating from its capture, the shark sank to the bottom of the tank and died.

When a six-foot white pointer was hooked off the north Sydney beach known as Warriewood and brought to the Marine Aquarium, it swam around for five days, attacking other fishes and a handler until the manager of the aquarium ordered the "berserk" animal destroyed. According to the headline in the *Australian Post* for May 23, 1968, "The White Pointer Was Mad. . . . It Had to Die Before It Emptied the Aquarium. . . ."

Aquariums in other parts of the world have also realized the drawing power of a captive white shark. In 1969 a young white shark was rushed to the aquarium in Durban, South Africa, but it died almost immediately. In October 1978, a 7-footer was captured in the nets off Umhlanga Rocks, a popular beach on South Africa's Natal Coast. (This is one of the Indian Ocean beaches where since the 1960's the Natal Sharks Board has set nets to keep the sharks—mostly bull sharks and duskies—from bothering or attacking the bathers.) The Umhlanga Rocks shark was in poor condition, having been immobilized and suffocating for several hours before the nets were hauled in, and it died the following day.

An 8-foot juvenile male photographed during its 36-hour captivity at Marineland of Florida in 1962.

The Okinawa Expo Aquarium in Japan has also tried to introduce white sharks into its tanks, with the same results. (In 1982, however, this aquarium became the first to capture and successfully display a *whale* shark, a 15-foot female that lived for six months.)

The American aquariums most likely to maintain a white shark in captivity are those on the West Coast, primarily in California. The large California aquariums, from north to south (with their dates of origin) are: Steinhart Aquarium of the California Academy of Sciences in San Francisco (1923); Monterey Bay Aquarium (1984); Marineland of the Pacific at Palos Verdes (opened in 1955, now closed); and Sea World at San Diego (1964). Each has, on various occasions, tried to maintain a living white shark. (The species is less common in Oregon, Washington, and British Columbia, and no such attempts have been made on those coasts.)

The Steinhart was the first California aquarium to attempt to exhibit a *Carcharodon,* but the efforts were half-hearted at best. W. Walter Schneebeli, collector for the aquarium from 1946 to 1979, made several attempts to revive white sharks that had been captured by fishermen in Bodega Bay, 50 miles north of San Francisco. On more than one occasion, these sharks had been seen with their sickle-shaped tails thrashing outside of a large box on the back of a truck on Highway 101. Schneebeli said that none of them lived for more than a day, because the aquarium did not have a tank truck large enough to transport them or an aquarium tank large enough to hold them. It was not until 1977, with the opening of the "Roundabout,"

In 1978, a white shark was trapped in the nets of the Natal Sharks Board at Umhlanga Rocks, Natal, South Africa, and brought to the Durban Aquarium, where it survived just one day.

a large toroidal (donut-shaped) tank that holds 100,000 gallons of slowly circulating seawater, that the Steinhart has had the facilities to support a living white shark.

Timing is everything in this business, and for the Monterey Bay Aquarium, the timing could not have been worse. The construction of this spectacular aquarium was already behind schedule in September 1984 when a call from an excited fisherman came in. The grand opening and accompanying festivities were planned for late October, and the prospect of a live white shark in the main tank was more than the staff could resist. Either they would have the first white shark on opening day, and thus garner even more worldwide publicity, or, if past experience was any indication, they would have on their hands a dead shark that would cast a pall of death and failure across the gala event.

Curator Dave Powell purchased the 4-foot 10-inch newborn shark from the Bodega Bay fisherman, and released it into the 345,000-gallon tank. To everyone's surprise, the fish responded well, swam without difficulty, and stayed alive for eleven days. Toward the end of the first week, however, it became obvious to Powell and his staff that it would not survive, and with the press sniffing out a story that had until then been a closely guarded secret, Powell decided to release the shark before it died in captivity. They debated returning it to Monterey Bay on Friday, September 14, hoping for a positive response from the public, but the shark died on the day they were planning to release it. Far from being a moment of shame, however, the death of the shark was one of the shining moments in the happy history of the aquarium, for on Saturday, an abalone diver named Omar Conger was killed by a white shark off Pigeon Point, at the north end of Monterey Bay. Had the original release plan been followed, the Monterey Bay Aquarium might have been held responsible for the release of a man-killer (notwithstanding that a white shark so small would scarcely be up to the job). The aquarium celebrated its incredible good fortune by using the image of their one-time resident on the label of their "Great White Wine."

The Southern California aquariums, Marineland at Palos Verdes and Sea World in San Diego, had little more than a passing interest in white sharks until the "Jaws" phenomenon exploded across the country. Both are located on the water—a clear advantage for anyone who would hope to transport and display a white shark—and they both possessed enormous display tanks. They had all the ingredients but the sharks.

Marineland of the Pacific was the first oceanarium on the West Coast, and, under the direction of Dr. Kenneth Norris, had pioneered the capture and successful exhibition of various species of pilot whales and dolphins, and was therefore not averse to trying another difficult species. In 1955, a 5-foot newborn white shark was trucked from the Scripps Institution at La Jolla to Marineland, but survived only a few hours. Curiously, young white sharks had been caught off Palos Verdes by sport and commercial fishermen for years, but it was not until 1981 that any of them made a serious attempt at keeping one. Don Zumwalt, then Curator, received a call from the sportfishing boat *Rebel* that a 58-inch white had been taken and was coming in. The fish was kept in a 540,000-gallon oval

At the Okinawa Expo Aquarium, the first *whale* shark ever exhibited swims serenely in its tank. It survived captivity for six months.

In a holding tank at the Steinhart Aquarium in San Francisco, Al Giddings and John McCosker contemplate a white shark rescued from a gill net.

tank for nearly a week, but finally succumbed to what the necropsy disclosed—gaff wounds in the gills and body.

Sea World, though a late arrival, quickly became Marineland's chief competitor. The effort was led by the redoubtable Dave Powell, already an industry legend in maintaining and exhibiting rare and difficult specimens. Powell and his staff experimented with transport slings, tranquilizing chemicals, pumping systems that would simulate the flow of water across the shark's gills, and capture techniques that would minimize stress. Powell left Sea World in 1974 to join the staff of the Steinhart Aquarium, but he left a handsome legacy in the form of a 400,000-gallon shark tank that had cost more than $2 million. By the time the movie "Jaws" was released in the summer of 1975, Sea World had opened its gigantic shark tank, but no white shark graced it.

Like a military operation, the Sea World staff established base camps in Ventura (just north of Los Angeles) and Marshall, a small fishing community 40 miles north of San Francisco. Cargo planes and trucks were at the ready, should a white shark be captured at either of these outposts. And indeed, several were caught between 1976 and 1980, but none survived the trip to San Diego. In 1981, three young sharks were caught off San Diego, and one of them lived for 16 days in the shark tank before it perished. The 5.5-foot juvenile never fed during its captivity.

Part of the problem at Sea World seems to have been temperature. The water had been heated to approximately 75 degrees Fahrenheit in order to meet the requirements of the bull sharks and the lemon sharks, which are warm-water species. The temperate-water white shark was thus at a physiological disadvantage. The presence of adult bull sharks probably contributed to the distress of the juvenile white, which was injured as a result of its capture and stressed because of its transport and strange surroundings. With the demise of the 16-day phenomenon, the campaign was cut back, and the emphasis shifted toward the display of dead sharks. Sea World nonetheless put out the word that it was willing to pay handsomely for white sharks, dead or alive, and the local fishermen were only too happy to oblige.

The Steinhart Aquarium, toward the other end of the state, has a long-standing reputation as a scientific institution as well as a display aquarium. It is part of the prestigious California Academy of Sciences, in San Francisco's Golden Gate Park, and an important center for biological research. On its staff are research ichthyologists as well as experts on fish husbandry and display. The aquarium was the first to display many rare species, such as the bioluminescent flashlight fishes and several rare and endangered American fishes. Despite its "serious" reputation—or perhaps because of it—the Steinhart joined the fray to become the first to exhibit

Sandy the shark, being resuscitated by Al Wilson, a gill-net fisherman out of Bodega Bay. Fishing from a small boat early in the morning, Al discovered Sandy in his net and returned with her to the wharf, where Aloysius O'Neill met the boat and helped with Sandy.

a live white shark. At this time, aquarists had begun to feel that their traditional attractions (brightly colored coral-reef fishes, electric eels, piranhas) were being overshadowed by the glamorous, ocean-oriented "theme parks" (of which Sea World in San Diego was the paradigm), and worse, that these new places, with their emphasis on gift shops, restaurants, and dolphin and killer whale razzle-dazzle, were siphoning off their visitors. It was obvious that an aquarium offering "educational" displays of symbiosis or pollution could not compete for the tourist dollar with a place that exhibited a trained killer whale (Sea World had begun its "Shamu" shows in 1966), and the Steinhart accordingly directed its efforts toward the thing it knew best: the display of fishes.

A shark bidding war commenced. The Steinhart offered $500 at the dock to anyone who could deliver a living white shark. Sea World doubled the bid. Steinhart countered with a complicated scheme that promised $1,000 if the shark lived 24 hours, and $250 more for each day that it remained alive until $5,000 had been reached. It was obviously in the best interests of the fishermen to capture and treat the sharks as gently as possible, in the hope that one of them might survive. Dave Powell, by then on the staff of Steinhart, designed large, self-contained, fiberglass transport boxes that could be hoisted onto a truck and filled with refrigerated seawater in a matter of minutes. On three occasions between 1976 and 1980, fishermen called from Bodega Bay to report the capture of a live white shark. Each time, the SWAT Team (Steinhart White Acquisition Team) sprang into action, hoping to beat Sea World to the punch, and the race was on. As the Steinhart task force headed for one shark, the Sea World detachment headed for another, but in every instance the results were the same: an exhausted team and an expired shark.

Al Wilson, a fisherman who had once been employed as a specimen collector for the Bodega Bay Marine Laboratory, a field station of the University of California, knew something about keeping animals alive. He also knew something about white sharks: earlier in the summer of 1980, he had snared a 600-pounder in his nets, and had to pump ten rifle slugs into it to slow it down. He delivered its carcass to the local fish market and its jaws to a curio dealer.

On August 12, however, the circumstances were different. Wilson was hauling in his flounder net when he realized that he had a white shark entangled in it. He slipped a rope around its tail and towed it to shore, "like the 'Old Man and the Sea,'" he was later to remark. The Sea World team had set up its headquarters at a local motel (where they were planning to use a plastic backyard swimming pool as a holding tank if the shark ever materialized), and Wilson knew they were there and were prepared to pay him $1,000 on the spot for the delivery. When he reached the dock, he called them, only to discover that they were all out, doing their laundry at the local laundromat. He then called Steinhart, and the SWAT team set out for Bodega Bay. Six hours later, the 300-pound, 7.5-foot shark was swimming groggily in the aquarium's Roundabout (see McCosker's account of her stay there, beginning on the following page). "Sandy" was different from every other white shark that had ever been kept in an aquarium: she's probably still alive.

# Sandy's Visit to the Steinhart Aquarium

Sandy was not the first great white shark to be kept in an aquarium, but she was the first that was "living" when placed in the tank, as opposed to "slowly dying." During the hell-for-leather ride from Bodega Bay to San Francisco, Ed Miller, an aquarist and shark expert, rode in the back of the Steinhart's truck, massaging Sandy's muscles and attending to the oxygen supply and water pumps in the transport box. At the aquarium, the 7.5-foot shark was carried gingerly up three flights of stairs on a stretcher and gently released into the Roundabout. She swam slowly with the current, "downstream" as it were, and everybody released the breath they'd been holding, it seemed, since Bodega Bay.

The donut-shaped Roundabout (the visitors stand in the "hole" and watch the fish circle around them) had been designed to eliminate the problems that open-water fish usually encounter in captivity—specifically, collisions with unseen and unexpected glass walls. (In the past, confrontations between an ir-resistible Great White Force and an immovable steel, concrete, and glass aquarium had invariably ended in favor of the aquarium.) Steinhart's Roundabout is 66 feet in diameter, with an 8-foot-wide, 10-foot-tall, open-topped raceway forming the donut. Pumps keep seawater constantly circulating around the raceway. Even without a maneater, it is one of the most popular exhibits in the aquarium, and the closest approximation of a pelagic environment that any aquarium has yet been able to develop. In addition to housing yellowtails, amberjacks, bluefish, rays, and leopard sharks, the Round-about has been a successful long-term habitation for other species of sharks that had never before been kept in captivity, such as the soup-fin and the sevengill cowshark. But it had not been built with the possibility of exhibiting a white shark in mind.

Sandy proved to be light-sensitive, having come from murky coastal waters that are considerably deeper than the Roundabout. So as to duplicate as closely as possible the circumstances from which she'd come, we reduced the light level and introduced filters. Video cameras and fast film enabled Al Giddings to film her behavior from underwater within the tank—the first time, so far as we know, that anyone had ever been in the water voluntarily with a healthy white shark without the protection of a cage. Subsequent examination of these films allowed us to study her swimming form and avoidance behavior (she seemed to show little interest in the divers or the other fish in the tank), as well as her breathing and tail-motion rates. For most of the remaining daylight hours of the first day, she swam against the current (as almost all other fish in the tank do), and seemed to improve her navigational skills, despite an occasional collision with a wall or window.

But the Roundabout is only donut-*shaped*; it is not a seamless torus of glass. Its design is complicated by three steel inner-edge abutments that are used to guide half-ton steel doors into gate tracks (the doors allow us to compart-

mentalize and drain portions of the tank). The abutments became a serious problem after dark, for they extend 4 inches into the tank, just enough to allow Sandy to stub her nose on them and stop her perpetual counterclockwise motion. Because she couldn't be allowed to stop moving—she would suffocate if she did—whenever she collided with one of these abutments, a wet-suited aquarist would enter the Roundabout and help her to get moving again.

Because it appeared that Sandy was either afraid of the dark or unable to navigate in total darkness, we left some of the lights on through the night. But as she improved and her swimming speed increased, the problem of the abutments became more critical, since she was now hitting them with greater force. Kevin O'Farrell, Chief Designer in the Exhibition Department (trained in Detroit as an automobile designer), quickly solved the problem by designing, fabricating, and installing a plexiglass shield that smoothed out the inner surface of the tank. Like everyone else involved in this extraordinary adventure (except Al Giddings and me), Kevin had never even seen a living white shark before, let alone gone for a swim with one. But his shield seemed, at least temporarily, to have solved the problem.

For most of that first day the Roundabout had been closed to the public, and the only people allowed to see the shark were the staff of the aquarium. Outside, a mob of reporters and photographers anxiously awaited the opportunity to see the maneater. Sandy obviously wasn't going to eat anyone, but we decided we'd better try to feed her something. We dumped slurries of blood, squid, and fish into the tank, hoping that would elicit the same feeding response in Sandy that we'd seen in white sharks off South Australia. We tried all kinds of fish, fresh and frozen, without success. A 5-foot skinned sturgeon was taken from the freezer and offered like a giant ear of corn to Sandy, but she wasn't interested.

For three days, Sandy swam slowly, as the crowds watched in awe. By the fourth day of her captivity, however, we began to notice some peculiarities in her behavior. Although she swam normally most of the time, slowly circling into the current, she would occasionally swim erratically through a particular 5-degree arc of the tank, and collide with the outer wall at pretty much the same point each time. There didn't seem to be any visible discontinuity in the tank's perimeter at that point, but she always seemed to react peculiarly there. We could see no differences in the levels of light, sound, or current in that area, and we finally decided that whatever was disturbing her movement was something beyond our landlocked observational skills.

Because white sharks are particularly sensitive to electrical discharges in the water, we called in an electrical engineer. Norm Buell arrived soon with a sensitive silver-silver chloride cell, which he employed like a sophisticated dowsing rod. After one trip around the tank's perimeter, he located the problem. There was a minute anomaly between two of the windows, a differential of 0.125 millivolt, an amount so tiny that the other sharks didn't notice it at all, or if they did, it didn't seem to bother them.

To correct this tiny electrical problem, we would have to drain the entire tank and implant an induced-current system, similar to those used on the undersides of some marine vessels to prevent ionization and corrosion. We'd have had to drill through the wall of the tank to implant the electrodes, and it would have taken more time than we thought we had to tune the system to electrical harmony. We couldn't empty the tank—aside from further traumatizing Sandy, we'd probably kill all the other fish in it—but it was clear that if we allowed her to keep bumping into the wall she would die.

There I was, with the aquarium director's dream—and the aquarium director's nightmare. We had worldwide media coverage, but it was depressingly contradictory. Some of the media people saw Sandy as a benign refutation of her own ominous reputation, but others saw her as a killer. Mayor Dianne Feinstein of San Francisco came to visit her, as did some 40,000 other visitors over the three-and-a-half-day period. Sandy made the wire services, the news magazines, and a double-page spread in *Life* magazine. Walter Cronkite dubbed her "the darling of San Francisco," and in a way, she was. Yes, she was the fabled "maneater" of "Jaws," but she was also a baby and, swimming slowly around the tank, she didn't look as if she was going to attack even the fish that swam with her, let alone the divers that hovered anxiously just out of sight of the crowds. For many people, it was hard to reconcile this graceful, black-eyed crea-

Very gingerly, the Steinhart team loads Sandy aboard the *Flying Fish*. John McCosker at center, with the dorsal fin.

ture with the vengeful monster of "Jaws," and yet that's exactly what they were being asked to do. Was she an unreconstructed killer, or simply a small shark that was so confused by her surroundings that she kept crashing into the wall? We were at a loss what to do, but if we did nothing at all, she would probably be dead in a week.

After endless cups of coffee, and endless circular discussions with Al and the others, I decided to release her. We could have trucked her to Tomales or Bodega Bay, up the coast, but we figured she'd probably just blunder into another fisherman's net and wind up either dead or back in the aquarium. We therefore decided to take her to the Farallon Islands, 26 miles out to sea, where she would encounter no nets and no swimmers—no swimmers because Sandy's adult relatives, which feed on the sea lions and elephant seals that breed there, had several years earlier discouraged swimming and diving around the islands (when one of them nearly did away with Al Giddings' partner while their scuba-school

The *Flying Fish* departs Sausalito for the Farallones.

students looked on, the appeal of the place took on a new character).

And so, with a proper police escort, sirens wailing, we drove her over the Golden Gate Bridge to the Sausalito wharf, where we boarded the *Flying Fish*, a 55-foot salmon-fishing boat. Through several hours of hammering seas and a stiff on-shore wind, the *Flying Fish* fought its way out to the Farallones. Al and his camera crew were seaworthy enough, but most of the reporters wished they had bid Sandy farewell from the dock.

The water sloshing in Sandy's box had been more than adequately oxygenated, and when we tipped her into the ocean, she exhibited the speed and power that we had not seen in the tank; she was off like a shot. Giddings, Terry Kerby, and I were in the chilly water to provide whatever help she needed, but it was clear that she needed no more help from people, and no more tanks, millivolts, or truck rides. Sandy was gone, but we were swimming in the white-sharkiest waters in Northern California, and none of us believed for a moment that she would tell her aunts and uncles how nice we'd been to her.

After it was all over, I felt good about what we'd done. In a limited sense, we'd been successful in keeping a white shark in captivity, and we'd learned a great deal about the species. An invisible defect in the tank had made it necessary for us to return Sandy to the wild. She had been with us for three and a half days.

Because I had the opportunity to explain what I had done and why I'd done it, I thought that the public would understand. Not everyone did. Bob Brumfield, a columnist for the *Cincinnati Inquirer*, wrote a piece that he entitled, "There Is No Reason to Spare the Sharks." In this ludicrous diatribe, he wrote,

It is hard for me to believe that anyone of sound mind would *capture* a shark when he could *kill* it, unless his purpose was to study the shark in order to develop an effective shark repellent or a way to eradicate the entire species once and for all.

And anyone *releasing* a captured shark *alive* [all these italics are his], once it had been studied, should have his head examined.

He went on to describe Sandy's captivity, and quotes me as saying that releasing her was better than watching her slowly die. This so enraged Mr. Brumfield that he howled, "Better than watching her slowly die? Why you dummy, there's *nothing* better than watching a shark slowly die! That's even better than watching one die *quickly*!"

He concluded by saying, "This isn't a Bambi movie, McCosker! You've let loose a relentless eating machine, with a life span of God only knows how long. You've released a dreadful, silent killer to stalk swimmers as well as its normal food supply of fish." Not content with condemning me for releasing what he called "a savage man-eating monster . . . that will spawn hundreds of other savage, man-eating monsters," he then (somewhat too enthusiastically, I thought) suggested that the first man to be eaten by Sandy should be me:

I hope that big booger gets *you*, McCosker. I hope one night you're swimming in the Pacific, and you feel something brush against your leg. Then I hope you look up and see a big, dark dorsal fin cutting through the ocean, leaving a sparkle of luminescence behind it—just before it slips below the surface—and WHAMMO! WHAMMO! WHAMMO!

Well, Mr. Brumfield, I'm sorry you felt that way. I rather hoped that we were doing the shark and science and our own kind a favor by releasing her. It troubles me to realize that there are still people who can get things so backward that they wish physical harm on someone who saves the life of a fish. I don't want anything bad to happen to you, Bob; I just wish you'd read something besides *Jaws*.

*John McCosker*

# 11

# The Predator as Protagonist

The great white shark has not been a popular subject in art. Copley's "Watson and the Shark" shows a strange-looking shark attacking a man in Havana Harbor, but in no way could this creature with its jaws on the outside of its lips be mistaken for a white shark—or any other known species, for that matter.* And although Winslow Homer's "Gulf Stream" depicts much better sharks, it does not show our subject either.

Charles R. Knight, best-known for his depictions of prehistoric animals in natural settings, painted Megalodon (see p. 46) at least twice during the 1930's: once as a sketch, and then as a small mural for the American Museum of Natural History in New York, giving it very much the look of a very large white shark. In his book *Before the Dawn of History*, Knight asked, "What must we think of the great fish shown in the picture—a vast creature some forty or fifty feet in length, with a mouth six feet in width, known only for its fossilized teeth which are from four to six inches long? Truly here is a brute to strike terror to the stoutest heart, and we may be thankful for its disappearance long before our era."

Aside from its occasional appearance in adventure stories—more often than not, simply as "a shark"—or its more frequent mention in scientific works, the great white shark was rarely identified by name or species in the literature of the past. A little literary detective work, however, turns up our subject in Jules Verne's *Twenty Thousand Leagues under the Sea*, written in 1870.

When Captain Nemo takes his prisoners for a stroll along the bottom

*In a discussion of the subject matter of the painting—which appeared as the cover illustration of the *Journal of the American Medical Association*—Dr. M. Therese Southgate wrote that "the critics of 1778 found several errors of logic in it, namely that the shark does not look like a shark and its tail is not lashing the water, that the figure of the boy is too large, that the men are not rowing correctly if they are trying to reach the boy, that their fingers are not in a proper position for grasping the boy, and that the wind that blows the harpooner's hair should also affect the sails of the ships in the harbor."

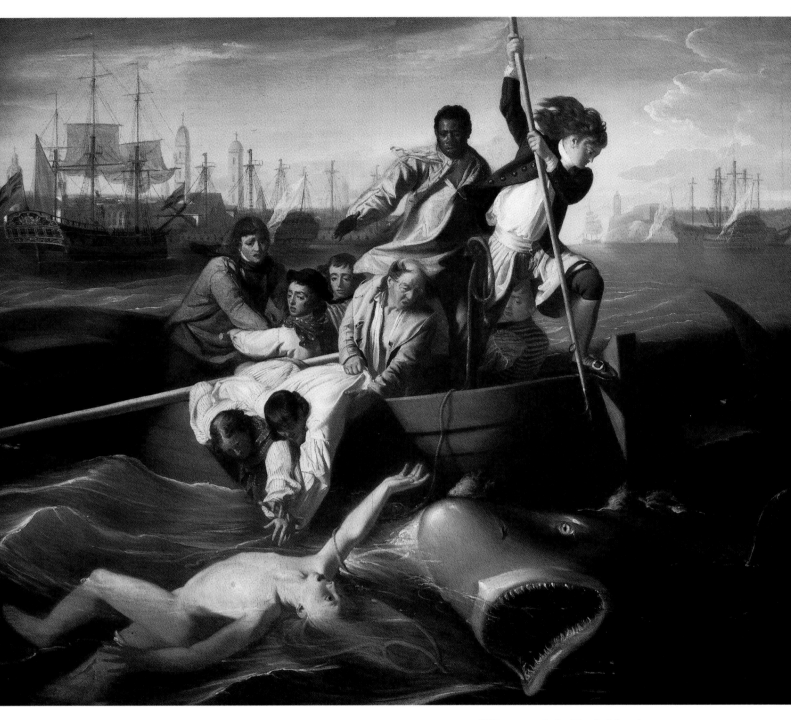

"Watson and the Shark," by the American artist John Singleton Copley (1738–1815). This curious shark—definitely *not* a white—was obviously painted from a set of jaws, which would explain the peculiar "lips" on the shark.

of the ocean, he exposes them to all sorts of dangers, not the least of which are the sharks. When Aronnax, Conseil, Ned Land, and Captain Nemo encounter their first sharks while returning from an underwater walk, they are made aware of these "huge shapes leaving streams of phosphorescense behind them." Aronnax, a "Professor of the Paris Museum" and an authority on marine life, then describes the climax of the expedition:

The blood froze in my veins. I saw we were being threatened by two formidable dogfish, those terrible sharks with enormous tails and dull glassy eyes, who secrete a phosphorescent substance through holes around their snouts. They are like monstrous fireflies who can crush an entire man in their jaws of iron! I don't know if Conseil was busy classifying them, but as for me, I was observing their silver bellies and huge mouths bristling with teeth from a not altogether scientific point of view—rather as a prospective victim than as a naturalist.

But the sharks pass harmlessly overhead ("very fortunately these voracious animals have bad eyesight"), and the hunters return to the *Nautilus* safe and sound. The "dogfish," however, previously described as "monstrous fireflies," put in another appearance in the South Atlantic, and from the

The *grand chien de mer* ("great sea-dog") from the orginal edition of *Twenty Thousand Leagues Under the Sea*. From the impressions of the fish that he offers in the text, it appears that Jules Verne was describing the great white shark—at least as it was known in 1870. Almost hidden in the gloom is the black-clad diver who is seeing to the unconscious swimmer's rescue.

references provided by Professor Aronnax, we are able to take an educated guess at the species.

We also saw some large dogfish, a voracious species of fish if ever there was one. Even though fishermen's stories are not to be believed, it is said that in one of these fish was found a buffalo head and an entire calf; in another, two tuna and a sailor still in uniform; in another, a sailor with his saber; and in yet another, a horse with its rider. It must be said, though, that these stories seem a bit doubtful. In any case, none of these animals ever allowed itself to be captured in the *Nautilus'* nets, and I therefore had no way of finding out how voracious they were.

Only one species of shark comes close to fulfilling these—and the earlier—critieria; only the great white, among the larger sharks, has the reputation for voraciousness and omnivorousness that Aronnax describes. It is doubtful that Verne ever saw a live one, but he may well have seen a dead one on the beach or in a taxidermist's shop. If indeed Verne's "dogfish" is a great white, it would explain the "enormous tail"—a full-grown white shark is an enormous fish—the glassy eyes (if it was a dead one), and finally, the "phosphorescent substance" they secrete "through holes around their snouts." Of course white sharks do not secrete a phosophorescent (actually, bioluminescent) substance, but they do have the ampullae of Lorenzini, a pronounced array of pores around their snouts, which could, in Verne's fertile imagination, exude phosphorescence.

The great white shark was originally known as *Canis carchariae*, which can be translated as "dog shark," and throughout the early history of popular ichthyology, sharks of all kinds were known as dog-fishes or seadogs. (In the original, Verne called this shark *grand chien de mer*, which can

*Megalodon*, the gigantic extinct relative of *Carcharodon*, scatters sharks, eagle rays, and small fry alike in this 1930's re-creation by Charles R. Knight. In *Before the Dawn of History*, Knight wrote, "Truly here is a brute to strike terror to the stoutest heart, and we may be thankful for its disappearance long before our era."

be translated as "great dog of the sea," not much help in determining the species.)

After making a film about blue sharks off Montauk, Long Island, in 1965, Peter Gimbel decided to mount an expedition to film white sharks. He had seen "Hunt for the Great White Shark," the 1964 film made by the Taylors and Rodney Fox, so there is no question that he knew from the start where white sharks could be found. (He did believe, however, that simply heading right for Australia and filming the sharks would not have made much of a feature film.) And because Gimbel had also heard that white sharks came to feed on whale carcasses off Durban, he first took his cages, his cameras, and his crew to South Africa. Gimbel, Ron and Valerie Taylor, and Stan Waterman filmed sharks feeding on a dead sperm whale, and although they got some of the most exciting undersea footage ever made—at one point, they were all out of the cages, filming oceanic white-tips, blues, duskies, and a tiger—the shark that Gimbel referred to as "Whitey" never appeared.

Several abortive attempts were made to find white sharks in the Indian Ocean, both off the Comoro Islands (where coelacanths live) and off Sri Lanka (south of India, and another location where there are no

LEFT: Peter Gimbel, the man who started it all.

OPPOSITE, ABOVE: Before Peter Gimbel's "Blue Water, White Death," there was Ron Taylor, filming "Giant White Death Sharks."

OPPOSITE, BELOW: The "Blue Water, White Death" film team: Peter Gimbel, Valerie and Ron Taylor, and Stan Waterman, with the cages aboard the *Terrier IV*, a South African whale-catcher.

known occurrences of white sharks), but finally, with only the Durban feeding frenzy in the can, they decided to head for South Australia. With Rodney Fox and Ron and Valerie Taylor as advisors, the "Blue Water, White Death" film team found their subject off Dangerous Reef, in January 1970. According to Peter Matthiessen (who chronicled the expedition with such skill in *Blue Meridian*), the footage shot at that time was "surely the most exciting film ever taken underwater [that] had been obtained without serious injury to anybody." It was the first time the great white had been the subject of a major film, but it would not be the last.*

"Blue Water, White Death" was an enormous success for a documentary. Both the expedition and the film won worldwide critical acclaim, and Gimbel, who had conceived the idea and sold it, and had produced and directed the film, deserves all the credit for introducing the great white shark to the world. Of course the white pointer was not an unknown quantity beforehand, but it was probably known mostly to a handful of ichthyologists, fishermen, and South Australians. Even along the California coast, it had not yet had much press. As of 1971, with the release of Gimbel's film, the seeds were planted for the growth of the phenomenon that became "Jaws." On May 12, 1971, Peter Gimbel's film opened in New York. Vincent Canby, *The New York Times*' film critic, wrote:

Sharks, however, are something else, often observed but until comparatively recently, little-known, the subjects of all sorts of old wives' tales, a symbol for everything from shylocking to every man's fate worse than death, an implacable, terrifying, disinterested power, an Old Testament tribulation, as well as a force of extraordinary grace, beauty, and serenity. Those of you who share my perhaps neurotic weekend skindiver's fascination with sharks will not, I think, be able to resist the quite jolly, sometimes awesome, new documentary movie that opened yesterday at the Festival Theater. . . .

* In 1936, Zane Grey made—and starred in—a movie he called "White Death," which was ostensibly about the white shark, but since the shark does not appear until the end, the film does not really qualify. In this movie, shot in New Zealand and Australia, a gent from an unspecified location on the Great Barrier Reef offers Grey the opportunity to catch a 20-foot white shark that has been terrorizing the local aborigines, and has eaten several of them along with the wife and son of the local missionary. Grey agrees to catch the shark, partly to win a bet with a rival fisherman, and partly to avenge the death of the missionary, who has also fallen victim to the shark. He hooks the shark, and, as in *Jaws*, to which this film bears no other resemblance, his boat is towed all over the place until the shark tires and can be gaffed. The film ends as the shark—a model painted white—is towed onto the beach, and the romantic leads, neither of whom is Zane Grey, gaze into the sunset.

It also contains some of the most beautiful and (there is no other way to describe it accurately) breathtaking underwater footage I've ever seen—truly remarkable, free-swimming encounters by Mr. Gimbel and his associates with sharks gorging themselves on newly caught whales, with barracudas, with fat pushy groupers, and finally, and triumphantly, with the great white sharks off the south coast of Australia. . . .

However, the heart of the film is its action, recorded with immense technical skill, and it is so pure that it's as poetic as anything I've seen on the screen in a long, long time.

So film has been kind, but fiction and the great white shark have proved to be uneasy bedfellows. With the singular exception of Peter Benchley, the author of "Jaws," very few writers have tried to tackle this intimidating subject in a serious work of fiction. Of course the great white shark appears in many books, but only rarely has the writer attempted to improve on reality—or what we think of as reality. *Carcharodon carcharias* is so awe-inspiring, so formidable, so majestic, that there seems to be no need and no way to make it better—or worse—by a well-turned phrase.

But in *Blue Meridian*, a nonfiction chronicle of an expedition, Peter Matthiessen has given us perhaps the most moving, accurate, literate, and beautiful description of the white shark that has been written. Matthiessen had been invited to join the "Blue Water, White Death" film team on its two-year, round-the-world quest for the great white shark. He accompanied Peter Gimbel to the Bahamas (where he learned to dive) and to South Africa (where he descended in a shark cage), and with the rest of the crew he wound up aboard the *Saori* off Dangerous Reef, South Australia. This is his description of his first view of a white shark underwater:

The bolder of the sharks, perhaps twelve feet long, was a heavy male, identifiable by paired claspers at the vent; a second male, slightly smaller, stayed in the background. The first shark had vivid scars around the head and an oval scar under the dorsal, and in the molten water of late afternoon it was a creature very different from the one seen from the surface. The hard rust of its hide had dissolved in pale transparent tones that shimmered in the ocean light on its satin skin. From the dorsal fin an evanescent bronze shaded down to luminous dark metallic gray along the lateral line, a color as delicate as the bronze tint on a mushroom which points up the whiteness of the flesh beneath. From snout to keel, the underside was a deathly white, all but the black tips of the broad pectorals.

Nicely done. But in the next paragraph, Matthiessen (in our view) all but transcends nature and literature. The paragraph is a match for its subject; it is the great white shark of shark writing.

The shark passed slowly, first the slack jaw with the triangular splayed teeth, then the dark eye, impenetrable and empty as the eye of God, next the gill slits like knife slashes in paper, then the pale slab of his flank, aflow with silver ripplings of light, and finally the thick short twitch of its hard tail. Its aspect was less savage than implacable, a silent thing of merciless serenity.

But this is not what we find elsewhere. Basically, the white shark literature takes one of two forms: scientific and sensational. In the former category are the myriad papers on its habits, size, distribution, body temperature, and such, many of which were used in the preparation of this book and are listed in the bibliography. In the latter a single work has

**"BLUE WATER, WHITE DEATH"**
The hunt for the Great White Shark

A CINEMA CENTER FILMS PRESENTATION
Produced by PETER GIMBEL · Directed by PETER GIMBEL and JAMES LIPSCOMB · TECHNICOLOR®
A NATIONAL GENERAL PICTURES RELEASE

The poster advertising "Blue Water, White Death," the sensational film by Peter Gimbel.

overwhelmed all else that has ever been written, and that, of course, is *Jaws*. It was this novel, published in 1974, that catapulted the white shark into the celebrity status that it retains to this day.

A good deal has been written about this novel since it emerged as the publishing sensation of 1974–75. Yes, Peter Benchley wrote it after being given a minimal advance, and no, it was not written by a committee of editors. Without background or pleasantries, the shark makes its appearance in the book's opening paragraph:

The great fish moved silently through the night water, propelled by short sweeps of its crescent tail. The mouth was open just enough to permit a rush of water over the gills. There was little other motion; an occasional correction of the apparently aimless course by the slight raising or lowering of the pectoral fins—as a bird changes direction by dipping one wing and lifting the other. The eyes were sightless in the black, and the other senses transmitted nothing extraordinary to the small, primitive brain. The fish might have been asleep, save for the movement dictated by countless millions of years of instinctive continuity: lacking the flotation bladder common to other fish and the fluttering flaps to push oxygen-bearing water through its gills, it survived only by moving. Once stopped, it would sink to the bottom and die of anoxia.

In 1973, Universal Studios bought the rights to Benchley's novel. Filmed on Martha's Vineyard, off the coast of Massachusetts, the story featured Richard Dreyfus, Roy Scheider, Robert Shaw, and Peter Benchley (in a bit part). Its star (actually, three separate units were required) was a model of a great white shark the film crews nicknamed "Bruce."

For anyone who has not read or seen "Jaws," we offer a brief synopsis. The story is a simple one. Off the beaches of a town called Amity, a large shark begins picking off swimmers and holing boats to get at their occupants. Mike Brody, the Amity police chief, becomes not a little con-

Peter Benchley, the author of "Jaws," the man who made us all shudder at the thought of entering the ocean—especially at night.

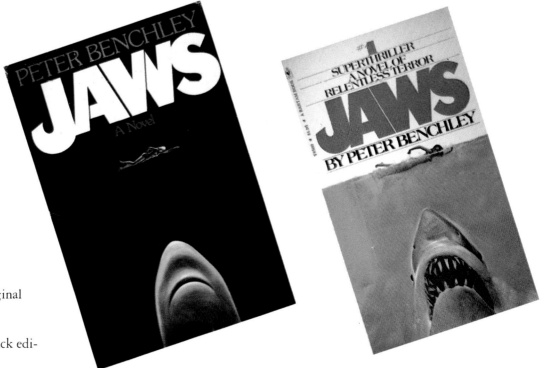

LEFT: Dust jacket of the original clothbound edition of *Jaws*.

RIGHT: Cover of the paperback edition of *Jaws*.

cerned, and because he can elicit no support whatever from the members of the town council, who are worried only about tourist income, he enlists the services of an ichthyologist named Matt Hooper. But Brody and Hooper are helpless as the shark continues its rampage. Enter Captain Quint, who offers to capture the shark for $10,000. Brody, Hooper, and Quint set out aboard Quint's boat to hunt the shark, and with harpoons, rifles, beer kegs, anesthetics, and macho determination, they succeed. In the book, Hooper is killed as the shark crushes the cage, but in the movie, he hides on the bottom until Brody dispatches the shark, which has eaten Quint. Then Hooper pops to the surface, and the two survivors swim off into the sunset and box-office history.

Produced by David Brown and Richard Zanuck and directed by Steven Spielberg, the movie version of "Jaws" was a fascinating exercise in movie-making. It required a location where the shark could be filmed in calm water (and one that suggested more the fictional island of Amity than Rarotonga); a re-write of the story to conform to various cinematic notions (because Benchley wrote his own first screenplay, this decision produced no real conflict); and most demanding of all, the fabrication of a shark that would perform on cue. According to Carl Gottlieb, the other screenwriter, the producers "had innocently assumed that they could get a shark trainer somewhere, who, with enough money, could get a great white shark to perform a few simple stunts on cue in long shots with a dummy in the water, after which they would cut to miniatures or something for the close-up stuff."

White sharks are notoriously uncatchable, not to mention untrainable, and the Special Effects Department was set to work designing a shark that could pass the scrutiny of the most demanding viewer. The three models—one to be shot from the left, one to be shot from the right, and one to be shot "in the round"—were built in California and trucked across the country to Martha's Vineyard, where they were kept carefully under wraps until they were to be used. After the second unit had filmed live great whites off Dangerous Reef, the three models were brought into play. Designed by Bob Mattey and Joe Alves, the model sharks were designed to run on a sunken trolley that had to be towed out to the shooting site every day, and the problems that attended the manipulation of these recalcitrant elasmo-mechanisms fill a good portion of Gottlieb's *Jaws Log*, published in 1975. The shark the models were supposed to represent was to be 25 feet long, longer than any known white shark.

The shark was also to be much longer than the live ones that Ron Taylor and Rodney Fox were concurrently filming in South Australia. Because all concerned knew that very few sharks sighted in South Australian waters were longer than 12 to 14 feet, a midget stuntman was to be placed in a scaled-down cage to compensate visually for the size difference. The stuntman, Carl Rizzo, had evidently never dived before, but with some trepidation he gamely entered the cage and descended for the filming. Later that day, Rizzo was halfway through the trapdoor of his tiny cage when a shark became entangled in the support cables. The agitated animal ripped the winch from its moorings and tossed Rizzo back into the boat. When the winch broke, its red hydraulic fluid drained out all over

Roy Scheider, who played Mike Brody, the Amity police chief, in "Jaws," chats with Valerie Taylor on the beach at Martha's Vineyard.

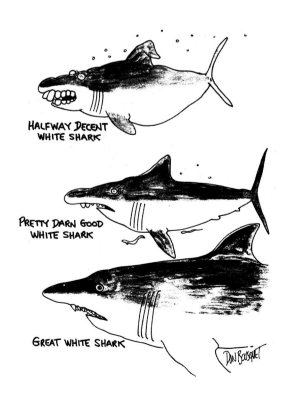

HALFWAY DECENT WHITE SHARK

PRETTY DARN GOOD WHITE SHARK

GREAT WHITE SHARK

the deck, and both Fox and Rizzo thought they were seeing their own blood.

The experience was unnerving, and when it came time to lower the cage for the next day's filming, Rizzo was nowhere to be found. Reports differ on where he had holed up, but Gottlieb (attributing the story to an anonymous source) says that he "was located cowering in the forward chain lockers with the anchor. . . ." He never dived again.

The film was released in the summer of 1975, and it was a huge success. In an uncredited piece, *Time* magazine for June 23 called it "technically intricate and wonderfully crafted, a movie whose every shock is a devastating surprise." On its cover, the issue carried an open-jawed shark with the caption "Super Shark." The film cost the (then enormous) sum of $8 million to make, and in its first ten weeks it grossed $21 million. It was the biggest money-maker in cinema history, and it spawned every conceivable spinoff, from plastic sharks' teeth necklaces and t-shirts to lame imitations of Benchley's novel and lurid picture books about "Jaws of Death!" and "Killer Sharks!" (The film soon had its imitators. The movie "Orca," made in 1977, had its protagonists—Richard Harris as a crusty fisherman, Charlotte Rampling as a marine biologist, and Bo Derek as a person who gets eaten—hunting white sharks, but instead they encountered killer whales, who, just as vengefully as the star of "Jaws," chased and sank boats all over the ocean.)

One of the more bizarre outgrowths of the "Jaws" phenomenon was the proposed "death match" between a great white shark and a diver. In

During the filming of "Jaws," the plan had been to use a half-sized cage and a small stunt man because none of the real sharks off South Australia was as big as the model shark.

late 1975, while the movie was still drawing well, a couple of Hollywood agents named Robby Wald and Jeff Cooper decided that what the public needed was a pitched battle between a white shark and a man. At first an Australian diver and shark hunter named Ben Cropp was to be the shark's opponent, but he withdrew, citing family problems. He was replaced by another Australian named Wally Gibbins, who was only too glad to offer his services for a million dollars. The contest was scheduled to take place in a specially constructed tank in Samoa (where, it might be pointed out, white sharks do not occur), and the diver was to retrieve a spear gun that had been thrown into the tank, before the battle commenced. Fortunately for everyone concerned, but especially the shark, this ridiculous "event" never came off.*

Given Hollywood's predilection for following good films with bad, it is hardly surprising that "Jaws II" was in the works almost as soon as the success of the original was assured. No more waiting to see if the book "had legs" (as the marketers describe a property that has its own momentum), for in this instance "Jaws II" the book was scheduled to appear simultaneously with the movie (in what the marketers called a "tie-in" sale). True, the studio had to license the name "Jaws" from the author—at a reputed price of a half million dollars, or $125,000 *per letter*—and state that their book was "based on characters created by Peter Benchley." For the rest, however, it was open season on maneating sharks and facts.

"Jaws II" takes place some four years later, and although the charac-

Valerie Taylor in Martha's Vineyard, Massachusetts, with "Bruce," one of the models used in the filming of *Jaws*.

* It would appear that the urge to do battle with a maneater is not new. Writing in 1919 of his adventures earlier, Russell J. Coles described his *voluntary* encounter in the water with a white shark, and because it is such an incredible story, it is reproduced here in its entirety, exactly as it appeared in the ichthyological journal *Copeia*:

My second adventure with the white shark [the first consisted of watching a 20-foot shark attack a sea turtle] occurred some years later, and although it contained an instant of close infighting, yet it was much less dangerous, for I was then trained and steadied by having won many knife fights with sharks and large rays. After trying for an hour to approach within harpooning distance of a large man-eater which was swimming in shallow water near the scene of my former encounter, I got over-board in a depth of five feet of water and had the boat retire to a distance of a hundred yards and with the coil of rope, which was attached to the harpoon which I had with me. I also

The cover of *Time* magazine, June 23, 1975.

* took with me a bushel of crushed and broken fish to attract the shark, which was then swimming on or near the surface, half a mile to the leeward of me. Soon the shark could be seen zig-zagging its course toward me, by crossing and re-crossing the line of scent from the broken fish, just as a bird-dog follows the scent of quail. With harpoon poised, I crouched low, trusting that its approach would be continued in this manner, until, by a long cast, I could fasten my harpoon in its side. The scent of the broken fish, however, was so strong that they were definitely located, and the shark charged from a hundred feet away with a speed which has to be seen to be appreciated. I met the onrushing shark by hurling my harpoon clear to the socket into it near the angle of the jaw, and as the iron entered its flesh, the shark leaped forward, catching me in the angle formed by its head and the harpoon shank, which caught me just under the right arm, bruising me badly, while my face and neck were somewhat lacerated by coming into contact with the rough hide of the side of its head. As my right arm was free, it was a great chance for using the heavy knife, with which I was armed, had my tackle been strong; but the force of the blow snapped the poorly made harpoon at the socket and the shark escaped, although it carried its death wound. I never again employed the same blacksmith to forge my harpoons, but that poorly made iron surely brought to a sudden ending a most exciting situation.

ters are the same, nobody seems to remember anything about a killer shark, even after the death of two divers, two water skiers, and a killer whale. Even when Chief Brody produces a *photograph* of the shark (taken by one of the divers just before the shark ate him), the town council—still determined to keep the beaches open and protect their tourist income—refuses to acknowledge the existence of the shark, and fires the chief. Brody gets drunk, mumbles "Four years shot to hell," and (never mind that he has just been fired) reinstates himself as police chief so he can rescue a bunch of dim-witted kids—including his own—who have gone for a little one-day sail. In the original "Jaws," Chief Brody had fired a shot into a scuba tank that had got jammed in the shark's mouth, producing the summary explosion of the shark. This time around, the intrepid and inventive Brody whacks on a loose high-voltage cable to gain the shark's attention (earlier in the film, he had learned that sharks are attracted by noise). As he dangles on the cable, he exhorts the shark to attack ("Come on, you son of a bitch"), and as the shark chomps down on the power line it electrocutes itself in an explosion of fire, sparks, and sizzling seaweed.

By 1983 the original cast was gone, and Brown and Zanuck had evidently had enough of sharks. Spielberg, having become Hollywood's *wunderkind* directing "Close Encounters of the Third Kind," "Raiders of the Lost Ark," and "E.T.," seems to have put terrestrial (or rather aquatic) monsters behind him. But there is no way to persuade Hollywood that if two things are good, three are not necessarily better. And if three are better, then 3-D promises to be even better than that. We therefore move

# The "Jaws" Phenomenon

THE FAR SIDE / Gary Larson

"O.K., Hank, Lower away!"

How cow documentaries are made

I have often been asked what I thought of "Jaws," and I think people expect me to say that it wasn't accurate, or that sharks don't get that big, or that you could tell when the fake shark was used. Well, it *wasn't* particularly accurate—white sharks really *don't* hang around beaches looking for more people to eat— and as far as we know, they don't get to be 25 feet long. And yes, if you look really closely, you can spot the model shark.

But people who look for the inconsistencies or the mistakes are missing the point. "Jaws" was not intended to be a factual PBS special on the habits of the great white shark (there have been several of those). It was made to be a thriller, and it succeeds superbly. Even after many viewings, I still find it riveting (McCosker agrees with me). The scene where Brody ladles the chum overboard and the shark rises up out of the water *with a roar* is one of the most electrifying scenes in all of filmdom. Without fail, it brings me out of my seat—never mind that I know it's coming, and that I know perfectly well that sharks don't roar. It was a brilliant movie, and the audience loved it. Until the "Star Wars" trilogy and "E.T.," it was the highest-grossing film in Hollywood history.

*Richard Ellis*

A gigantic white shark model with
carrot-sized teeth roars out of the
water, unnerving visitors to the Universal Studios tour in Hollywood.

THE PREDATOR AS PROTAGONIST    231

the shark rig and a new cast of actors, directors, and technicians to Florida, where an oceanarium is to be the site of "Jaws 3-D." Joe Alves, the production designer of Jaws I and the Assistant Director of II, has now become a full-fledged director. The Brody brothers have grown up, and one of them, Mike, is now a supervisor at Sea World in Florida, while the other, "who hates the ocean," has gone off to college in Colorado.

In an oceanarium setting, then, with a very stiff and tired-looking mechanical shark, the story continues. A 10-foot shark has managed to sneak into an enclosure, and proceeds to gobble up a maintenance man. After a heated discussion about whether it would be better to capture the 10-footer (and thus be "the first aquarium ever to exhibit a great white") or to kill it on camera for the publicity, the sentimentalists prevail, and the shark is captured. After it nonetheless dies, the biologists realize (a) that "because it doesn't have all its teeth" it is just a baby, and (b) that its mother, a 35-footer, is right outside. Panic ensues as the enraged mother speeds around the oceanarium's lagoon hunting down water skiers, swimmers, and bumper-boaters, finally smashing its canvas snout through an underwater tunnel. More roaring, smashing, and gnashing. Finally, the shark blunders into the aquarium's underwater control room with the body of a would-be hero in its mouth. But the dead hero, it seems, had provided himself with a couple of grenades, and Mike Brody (who had cleverly slipped into his scuba gear as the shark burst into the control room) sees one in the dead man's hand. With a skewer of some sort that happens to be close to hand, he hooks the ring of the grenade and pulls the pin. This preposterous resolution explodes the shark, and makes the score Brodies 3, Sharks 0.

By 1987, young Mike Brody has been installed as Amity police chief, but we will not linger in the cold waters of New England for long. In this masterpiece, "Jaws IV: The Revenge," the shark—or its mechani-

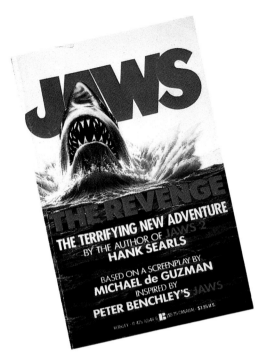

*Jaws—the Revenge* dust jacket.

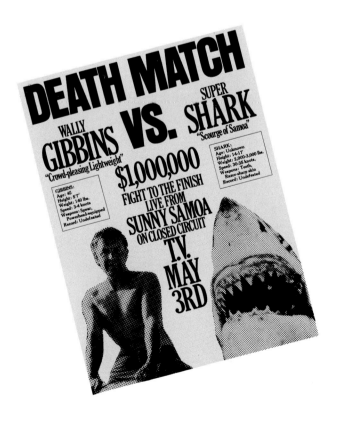

The ad for the unrealized encounter between Wally Gibbins and a white shark.

John McCosker (left) and California diver Dick Anderson with the model of a white shark that was used in the filming of "Jaws—the Revenge" in the Bahamas, April 1987.

cal descendant—seeks revenge on the whole Brody family. After all, one or another of them has been blowing up the shark's family since 1974. When it kills Chief Brody, Jr., as he checks on a disturbance in the harbor, his mother decides that she can no longer live in a place where malevolent sharks are after her family, and everybody—including the shark—goes off to the Bahamas. (The Brody family flies down in a 747, but the shark seems to arrive at the same time they do.) Mama Brody now has her granddaughter to worry about, and naturally, the kid spends a lot of time in the water. She also has Michael Caine to worry about, since Papa Brody—the original chief, that is—seems to have died of a heart attack. But never mind. After gobbling up the requisite number of swimmers, boats, and divers, the shark is hunted down and this time (did they run out of explosives?) it dies impaled on the bowsprit of a boat.

The success of the later "Jaws" movies—considerable, even as it diminished from film to film—certainly cannot be attributed to the filmmakers' craft. Though the original "Jaws" was a well-made film, with reasonably developed characters and a more or less logical storyline, the sequels lack even a modicum of structure, and the cardboard characters speak in comic-book lines and act with no rational motivation. They are, to put it simply, bad movies.

Why, then, would anyone want to make these films, again and again? Certainly the first motivation is greed. "We made such a bundle on the first one, why not make another?" And another and another. But there is more to it than that. Unlike the giant gorilla in "King Kong," or the assorted "Godzilla" monsters, the villain of the "Jaws" movies *really exists*. There *are* very large great white sharks swimming in our offshore waters, and though they do not reach 35 feet, work their evil ways on selected families, or cleave the water with the speed of a torpedo boat, they do occasionally attack people, with appalling and often fatal results. It is the *reality* of this creature that produces the nightmares, and leads the producers, ever mindful of signals in the marketplace, to make more nightmare films. The novel and the films, or perhaps just the mass mindset established by the films, sustained in large measure by the reality of the great white shark, have made each of us pause—if only for a moment—before going into the sea for a swim. And anything that can provoke that same brief, dark thought in all of us is a powerful force indeed.

# Can We Save the Great White Shark?

*12*

No one knows how many great white sharks there may be. We cannot make even an educated guess. Within their known, extensive range, white sharks seem to show up wherever and whenever it suits them, sometimes singly, sometimes in pairs or larger numbers. In some reaches of the world's oceans, such as the southern coast of Africa, they are moderately plentiful—sufficiently so, at least, that some fishermen regard them as a nuisance. In a few other locales, notably South Australia, the Mid-Atlantic Bight, and central California, people can fish for them with a fair expectancy of catching one. But in other parts of the world, they occur so infrequently that the appearance of a single individual is newsworthy. A great white shark (especially one that bites people) in Cuba, Hawaii, Malta, or Buzzard's Bay becomes—not surprisingly—a local celebrity.

Researchers and photographers have devised methods of identifying individual elephants (by the ears), humpback whales (by the pattern on the underside of the flukes), gorillas, chimpanzees, lions, bottlenose dolphins, and even hyenas. By such means, researchers like Jane Goodall are able to follow the doings of individual animals, and even to maintain an accurate, changing count of a given population over time. But until now, no one has seemed to think the identification of individual sharks particularly important, even though individuals may prowl the same coast for 20 years or more. In South Australia, where various darts and transmitters have occasionally been attached to sharks for research purposes, one might be able to recognize an individual from one month to the next, but by the next season the marker has fallen off and all the sharks look alike again.

Or do they? Look again at the photographs in this book. Yes, they all show a massive, bullet-nosed creature with a black eye and white undersides, but now look at the pictures of living sharks underwater. . . . Notice the way the dorsal coloration intersects with the white underbelly in varying ragged patterns, or the point where the white coloration appears on the lower leading edge of the tail fin. Some white sharks have a broken

*In 1990 and 1991, researchers from the Cousteau Society, working with the South Australian Department of Fisheries, put in over six months of sea time at Dangerous Reef and the South Neptune Islands, tagging and counting white sharks. As of this writing, their data has not been published, but preliminary reports indicate that although the sharks there are indeed reduced in overall numbers, more individuals may congregate farther offshore.

Al Giddings brought an ROV (remotely operated vehicle) to South Australia to shoot white sharks for the filming of *Ocean Quest* for NBC in 1985. The shark seems to ignore the bright-eyed intruder.

line that extends down to the pelvic fins, while others have white all the way up the sides. Perhaps, then, it *is* possible to identify individuals. With sharks, as compared to most other fishes, separating the males from the females is a simple task, at least if the undersides can be seen. Now examine the dorsal fins. Some are higher, more vertical, while others lean tailwards. And the caudal details, too, vary from fish to fish. Finally, we can call upon simple gestalt recognition, as we would distinguish our cousins at a family picnic: this one just *looks* different from that one, in an instant.

But because no one has devised an actual system for identifying individuals or developed a proper way of counting them, we have no way of estimating local or worldwide population.* For some, of course, any number of white sharks is too many, but by now it has become clear that *Carcharodon carcharias* is not a mindless assassin. It is also not an affable teddy-bear whose reputation is completely undeserved. Somewhere between these extremes the white shark swims along, impassive and implacable, and its numbers worldwide appear to be declining.

Since we have no idea of how many there are, we have no way of knowing with confidence whether their numbers are increasing or decreasing. In some parts of the world, they may be on the increase. The Marine Mammal Protection Act, passed in 1972, accords blanket protection to seals and sea lions in American waters, and some believe that the exploding pinniped populations are being matched by a concurrent increase in

the white sharks that feed on the pinnipeds. If this is indeed the case, it might explain the increase in shark attacks in California waters: more seals, more sharks; more sharks, more attacks on people. But of course the increase in California's human population puts more humans in the water too: more sharks and more people, then surely more attacks.

Great whites have never been common anywhere, but their ancient relative, *Carcharodon megalodon*, is now extinct, and the disappearance of what was quite possibly the most powerful, fearsome predator that ever lived must give us pause. Certainly, if it is possible for Megalodon to disappear, even though its generic prey did not disappear, then its much smaller relative, notwithstanding its current reputation and prodigious predatory skills, has no guarantee of immortality. There were no fishermen to hunt Megalodon, but today, from Cape Town to Port Lincoln, from Montauk to Malta, intrepid anglers strap on their harnesses and oil their reels to hunt the most powerful big-game fish of all. As far as we know, the white shark is not an endangered species, but there is obviously a class of people who would like to change that. Vic Hislop, for one, the self-proclaimed Shark Hunter, believes that every shark he kills makes the world a little bit safer for swimmers and sea lions.

After 1975, in the wake of *Jaws* the novel and "Jaws" the movie, there was a phenomenal increase in white shark fishing. Whole gaggles of trophy hunters raced to see who among them would be first to display the head or the jaws of the maneater over the fireplace. Can the species with-stand such an assault on its numbers? And if it cannot, should we care?

Al Giddings films a tagged shark from a cage.

RIGHT: Men whose lives have been affected by white sharks. Left to right, Henri Bource, whose leg was bitten off; Alf Dean, world's record holder for a fish caught on rod and reel; and Rodney Fox, who survived a savage attack in 1963. The badly mangled shark was attacked by another white shark as it was being reeled in.

BELOW, LEFT: In 1976, following the release of the movie "Jaws," fishermen began harpooning every white shark they could find. This one was killed in Southern California waters and brought to Sea World in San Diego.

BELOW, RIGHT: The self-styled "Shark Hunter," Vic Hislop of Queensland, Australia, grins beside the gaping jaws of a 22-foot white pointer.

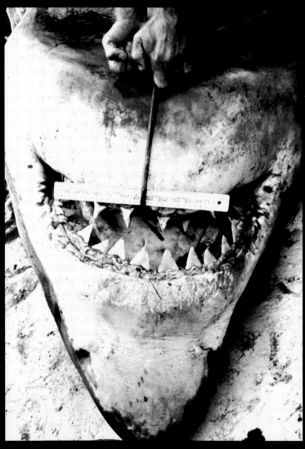

The man who had the most to do with initiating the onslaught thinks we should. When a 2,800-pound great white was caught in Long Island Sound in the summer of 1983, Peter Benchley rebuked the fishermen for killing it. The fishermen claimed they had collected it for science, but in a local newspaper interview, Benchley was quoted as saying, "I find it difficult to believe that they were on some great scientific study. If you believe that, then I suggest that you also believe in the tooth fairy."

In South Australia, where white shark fishing has been popular for more than 50 years, the publication and release of *Jaws* increased interest in the white pointer exponentially. In her journal for 1976, recalling that twelve great whites had been caught early that year, Valerie Taylor wrote that that "is a lot to take from one area, and it will be a long time before the great white sharks return to Dangerous Reef in anything like their former numbers." To date, there has been no restriction on the number of whites that can be taken from South Australian waters, and the fishing goes on, unchecked and uncontrolled.

In early 1989, a team from the Cousteau Society traveled to South Australia to shoot yet another film about this photogenic creature. For three weeks the crew chummed the waters around Dangerous Reef and the Neptune Islands, but for their efforts, all they attracted were three smallish whites that failed to stay around long enough for the cages to be put in the water. Describing the expedition in a game-fishing newsletter, Nicolas Dourassoff said, "The way things are going, the great white will be extinct in 20 years. . . . Game fishermen should not be allowed to catch them, and fishermen should be more careful not to catch them in nets."

In California, despite an increase in its preferred prey, the prognosis for the white shark is tenuous at best. A commercial fisherman named Michael McHenry captured four adult white sharks near the Farallon Islands on a single day in 1982. (The Farallones are an important study site for San Francisco Bay area biologists, who have continuously studied the marine life and seabird populations on and around these islands since 1972.) With just these four sharks removed from the waters, observations of white sharks attacking pinnipeds decreased by nearly half, and several years passed before the shark sightings returned to their previous level. Such studies suggest that populations of white sharks, even at prime locations, are relatively small, and, further, that it is difficult for such a long-lived, slow-growing, late-maturing species with such small broods and such a low fecundity rate to reinvade a habitat once occupied.

Indeed, many shark species appear to be threatened nowadays, since commercial shark fishing has taken a marked upturn in recent years. Elasmobranchs, by their very nature, are inappropriate candidates for a fishery. In their evolutionary strategy, sharks and rays count on few, well-developed young, negligible infant mortality, slow growth, and late sexual maturity. Combining modern fishing techniques with this life history—known as "k-selected" by ecologists—is a recipe for disaster. After considerable investment in boats and equipment, fishermen soon find themselves working harder but catching fewer and younger (smaller) sharks. Ultimately, the shark fishery will collapse, but by then it might be too late for

The Farallon Islands of California, the habitat of seals, sea lions, elephant seals, and great white sharks.

a particular population of one species or another—or even an entire species, worldwide.

In the past, sharks were considered trash fish, but now that traditional concerns about consuming shark meat have abated, clever marketing has made it fashionable. Twentieth-century affluence in the Orient has added additional stress on many species of sharks, which are now the target of high-seas and coastal fisheries where only the fins are saved and the carcasses discarded. Shark-fin soup, which uses the fin's gelatinous elements as a base, has long been a desirable and expensive delicacy. In early 1991, dried fins were fetching $53.00 per pound, and in Hong Kong the soup was selling for $50.00 a bowl. In a 1991 article in *Time* entitled "Are Sharks Becoming Extinct?", Philip Elmer-Dewitt wrote, "The fishing is extraordinarily wasteful . . . shark meat spoils so quickly that fin hunters would rather toss it overboard than be bothered with the necessary processing and refrigeration."

Leonard Compagno, a shark scientist singlemindedly devoted to studying and protecting sharks and their relatives, has taken a very strong position in the shark/human debate. In 1984, he stated that

From the white shark's viewpoint, human beings are much more dangerous to it than vice versa. Off California 10 or 20 or more white sharks are killed each year as a by-catch of fisheries, vs. 0.13 humans per year killed (in California) by white sharks. As the number of white sharks present in these waters is very small and probably vastly less than the herd of swimmers, divers, surfers, and other people at risk from white shark attack, the sharks are sustaining a greatly higher *per capita* loss from human attack than people are from them. *

Rodney Fox is a man whose life has been all but defined by the white pointer. The 1963 attack (pp. 149–50) left him with a great fold in his left side where he was sewn together, but he nonetheless chose to devote much of his life to the pursuit (with camera and tourists) of *Carcharodon*, and he probably knows more about the behavior of the white shark than any other man or woman alive. There has scarcely been an expedition, movie, book, or scientific study of the great white shark in which Rodney was not involved. Other people in other places have tried to duplicate his expertise, but somehow, trying to chum up sharks off South Africa, Montauk, or California produces limited results at best, or, frequently, no results at all. It is only in South Australia, where Rodney (and the other Aussies, like Ron and Valerie Taylor), designed the cages, developed the chum, and located the sharks' favorite haunts, that others have succeeded. And now, Rodney Fox is worried about the fate of the fish that nearly killed him.

* By 1991, Compagno and his associates had taken even stronger steps. The Great White Shark Research Unit, associated with the South African Museum at Cape Town, and directed by Compagno, has recently proposed legislation that would protect the white shark in South African waters, meaning that fisheries and private citizens alike would be prohibited from catching them. By April, the measure had become the law of the land. A venture to promote cage diving with white sharks has also been developed in Cape coast communities, suggesting that at least some South Africans recognize that the white shark is more than a dangerous fish that must be eradicated.

Where the dark back of a white shark meets the light underside, the border is ragged and variable, often allowing researchers to distinguish individuals.

Fox in fact wants to see the great white shark declared a protected species in South Australian waters, and not necessarily because his livelihood would be affected if the sharks disappeared. (He does believe they are becoming scarcer in South Australian waters, however, and the expeditions he has led in recent years have drawn fewer sharks to the chum slick.) As with most people who have studied great white sharks, Rodney Fox has great respect and admiration for the species, and he has begun a campaign to protect them. In a series of unpublished letters to the South Australian Department of Fisheries (he has made both the letters and the replies available to us), he has written, "Over the years, since my shark attack and direct involvement with the species, I have become increasingly concerned with their future. To this end, I propose that there is a strong case for the protection of the great white shark."

Unlike gorillas or lions, sharks do not easily lend themselves to field observations: we must lure them away from their natural behavior if we are to see them at all. Fox advocates the development of new methods of studying the behavior of the great white because he believes that the conditions under which they are usually observed are so anomalous as to be of little benefit for scientific purposes: "All we do is draw them in and feed them; no wonder they behave like crazy monsters. Any animal would behave crazily if you drenched it in blood and threw food at it." The South Australian Fisheries' response to Rodney Fox's recommendations is supportive but equivocal:

Unfortunately, the necessary biological data to quantify the limits of exploitation for great whites are extremely difficult and expensive to obtain. This is because the species is extremely long-lived; has territorial areas ranging over large distances; being large and a carnivore, it is difficult to handle when trying to obtain accurate data such as length measurements etc.; and being a pelagic species requires extensive sea time on large research vessels to obtain any meaningful results. Despite the lack of data, responsible fisheries managers and the community should be conservative to ensure the species' survival.

Diving with sharks does not endanger the sharks, and should be allowed to continue, but the publicity surrounding the divers (and the "Jaws" movies) encourages deep-sea anglers to test their mettle and skill against the maneaters. Even though the shark occasionally wins—usually when both contenders are in the sharks' element and *never* when the hunter remains above the water—the final score is decidedly in favor of *Homo sapiens*, the most efficient, most ruthless, and most wasteful predator in history.

When Mrs. Durdin was bitten in half and eaten in 1985, a veritable navy of shark hunters took to the boats in South Australia. Armed with guns, harpoons, and a righteous cause, they scoured the waters and set out nets, baits, and buoys in an all-out effort to capture the killer. Against the collective skills and weapons of such an armada, the only defense for even a super-predator like the white shark is a quick retreat, and only the normal behavior of the species—great whites probably eat infrequently—saved this individual. For all their equipment and dedication, the hunters never found the shark that savaged Mrs. Durdin.

If we have learned anything from this incident, it is that, in life,

Most South Australian dives with
white sharks have originated from
the dive boat *Nenad*, owned and
operated by Bob Britcher and
Mateo Ricov.

white sharks do not behave as they do in Peter Benchley's fiction: having once tasted human flesh, they do not immediately forsake their normal prey items and rewrite their menu in favor of swimmers. No one is suggesting that a killer shark should not be dispatched, lest it kill again, but the argument can be made that the ocean is the shark's element and we enter it at our peril.

The great white shark has become a totem for our times: the embodiment of evil and terror. From its first, shadowed appearance in our collective consciousness, the white shark has been threateningly larger than life. In the summer of 1916, as French and German soldiers were fighting the terrible, bloody battle of the Somme, a series of shark attacks in New Jersey effectively displaced the war from the headlines. (As it turned out, the attacker was probably not a white shark, but people thought it was.) After a succession of white shark attacks in South Africa and Australia had amplified the terror in the 1960's, Peter Gimbel decided to look that terror in the eye, and made "Blue Water, White Death." The white shark was on its way to the pantheon of legendary beasts, and when Peter Benchley published *Jaws* in 1974, its place in the front rank was assured.

In the new mythology of the shark, there is a single great presence, *Carcharodon carcharias*. The great white shark swims alone in cool waters—in science, in literature, in infamy. It is the selachian definition of *sui generis*, but it has come to represent all sharks, because in a sense it *is* all sharks: it is big, powerful, dangerous, unheeding, and frightening to behold, and it is equipped with all the fixtures of the quintessential shark: rows of razor-sharp teeth in a gaping maw, a soul-less black eye, a bullet nose, and of course the great triangular dorsal fin, always "knifing" through the water.

Of all large, predatory animals, the white shark is probably the most dangerous to man and woman. Various smaller predators—like cobras in Asia and scorpions around the globe—kill vastly more people each year than all the sharks in the seas, *but they do not eat their victims*, and they assuredly have not acquired the same reputation, at least not in Western countries.

Lions, tigers, leopards, polar bears, and grizzlies also attack people on occasion, but their attacks are rare, probably because the big land carnivores themselves are rare. The big cats and bears are seldom singled out as a threat to our existence, or even our safety. In fact, we tend to regard these powerful apex predators as relatively harmless residents of zoos or circuses. But although some species of sharks, such as nurses, lemons, leopards, and sand tigers, have been successfully maintained in aquariums, all attempts to keep whites have met with complete or barely qualified failure. The only impression of *Carcharodon* permitted us is the giant offshore menace, unreachable even by those of us who have studied its ways and simply want to learn a little more about it.

The shark occupies a habitat that is not of our terrestrial understanding. Despite the technological advances that have enabled us to enter the water, or even to *stay* in the water, we do so as maladroit trespassers in an

Andrew Guest wearing a "Save the Shark" t-shirt; a gift from Valerie Taylor.

One of Ron Taylor's spectacular portraits, taken near the surface in South Australia in 1967.

alien and unwelcoming world. Even the medium itself is hostile: we cannot breathe it as the fishes do, and without a face-mask we can barely see through it; it can so drain the heat from our landlubberly bodies that without protection we succumb to hypothermia in minutes. In this thick, liquid environment, we are outclassed and outmaneuvered; we are awkward, slow, and above all, terribly, hopelessly *vulnerable*. Perhaps it is this recognition of our own frailty that disturbs us so; how can a *fish* be so threatening?

We admire these great apex predators for their graceful form, their spare economy, their smooth, sleek power, and their ancient efficiency, and yet we have mobilized a small war against them. What are the elements in this love-hate relationship? Is it that these big fish with small brains have eluded—utterly ignored—our every effort to control or even understand them? Is there something beyond that goes deeper into our collective psyche? A glimpse of some dark, unreasoning, but beckoning evil, heedless of all notions of restraint, emerging unpredictably from the blackness and returning just as silently whence it came? Is it our atavistic fear of being eaten that lends both distance and a disturbing proximity to our relationship with the shark? The great white is the only beast in our reckoning that we fear can—or worse, *will*—eat us, and that is the stuff of legends.

Since the days when the first seafarers saw—and learned to fear—the gaping jaws of this great fish, it has symbolized the quintessence of malice. In novels and films, in record books and scientific texts, occasionally and briefly even in aquariums, and of course in the sea, the unblinking black eye of the great white shark has stared at us as if to challenge our alleged dominion over the animals. We have now confirmed our rank as the planet's predominant pillager and predator, subduing the forests, the plains, the jungles, and the deserts, along with the flora and fauna that inhabit these realms. Our technological prowess has also enabled us to poison the land, the lakes and rivers, the atmosphere, and, to a lesser extent, even the ocean, which—so far—has resisted our depredations only by virtue of its vast expanse, its great depth, and its resilience. Extinctions and endangerment are our legacy, and included on the long list of the world's depleted species is the great white shark.

Is it too late to save the white shark? Perhaps not. The South Africans, long in the vanguard of the battle waged *against* the white shark—think of the Durban Shark Anglers, Danie Schoeman, and the Natal Anti-Sharks Board—have now taken the first steps to protect this great predator. Encouraged by American-born scientist Leonard Compagno, the South Africans, on the heels of their monumental political reforms, are reversing their policies against the great white shark. On April 11, 1991, at a press conference in the South African Museum in Cape Town, Environment Minister Louis Pienaar announced that "the numbers of the Great White Shark are known to have declined alarmingly in some parts of the world . . . while commercial and trophy hunters have decimated populations of these sharks," and that it "will now be a crime to hunt the great white shark within 200 miles of the South African coast." According to legislation scheduled for introduction in the near future, "it will be illegal to sell or offer for sale any Great White Shark or part thereof. It will also be illegal to catch or kill any Great White Shark except on the authority of a permit issued by the Director General of Environment Affairs." Pienaar concluded by asserting that "these measures are justified and necessary to protect the great white shark and its important role in the ecosystem from the threat of overexploitation." With the passage of this legislation, South Africa will become the first nation to ban the killing of white sharks, whether for fish markets, for sport, or for the trade in their jaws and other souvenirs.

After a thousand years of darkness, we may be seeing the first inklings of a healthy concern for this unreasonably maligned and misunderstood creature. It is not a cruel killer; not a man-eating monster; not a seagoing homicidal maniac. It is a powerful, magnificently adapted creature of ancient lineage that has resisted our understanding and control, mindless of our attempts to eradicate it; mindless of the concern that some have shown for its food preferences and its welfare; mindless too of the calumny that has attended its silent journey through the eternity of life and time.

# BIBLIOGRAPHY

In addition to some of the fundamental references on ichthyology and paleontology, this Bibliography attempts to include virtually every serious English-language work, long or short, dealing with the white shark (excluding brief passing references of no particular interest here), as well as many key references in other languages. The entries range from scientific papers (generally recognizable from the name of the journal after the title of the paper) to book-length treatments and recollections, newspaper accounts, novels, and articles in popular magazines.

It would have been relatively simple to address our task in purely scientific terms, but this large fish tends to force itself into our popular consciousness, and therefore into the popular literature. Unlike the subjects of most biological papers, *Carcharodon* has made guest appearances in mass-circulation magazines like *Time*, and has been prominently featured on posters outside movie theaters. There is, therefore, a large body of work on *Carcharodon carcharias* that is solidly rooted in the popular, or even the sensational, idiom. Some of this literature, such as Peter Matthiessen's *Blue Meridian* or David Baldridge's *Shark Attack*, successfully bridges the gap between the scientific and the popular, but, generally speaking, the lines are sharply drawn.

There is also a category of materials, the so-called "trash literature," that defies inclusion in a serious work. In the years since the "Jaws" phenomenon, there have been many cheaply produced rip-offs, with titles like "Jaws of Death!" and "Killer Sharks!" These have not been listed in the Bibliography, since their only value is to students of popular culture and those who would study the "bandwagon" phenomenon: if it seems that money can be made from exploiting a current fad, there will be those who immediately go after it.

The many first-hand accounts of fishing for white sharks, diving among them, or even being attacked by them have been extremely useful in assembling this composite portrait of the white shark. Some of the fish's habits, too, have been revealed to us by fishermen and -women, divers, and photographers, people who do not normally submit their observations to learned journals.

Many of the works listed below are general books about sharks that accord the white shark a chapter or a section of its own. The scientific papers are usually devoted to a single species, but there are some papers that discuss all or several of the lamnid sharks or, occasionally, sharks in general. For the chapter on Close and Distant Relatives, it was necessary to include many items that refer, not to the white shark at all, but to those species that we used for comparative purposes, or to make a particular point.

Agassiz, L. 1833–43. *Recherches sur les poissons fossiles*. Vol. 3. Contenant l'histoire de l'Ordre des Placiodes. Text and Atlas. Neuchâtel.

Ainley, D. G., and R. J. Boekelheide. 1990. *Seabirds of the Farallones: Ecology, Dynamics, and Structure of an Upwelling-System Community*. Stanford, Calif.: Stanford University Press.

Ainley, D. G., R. P. Henderson, H. R. Huber, R. J. Boekelheide, S. G. Allen, and T. L. McElroy. 1985. Dynamics of White Shark/Pinniped Interactions in the Gulf of the Farallones. *Memoirs of the Southern California Academy of Sciences* 9: 109–22.

Ainley, D. G., C. S. Strong, H. R. Huber, T. J. Lewis, and S. H. Morrell. 1981. Predation by Sharks on Pinnipeds at the Farallon Islands. *Fisheries Bulletin* 78: 941–45.

Aldrovandi, U. 1613. *De Piscibus libri V et de Cetis liber unus*. Bologna: J. C. Unterverius.

Ames, J. A., and G. V. Morejohn. 1980. Evidence of

White Shark, *Carcharodon carcharias*, Attacks on Sea Otters, *Enhydra lutris*. *California Fish and Game* 66: 196–209.

Anon. 1891. [Great white shark in the Mediterranean]. *Mediterranean Naturalist* 1(4): 76.

Anon. 1916a. Harlem Man in Tiny Boat Kills a 7 ½-Foot Man-Eating Shark. *The Home News* (New York) July 16: 1.

Anon. 1916b. Man-Eating Shark, Displayed in *Home News* Window, Thrills Many Thousands. *The Home News* (New York) July 23: 1.

Anon. 1960. Look Out for Dangerous Sharks. *Life* 42(2): 58–72.

Anon. 1971. In Quest of the Deadliest Creature in the Seas: Great White Shark. *Life* 70(1): 56–61.

Anon. 1975. The Summer of the Shark. *Time* June 23.

Anon. 1976. Is the Record White Pointer a Fairy Story? *Australian Fisheries* 35(7): 2–3.

Anon. 1980a. Brief Captivity for a Great White. *Life* 3(10): 124–25.

Anon. 1980b. The Fishing Family Simms. *SAFIC (Magazine of the South Australian Fishing Industry Council* 4(5): 3–6.

Anon. 1982. A Warning Dressed in White. *Surfer* 23(5): 24.

Anon. 1990. [Greg Norman's sporting image]. *Adelaide Advertiser*, Feb. 7: 16.

Applegate, S. P. 1967. A Survey of Shark Hard Parts. Pp. 37–64 *in* P. W. Gilbert, R. F. Mathewson, and D. P. Rall, eds. *Sharks, Skates and Rays*. Baltimore: Johns Hopkins Press.

Applegate, S. P., and A. E. Daugherty. 1966. The Mystical Fascination of the Shark. *Los Angeles County Museum Quarterly* 5(2): 4–10.

Arnold, P. W. 1972. Predation on Harbor Porpoise, *Phocoena phocoena*, by a White Shark, *Carchardon carcharias*. *Journal of the Fisheries Research Board of Canada* 29(8): 1213–14.

Artedi, P. 1788–1792. *Bibliotheca ichthyologica . . . emendata et aucta a Iohanne Iulio Walbaum*. Grypeswaldae.

Backus, R. H. 1963. Hearing in Elasmobranchs. Pp. 243–54 *in* P. W. Gilbert, ed. *Sharks and Survival*. Boston: D. C. Heath.

Balazs, G. H., and A. K. H. Kam. 1981. A Review of Shark Attacks in Hawaiian Islands. *'Elepaio* 41(10): 97–105.

Baldridge, H. D. 1970. Sinking Factors and Average Densities of Florida Sharks as Functions of Liver Buoyancy. *Copeia* 1970(4): 744–54.

———. 1972. Accumulation and Function of Liver Oil in Florida Sharks. *Copeia* 1972(2): 306–25.

———. 1974a. Shark Attack: A Program of Data Reduction and Analysis. *Contributions of the Mote Marine Laboratory* 1(2).

———. 1974b. *Shark Attack*. New York: Berkley.

———. 1982. Sharks Don't Swim—They Fly. *Oceans* 15(2): 24–26.

———. 1987. Antishark Warfare? *Proceedings of the U.S. Naval Institute* Dec. 1987: 119–20.

———. 1988. Shark Aggression Against Man: Beginnings of an Understanding. *California Fish and Game* 74(4): 208–17.

———. 1990. Shark Repellent: Not Yet, Maybe Never. *Military Medicine* 155(8): 358–61.

Baldridge, H. D., and J. Williams. 1969. Shark Attack: Feeding or Fighting? *Military Medicine* 134(2): 130–33.

Bartsch, P., and A. R. Barwick. 1941. Vertebra of *Carcharodon megalodon*. *Copeia* 1941(1): 40–41.

Bass, A. J., J. D. D'Aubrey, and N. Kistnasamy. 1975. Sharks of the East Coast of Southern Africa. IV. The families Odontaspididae, Scapanorhynchidae, Isuridae, Cetorhinidae, Alopiidae, Orectolobidae, and Rhiniodontidae. *Oceanographic Research Institute Investigational Report* 39: 2–88.

Bates, T. 1984. The Great White Hope. *California Magazine* 9(3): 67–71; 126–31.

Baughman, J. L. 1948. Sharks, Sawfishes, and Rays: Their Folklore. *American Midland Naturalist* 39(2): 373–81.

———. 1955. The Oviparity of the Whale Shark, *Rhineodon typus*, with Records of This and Other Fishes in Texas Waters. *Copeia* 1: 54–55.

Belayaev, G. M., and L. S. Glikman. 1970. On the Geological Age of the Teeth of the Shark *Megaselachus megalodon*. *Transactions of the Shirskov Institute of Oceanology* 88.

Benchley, P. 1974. *Jaws*. New York: Doubleday.

Berg, L. S. 1947. *Classification of Fishes, Both Recent and Fossil*. (English and Russian.) Ann Arbor, Michigan: J. W. Edwards.

Bergman, D. 1969. The Great Shark Hoax. *Skin Diver* 18(11): 55–59.

Beston, H. 1928. *The Outermost House*. New York: Holt, Rinehart and Winston.

Bigelow, H. B. 1958. A Large White Shark, *Carcharodon carcharias*, Taken in Massachusetts Bay. *Copeia* 1958(1): 54–55.

Bigelow, H. B., and W. C. Schroeder. 1948. Sharks. Part I of *Fishes of the Western North Atlantic*. Memoirs of the Sears Foundation for Marine Research. Yale University.

——— 1951. Fishes of the Gulf of Maine. *U.S. Fish and Wildlife Service Fisheries Bulletin* 53: 577.

———. 1953. Sawfishes, Guitarfishes, Skates and Rays. Part II of *Fishes of the Western North Atlantic*. Memoirs of the Sears Foundation for Marine Research. Yale University.

Bigg, M. A. 1981. Harbor Seal—*Phoca vitulina* and *P. largha*. Pp. 1–27 *in* S. H. Ridgway and R. J. Harrison, eds. *Handbook of Marine Mammals. Volume 2: Seals*. New York: Academic Press.

Blainville, H. M. D. 1816. Prodrome d'une nouvelle distribution systématique du règne animal. *Bulletin Société Philomathique Paris* 8: 105–24.

Block, B. A., and F. G. Carey. 1988. Warm Brains in Lamnid Sharks. *Journal of Biochemistry and Physiology* 212: 209–57.

Boggs, R. F. 1976. *Captain Frank Mundus: Monster Man*. New York: Cricket II.

Bolin, R. L. 1954. Report on a Fatal Attack by a Shark. *Pacific Science* 8(1): 105–8.

Boly, W. 1981. The Great White Shark Invasion. *New West* 6(2): 47–48.

Bonaparte, C. L. J. L. 1832–41. *Iconografia della fauna italica*. Vol. 3, Pesci. Roma.

Bonham, K. 1942. Records of Three Sharks on the Washington Coast. *Copeia* 1942(4): 264–66.

Bonner, W. N. 1981. Southern Fur Seals—*Arctocephalus*. Pp. 161–208 *in* S. H. Ridgway and R. J. Harrison, eds., *Handbook of Marine Mammals: Volume 2: The Walrus, Sea Lions, Fur Seals and Sea Otter*. New York: Academic Press.

Boord, R. L., and C. B. G. Campbell. 1977. Structural and Functional Organization of the Lateral Line System of Sharks. *American Zoologist* 17(2): 431–40.

Bory de Saint-Vincent, J. B. G. M. 1829. *Dictionnaire classique d'histoire naturelle*. Paris.

Boxall, B., and M. Corwin. 1989. Coast Scoured for Friend of Shark Victim. *Los Angeles Times*. February 1: 3, 23.

Boyd, E. 1975. Monster Teeth of Chesapeake Bay. *Skin Diver* 24(1): 5–9.

Breder, C. M., and D. E. Rosen. 1966. *Modes of Reproduction in Fishes*. Jersey City, N.J.: T. F. H. Publications.

Bright, M. 1984. Sharks, Surfboards, and Sea Elephants. *BBC Wildlife* 2(2): 83–89.

Brodie, P., and B. Beck. 1983. Predation by Sharks on Grey Seal (*Halichoerus grypus*) in Eastern Canada. *Canadian Journal of Fisheries and Aquatic Sciences* 40: 267–71.

Brown, R. 1981. *Megalodon*. New York: Coward, McCann & Geohegan.

Bruce, B. 1989. Biology of the White Shark. *SAFISH* 14(1): 4–7.

———. 1991. Preliminary Observations on the Biology of the White Shark, *Carcharodon carcharias*, in South Australian Waters. Abstract of presentation at *"Sharks Down Under" Symposium, February 24–March 1, 1991*. Sydney.

Brumfield, B. 1980. There Is No Reason to Spare the Sharks. *Cincinnati Inquirer* August 29: A-19.

Bryson, J. 1976. The $1-Million Death Match in Samoa. *New York Magazine* April 5: 40–43.

Buck, J. D., S. Spotte, and J. J. Gadbaw. 1984. Bacteriology of the Teeth from a Great White Shark: Potential Medical Implications for Shark Bite Victims. *Journal of Clinical Microbiology* 20(5): 849–51.

Budker, P. 1971. *The Life of Sharks*. New York: Columbia University Press.

Burton, E. M. 1935. Shark Attacks Along the South Carolina Coast. *The Scientific Monthly* 40: 279–83.

Cadenat, J., and J. Blanche. 1981. *Requins de Mediterranée et d'Atlantique (Plus Particulierement de la Côte Occidentale d'Afrique)*. Paris: Editions de l'Office de la Recherche Scientifique et Technique Outre-mer.

Cailliet, G. M., L. J. Natanson, B. A. Welden, and D. A. Ebert. 1985. Preliminary Studies on the Age and Growth of the White Shark, *Carcharodon carcharias*, Using Vertebral Bands. *Memoirs of the Southern California Academy of Sciences* 9: 49–60.

Canby, V. 1971. Dramatic Pursuit of Elusive Killer Shark. *The New York Times* May 12: 29.

Cappetta, H. 1987. Chondrichthyes II: Mesozoic and Cenozoic Elasmobranchii. Vol. 3B *in Handbook of Paleoichthyology*. Stuttgart & New York: Gustav Fischer Verlag.

Cappo, M. 1988. Size and Shape of the White Pointer Shark, *Carcharodon carcharias* (Linnaeus); Was Peter Riseley's White Pointer a World Record? *South Australian Fisheries Magazine* 13(1): 11–13.

Carey, F. G. 1973. Fishes with Warm Bodies. *Scientific American* 228(2): 36–44.

Carey, F. G., J. G. Casey, H. L. Pratt, D. Urquhart, and J. E. McCosker. 1985. Temperature, Heat Production, and Heat Exchange in Lamnid Sharks. *Memoirs of the Southern California Academy of Sciences* 9: 92–108.

Carey, F. G., J. W. Kanwisher, O. Brazier, G. Gabrielson, J. G. Casey, and H. L. Pratt. 1982. Temperature and Activities of a White Shark, *Carcharodon carcharias*. *Copeia* 1982(2): 254–60.

Carey, F. G., and J. M. Teal. 1969. Mako and Porbeagle: Warm-Bodied Sharks. *Comparative Biochemistry and Physiology* 28: 199–204.

Carey, F. G., J. M. Teal, and J. W. Kanwisher. 1981. The Visceral Temperature of Mackerel Sharks (Lamnidae). *Physiological Zoology* 54(3): 334–44.

Case, G. R. 1973. *Fossil Sharks: A Pictorial Review*. New York: Pioneer Litho.

Casey, J. G. 1964. Angler's Guide to the Sharks of the Northeastern United States, Maine to Chesapeake Bay. *U.S. Fish and Wildlife Service, Bureau of Sport Fisheries and Wildlife*, Circular 179. Narragansett, R.I.

Casey, J. G., and H. L. Pratt. 1985. Distribution of the White Shark, *Carcharodon carcharias*, in the Western North Atlantic. *Memoirs of the Southern California Academy of Sciences* 9: 2–14.

Castro, J. I. 1983. *The Sharks of North American Waters*. College Station: Texas A&M University Press.

Cione, A. L. 1983. Registros Fosiles de *Carcharodon carcharias* (Linne, 1758) (Elasmobranchii, Lamniformes) en Argentina. Ameghiniana 20 (3-4): 261–64.

Clark, E. 1963. The Maintenance of Sharks in Captivity with a Report on Their Instrumental Conditioning. Pp. 115–46 in P. W. Gilbert, ed., *Sharks and Survival*. Boston: D. C. Heath.

———. 1969. *The Lady and the Sharks*. New York: Harper & Row.

———. 1981. Sharks: Magnificent and Misunderstood. *National Geographic* 160(2): 138–86.

Clark, E., and S. Chao. 1973. A Toxic Secretion from the Red Sea Flatfish *Pardachirus marmoratus* (Lacépède). *Bulletin of the Sea Fisheries Research Station (Haifa)* 60: 53–56.

Clark, J. F. 1968. Serpents, Sea Creatures and Giant Sharks. (unpublished ms.).

Cliff, G., S. F. J. Dudley, and B. Davis. 1989. Sharks

Caught in the Protective Gill Nets off Natal, South Africa. 2. The Great White Shark *Carcharodon carcharias* (Linnaeus). *South African Journal of Marine Science* 8: 131–44.

Cliff, G., and R. B. Wilson. 1986. *Natal Sharks Board's Field Guide to Sharks and Other Marine Animals*. Durban: Natal Sharks Board.

Cloquet, H. 1822. *Considerations générales sur l'ichthyologie*. Paris.

Cohen, J. L. 1981. Vision in Sharks. *Oceanus* 24(4): 17–22.

Colbert, E. H. 1955. *Evolution of the Vertebrates*. New York: John Wiley.

Coles, R. J. 1915. Notes on the Sharks and Rays of Cape Lookout, N.C. *Proceedings of the Biological Society of Washington* 28: 89–94 (1914).

————. 1919. The Large Sharks of Cape Lookout, North Carolina: The White Shark or Maneater, Tiger Shark and Hammerhead. *Copeia* No. 69: 34–43.

Colinvaux, P. 1978. *Why Big Fierce Animals Are Rare*. Princeton, N.J.: Princeton University Press.

Collier, R. S. 1964. Report on a Recent Shark Attack off San Francisco, California. *California Fish and Game* 50(4): 261–64.

Compagno, L. J. V. 1977. Phyletic relationships of living sharks and rays. *American Zoologist* 17(2): 303–22.

————. 1981. Legend versus Reality: The Jaws Image and Shark Diversity. *Oceanus* 24(4): 5–16.

————. 1984a. *FAO Species Catalogue. Vol. 4, Sharks of the World. An Annotated and Illustrated Catalogue of the Shark Species Known to Date*. Part I, Hexanchiformes to Lamniformes. Rome: UN Development Programme.

————. 1984b. *FAO Species Catalogue. Vol. 4. Sharks of the World. An Annotated and Illustrated Catalogue of the Shark Species Known to Date*. Part II. Carchariniformes. Rome: UN Development Programme.

————. 1987a. Kinds of Sharks. Pp. 170–85 *in* J. D. Stevens, ed. *Sharks*. Drummoyne, Australia: Golden Press.

————. 1987b. Shark Attack in South Africa. Pp. 134–47 in J. D. Stevens, ed. *Sharks*. Drummoyne, Australia: Golden Press.

Cook, S. F. 1990. Trends in Shark Fin Markets: 1980, 1990, and Beyond. *Chondros* 2(1): 3–5.

Coppleson, V. 1958. *Shark Attack*. Sydney: Angus & Robertson.

————. 1963. Patterns of Shark Attack for the World. Pp. 389–421 *in* P. W. Gilbert, ed. *Sharks and Survival*. Boston: D. C. Heath.

Couch, J. 1867. *A History of the Fishes of the British Islands*. Vol. I. London: Groombridge.

Cousteau, J-Y., and P. Cousteau. 1970. *The Shark: Splendid Savage of the Sea*. New York: Doubleday.

Cousteau, J-Y., and F. Dumas. 1953. *The Silent World*. New York: Harper & Row.

Crockett, J. 1989. *The Great White Shark*. New York: Arch Cape Press.

Czerkas, S. M., and D. R. Glut. 1982. *Dinosaurs, Mam-*

*moths and Cavemen: The Art of Charles R. Knight*. New York: E. P. Dutton.

Daniel, J. F. 1934. *The Elasmobranch Fishes*. Berkeley: University of California Press.

D'Aubrey, J. D., and D. H. Davies. 1961. Shark Attack off the East Coast of South Africa 24 December 1960. *Oceanographic Research Institute Investigational Report No. 5*.

Davidson, R. 1988. *Whalemen of Twofold Bay*. Eden, N.S.W. Australia: René Davidson.

Davies, D. H. 1960. Recent Shark Attack off the East Coast of South Africa, April, 1960. *Copeia* 1960(4): 350–51.

————. 1961a. *About Sharks and Shark Attack*. Pietermaritzburg, South Africa: Shuter & Shooter.

————. 1961b. Shark Attack off the East Coast of South Africa, 22nd January 1961. *Oceanographic Research Institute Investigational Report No. 4*.

————. 1961c. Shark Attack on Fishing Boat in South Africa. *Oceanographic Research Institute Investigational Report No. 1*.

————. 1962. The Shark Problem. *South African Journal of Science* 58(9): 253–57.

————. 1963a. Shark Attack and Its Relationship to Temperature, Beach Patronage and the Seasonal Abundance of Dangerous Sharks. *Oceanographic Research Institute Investigational Report No. 6*.

————. 1963b. The Shark Problem and What Is Being Done about It. *Nucleon* 5: 78–87.

————. 1964. The Miocene Shark Fauna of the Southern St. Lucia Area. *Oceanographic Research Institute Investigative Report No. 10*.

Davies, D. H., and G. D. Campbell. 1962. The Aetiology, Clinical Pathology and Treatment of Shark Attack. *Journal of the Royal Naval Medical Service* 68(3): 1–27.

Davies, D. H., and J. D. D'Aubrey. 1961a. Shark Attack off the East Coast of South Africa 24 December 1960, with Notes on the Species of Shark Responsible for the Attack. *Oceanographic Research Institute Investigational Report No. 2*.

————. 1961b. Shark Attack off the East Coast of South Africa, 6 January 1961. *Oceanographic Research Institute Investigational Report No. 3*.

Davis, B., and T. S. Wallett. 1975. Anti-Shark Measures as Practiced in Natal, Republic of South Africa. Unpublished ms. of a paper given at the Seminar for Community First Aid and Accident Prevention; Faculty of Anaesthetists of the Royal Australasian College of Surgeons. April 9–12, 1975. Sydney.

Day, L. R., and H. D. Fisher. 1954. Notes on the Great White Shark, *Carcharodon carcharias*, in Canadian Atlantic Waters. *Copeia* 1954(4): 295–96.

de Muizon, C., and T. J. DeVries. 1985. Geology and Paleontology of Late Cenozoic Marine Deposits in the Sacaco Area (Peru). *Geologische Rundschau* 74(3): 547–63.

Diamond, J. M. 1986. How Great White Sharks, Sabre-Toothed Cats and Soldiers Kill. *Nature* 322(28): 773–74.

Dinkergus, G. 1985. *The Sharkwatchers' Guide*. New York: Simon & Shuster.

Dourassoff, N. 1989. Is the Great White Shark Facing Extinction? *International Game Fish Association Newsletter* 51(3): 3

Edwards, H. 1975. *Sharks and Shipwrecks*. New York: Quadrangle.

Egaña, A. C., and J. E. McCosker. 1984. Attacks on Divers by White Sharks in Chile. *California Fish and Game* 70(3): 173–79.

Ellis, R. 1975. *The Book of Sharks*. New York: Grossett & Dunlap (1989 edition, Alfred A. Knopf).

———. 1983. Chiller from the Depths. *Geo* 5(3): 90–97.

———. 1987a. Australia's Southern Seas. *National Geographic* 171(3): 286–319.

———. 1987b. The Great White Shark. *Underwater Naturalist*. 16(3): 3–11.

———. 1987c. The Legendary Shark. Pp. 170–85 in J. D. Stevens, ed. *Sharks*. Drummoyne, Australia: Golden Press.

———. 1989. The Great White Shark. *Nautical Quarterly* 48: 64–75.

Ellis, R., and J. E. McCosker. 1985. Speaking of Sharks. *Oceans* 19(3): 24–29; 58–60.

Elmer-Dewitt, P. 1991. Are Sharks Becoming Extinct? *Time* 137(9): 67.

Elton, C. 1935. *Animal Ecology*. London: Sidgwick & Jackson.

Emery, S. H. 1985. Hematology and Cardiac Morphology in the Great White Shark, *Carcharodon carcharias*. *Memoirs of the Southern California Academy of Sciences* 9: 73–80.

Eskelund, C. S. 1983. The Great White Shark. *Redwing* 1983: 21–23.

Eyles, V. A. 1954. Nicolaus Steno, Seventeenth-Century Anatomist, Geologist and Ecclesiastic. *Nature* 174: 8–10.

Farquhar, G. B. 1963. Sharks of the Family Lamnidae. *Technical Reports, U.S. Navy Oceanographic Office* (TR-157): 22 pp.

Fast, T. N. 1955. Second Known Attack on a Swimmer in Monterey Bay. *California Fish and Game* 41: 348–51.

Fernicola, R. G. 1987. *In Search of the "Jersey Man-Eater."* Deal, N.J.: George Marine Library.

Fish, C. J., and M. C. Cobb. 1954. *Noxious Marine Animals of the Central and Western Pacific Ocean*. Research Report 36. Washington, D.C.: U.S. Department of the Interior Fish and Wildlife Service.

Fitch, J. E. 1949. The Great White Shark *Carcharodon carcharias* (Linnaeus) in California Waters During 1948. *California Fish and Game* 35: 135–38.

Follett, W. I. 1966. Man-Eater of the California Coast. *Pacific Discovery* 29(1): 18–22.

———. 1974. Attacks by the White Shark, *Carcharodon carcharias* (Linnaeus), in Northern California. *California Fish and Game* 60: 192–98.

Garrick, J. A. F., and L. P. Schultz. 1963. A Guide to the Kinds of Potentially Dangerous Sharks. Pp. 3–60 *in*

P. W. Gilbert, ed., *Sharks and Survival*. Boston: D.C. Heath.

Gesner, C. 1560. *Historia Animalium*. Zurich.

Gilbert, P. W. 1963. ed. *Sharks and Survival*. Boston: D.C. Heath.

———. 1981. Patterns of Shark Reproduction. *Oceanus*. 24(4): 30–39.

Gilbert, P. W., and C. Gilbert. 1973. Sharks and Shark Deterrents. *Underwater Journal* 5(2): 69–79.

Gilbert, P. W., R. F. Mathewson, and D. P. Rall, eds. 1967. *Sharks, Skates and Rays*. Baltimore: Johns Hopkins University Press.

Gill, T. 1861. Analytical Synopsis of the Order Squali. *Annals of the Lyceum of Natural History in New York* 7: 1–47.

Goadby, P. 1970. *Big Fish and Blue Water: Gamefishing in the Pacific*. New York: Holt, Rinehart and Winston.

Goodson, G. 1988. *Fishes of the Pacific Coast*. Stanford, Calif.: Stanford University Press.

Gorman, T. B., and D. J. Dunstan. 1967. Report on an Attack by a Great White Shark off Coledale Beach, N.S.W., Australia, in Which Both Victim and Attacker Were Recovered Simultaneously. *California Department of Fish and Game* 55(3): 219–23.

Goto, M., and M. Goto. 1987. Three Fossil Teeth of the Lamnoid Shark *Carcharocles* and *Carcharodon* from the Hokuriku Group (Late Miocene—Early Pleistocene) of Takaoka City, Toyama Prefecture, Central Japan. *Bulletin of the Toyama Science Museum* 11: 123–32.

Goto, M., T. Kikuchi, S.-I. Sekimoto, and T. Noma. 1984. Fossil Teeth of the Great White Shark, *Carcharodon carcharias*, from the Kazusa and Shimosa Groups (Pliocene to Pleistocene) in the Boso Peninsula and Shimosa Upland, Central Japan. *Earth Sciences* (Tokyo) 38(6): 420–26.

Gottlieb, C. 1975. *The Jaws Log*. New York: Dell.

Grady, D. 1982. *The Perano Whalers of Cook Strait*. Wellington, N.Z.: A. H. & A. W. Reed.

Green, J. 1988. A Shark of a Story: Keys Fisherman Hauls in a Great White. *Broward County Sun-Tattler* April 21: 1.

Green, L. 1958. *South African Beachcomber*. Cape Town: Howard Timmins.

Grey, L., ed. 1976. *Zane Grey: Shark*. New York: Belmont Turner Books.

Grey, Z. 1928. Big Game Fishing in New Zealand Seas. *Natural History* 28(1): 46–52.

———. 1937. *An American Angler in Australia*. New York: Harper & Brothers.

Gruber, S. H. 1977. The Visual System of Sharks: Adaptations and Capability. *American Zoologist* 17(2): 453–69.

———. 1978. Sharks: Good Vision or Poor? *Sea Frontiers* 24(4): 229–36.

———. 1982. Shark Repellents: Perspectives for the Future. *Oceanus* 24(4): 72–76.

———. 1988. Why do Sharks Attack Humans? *Naval Research Reviews* 60(1): 2–13.

Gruber, S. H., and J. L. Cohen. 1978. Visual System of the

Elasmobranchs: State of the Art 1960–1975. Pp. 11–105 in E. S. Hodgson and R. F. Mathewson, eds. *Sensory Biology of Sharks, Skates, and Rays.* Arlington, Va.: U.S. Office of Naval Research.

————. 1985. Visual System of the White Shark, *Carcharodon carcharias*, with Emphasis on Retinal Structure. *Memoirs of the Southern California Academy of Sciences* 9: 61–72.

Gruber, S. H., and C. A. Manire. 1989. Challenge of the Chondrichthyans. *Chondros* 1(1): 1, 3.

Gruber, S. H., and J. F. Morrissey, 1990. Shark vs. Man: Are Sharks Losing the Battle? *Underwater Naturalist* 19(1): 3–7.

Gruber, S. H., and E. Zlotkin. 1982. Bioassay of Surfactants as Shark Repellents. *Naval Research Reviews* 32: 1–10.

Gudger, E. W. 1950. A Boy Attacked by a Shark, July 25, 1936, in Buzzard's Bay, Massachusetts, with Notes on Attacks by Another Shark Along the New Jersey Coast in 1916. *American Midland Naturalist* 44(3): 714–19.

Guitart-Manday, D., and J. F. Milera. 1974. El monstruo marino de Cojimar. *Mar y Pesca* 104: 10–11.

Günther, A. 1870. *Catalogue of the Fishes of the British Museum.* Vol. 8. 549 pp.

Hall, H. 1990. Safe Passage in Shark Territory. *International Wildlife* 20(2): 42–45.

Harrison, D. 1978. Fossil Fever Hits Florida. *Skin Diver* 27(6): 68–70.

Hauser, H. 1983a. Life After Jaws: An Appreciation of Sharks. *Oceans* 16(6): 8–10.

————. 1983b. Filming Great White Sharks. *Oceans* 16(6): 3–7.

Hedges, F. A. M. 1925. *Battles with Giant Fish.* London: Duckworth.

Heezen, B., and C. D. Hollister. 1971. *The Face of the Deep.* New York: Oxford University Press.

Helm, T. 1963. *Shark: Unpredictable Killer of the Sea.* New York: Collier Books.

Henschel, U. 1983. Das Perfekte Ungeheuer. *Geo* (Germany) 4: 98–112.

Herald, E. S. 1961. *Living Fishes of the World.* New York: Doubleday.

Hewitt, J. C. 1984. The Great White Shark in Captivity: A History and Prognosis. *AAZPA Conference Proceedings 1984:* 140–46, 317–24.

Hodgson, E. S., and R. F. Mathewson, eds. 1978. *Sensory Biology of Sharks, Skates, and Rays.* Arlington, Va.: U.S. Office of Naval Research.

Homer, S. 1984. Jaws IV: Great White Shark Netted off Maritime Tourist Beaches. *Equinox* 3(14): 127–28.

Hughes, R. 1987. Shark Attack in Australian Waters. Pp. 108–21 in J. D. Stevens, ed. *Sharks.* Drummoyne, Australia: Golden Press.

Hussakof, L. 1912. An Extinct Giant Shark: The Race Probably Died Out Through Its Own Rapacity. *Scientific American Supplement* 73: 225.

International Game Fish Association. 1987. *World Record Game Fishes.* Ft. Lauderdale, Fla.: IGFA.

Johnson, C. S., and H. D. Baldridge. 1985. Analytic Indication of the Impracticability of Waterborne Chemicals for Repelling an Attacking Shark. *Naval Oceans Systems Center* Technical Document 843.

Johnson, R. H. 1978. *Sharks of Polynesia.* Papeete, Tahiti: Les Editions du Pacifique.

Johnson, R. H., and D. R. Nelson. 1978. Copulation and Possible Olfaction-Mediated Pair Formation in Two Species of Carcharhinid Sharks. *Copeia* 1978(3): 539–42.

Jones, E. C. 1971. *Isistius brasiliensis,* a Squaloid Shark, the Probable Cause of Crater Wounds in Fishes and Cetaceans. *Fisheries Bulletin* 69(4): 791–98.

Jonstonus, J. 1649. *Historia Naturalis. Libri V de Piscibus et Ceti.* Frankfurt.

Jordan, D. S. 1925. The Generic Name of the Great White Shark, *Squalus carcharius* L. *Copeia* No. 140: 17–20.

————. 1928. Notes on *Carcharias, Carcharhinus,* and *Carcharodon. Copeia* 1928(1): 1–4.

Joseph, M. 1986. Dog Named "Lucky" Survives Shark Attack. *West County Times* (Richmond, Calif.) October 16: 1a–2a.

Kalmijn, A. J. 1971. The Electric Sense of Sharks and Rays. *Journal of Experimental Biology* 55: 371–83.

————. 1977. The Electric and Magnetic Sense of Sharks, Skates, and Rays. *Oceanus* 20(3): 45–52.

————. 1978. Electric and Magnetic Sensory World of Sharks, Skates, and Rays. Pp. 507–28 in E. S. Hodgson and R. F. Mathewson, eds. *Sensory Biology of Sharks, Skates, and Rays.* Arlington, Va.: U.S. Office of Naval Research.

————. 1982. Electric and Magnetic Field Detection in Elasmobranch Fishes. *Science* 218 (4575): 916–18.

Kalmijn, A. J., and K. J. Rose. 1978. The Shark's Sixth Sense. *Natural History* 87(3): 76–81.

Kato, S. 1965. White Shark, *Carcharodon carcharias* from the Gulf of California with a List of Sharks Seen in Mazatlan, Mexico, 1964. *Copeia* 1965(3): 384.

Kean, B. H. 1944. Death Following Attack by Shark, *Carcharodon carcharias. Journal of the American Medical Association* 125(12): 845–46.

Kenney, N. T. 1968. Sharks: Wolves of the Sea. *National Geographic* 133(2): 222–57.

Kenyon, K. W. 1959. A 15-Foot Maneater from San Miguel Island, California. *California Fish and Game* 45(1): 58–59.

Keyes, I. W. 1972. New Records of the Elasmobranch *Carcharodon megalodon* and a Review of the Genus *Carcharodon* in the New Zealand Fossil Record. *New Zealand Journal of Geology and Geophysics* 15(2): 228–42.

Khalaf, N.-A. B. 1987. The Great White Shark *Carcharodon carcharias* from the State of Kuwait, Arabian Gulf. *Gazelle* 16: 1–7.

King, J. E. 1983. *Seals of the World.* Ithaca, N.Y.: Cornell University Press.

Klimley, A. P. 1974. An Inquiry into the Causes of Shark Attacks. *Sea Frontiers* 20(2): 66–76.

———. 1976. The White Shark—A Matter of Size. *Sea Frontiers* 22(1): 2–8.

———. 1980. Observations of Courtship and Copulation in the Nurse Shark, *Ginglymostoma cirratum*. *Copeia* 4: 878–82.

———. 1985. The Areal Distribution and Autoecology of the White Shark, *Carcharodon carcharias*, off the Western Coast of North America. *Memoirs of the Southern California Academy of Sciences* 9: 15–40.

Knight, C. R. 1935. *Before the Dawn of History*. New York & London: Whittlesey House and McGraw-Hill.

———. 1946. *Life Through the Ages*. New York: Knopf.

Lake, P. A. 1978. Face to Face with White Death. *Skin Diver* 27(1): 36–41.

Larson, P. L. 1990. The Fauna of the Marine Tertiary Pisco Formation of Southwestern Peru. Paper presented at the Society of Vertebrate Paleontologists Meeting, 11 October, 1990. Lawrence, Kansas.

Last, P., and J. Stevens. 1991. *Sharks and Rays of Australia*. Sydney: CSIRO Publishing.

Lea, R. N., and D. J. Miller. 1985. Shark Attacks off the California and Oregon Coasts: An Update, 1980–84. *Memoirs of the Southern California Academy of Sciences* 9: 136–49.

Le Boeuf, B. J. 1981. Elephant Seals. Pp. 326–74 in B. J. Le Boeuf and S. Kaza, eds. *The Natural History of Año Nuevo*. Pacific Grove, Calif.: Boxwood Press.

Le Boeuf, B. J., M. Riedman, and R. S. Keyes. 1982. White Shark Predation on Pinnipeds in California Coastal Waters. *Fisheries Bulletin* 80: 891–95.

Leim, A. H., and L. R. Day. 1959. Records of Uncommon and Unusual Fishes from Eastern Canadian Waters. *Journal of the Fisheries Research Board of Canada* 16: 503–14.

LeMier, E. H. 1951. Recent Records of the Great White Shark, *Carcharodon carcharias*, on the Washington Coast. *Copeia* 1951(3): 249.

Levine, M. 1991. *Sharks and Shark Attacks: Southern Africa*. Cape Town: Struik. [In press.]

Limbaugh, C. 1963. Field Notes on Sharks. Pp. 63–94 *in* P. W. Gilbert, ed. *Sharks and Survival*. Boston: D. C. Heath.

Lineaweaver, T. H., and R. H. Backus. 1969. *The Natural History of Sharks*. New York: Lippincott.

Linnaeus, C. 1758. *Systema naturae*. 10th edition. Vol. 1, Regnum animale. Holmiae.

Lissau, S. 1977. The Jaws of "Jaws." *Oceans* 10(6): 31–33.

Llano, G. A. 1975. *Sharks: Attacks on Man*. New York: Tempo Books.

Lupica, M. 1990. Shark Bites Back. *Esquire* 113(6): 75–76.

Mara, J. 1986. *A Fisherman's Tale: Fifty Years of Angling Along the Natal Coast*. Umhlanga Rocks, South Africa: Angler Publications.

Marshall, T. C. 1966. *Tropical Fishes of the Great Barrier Reef*. Sydney: Angus & Robertson.

Matthiessen, P. 1971. *Blue Meridian: The Search for the Great White Shark*. New York: Random House.

Maunder, S. 1852. *The Treasury of Natural History, or, A Popular Dictionary of Animated Nature*. London: Longman, Brown, Green & Longmans.

McAllister, D. E. 1987. The Biggest Great White Shark. *Sea Wind* 1(4): 11–14.

McCormick, H. W., T. Allen, and W. E. Young. 1963. *Shadows in the Sea*. New York: Chilton Books.

McCosker, J. E. 1980. Sandy, the Great White Shark. *Animal Kingdom* 83(6): 11–13.

———. 1981a. Great White Shark. *Science/81* 2: 40–51.

———. 1981b. Reflections of Sandy, the Great White Shark. *Pacific Discovery* 34(2): 1–9.

———. 1985. White Shark Attack Behavior: Observations of and Speculations about Predator and Prey Strategies. *Memoirs of the Southern California Academy of Sciences* 9: 123–35.

———. 1987a. The White Shark, *Carcharodon carcharias*, Has a Warm Stomach. *Copeia* 1987(1): 195–97.

———. 1987b. Building a Better Bruce. *Los Angeles Times Magazine* 3(29): 16–19.

———. 1988. Tod aus der Tiefe. *Geo* 1988(9): 82–94.

McGinnis, S. M., and R. J. Schusterman. 1981. Northern Elephant Seal—*Mirounga angustirostris*. Pp. 329–49 *in* S. H. Ridgway and R. J. Harrison, eds. *Handbook of Marine Mammals. Volume 2: Seals*. New York: Academic Press.

Mead, T. 1961. *Killers of Eden*. Sydney: Angus & Robertson.

Miles, P. 1971. The Mystery of the Great White Shark. *Oceans* 4(5): 51–59.

Miller, D. J., and R. S. Collier. 1981. Shark Attacks in California and Oregon, 1926–1979. *California Fish and Game* 67(2): 76–104.

Moss, S. A. 1982. Shark Feeding Mechanisms. *Oceanus* 24(4): 23–29.

———. 1984. *Sharks—An Introduction for the Amateur Naturalist*. Englewood Cliffs, N.J.: Prentice-Hall.

Müller, J., and F. G. J. Henle. 1838. On the Generic Characters of Cartilaginous Fishes with Descriptions of New Genera. *Annals and Magazine of Natural History* Vol. 2: 33–37, 88–91.

———. 1841. *Systematische Beschreibung der Plagiostomen*. Berlin.

Mundus, F., and B. Wisner. 1971. *Sportfishing for Sharks*. New York: Macmillan.

Murray, J. 1891. *Voyage of the Challenger: Deep Sea Deposits*. London: Eyre-Spottiswoode.

Myrberg, A. A. 1974. Research on the Behavior and Sensory Physiology of Sharks. *Annual Report, Office of Naval Research*. 29 pp.

———. 1978. Underwater Sound—Its Effect on the Behavior of Sharks. Pp. 391–417 *in* E. S. Hodgson and R. F. Mathewson, eds. *Sensory Biology of Sharks, Skates, and Rays*. Arlington, Va.: U.S. Office of Naval Research.

Myrberg, A. A., A. Banner, and J. D. Richard. 1969.

Shark Attraction Using a Video-Acoustic System. *Marine Biology* 2(3): 264–76.

Myrberg, A. A., R. Gordon, and A. P. Klimley. 1976. Attraction of Free-Ranging Sharks by Acoustic Signals in the Near Sub-sonic Range with Comments on Biological Significance. Pp. 205–28 in A. Schuijf and A. D. Hawkins, eds. *Sound Reception in Fishes*. New York: Elsevier.

Myrberg, A. A., and J. Ha, S. Walewski, and J. C. Banbury. 1972. Effectiveness of Acoustic Signals in Attracting Epipelagic Sharks to an Underwater Sound Source. *Bulletin of Marine Science* 22(4): 926–49.

Nakano, H., and K. Nakaya. 1987. Records of the White Shark *Carcharodon carcharias* from Hokkaido, Japan. *Japanese Journal of Ichthyology* 33(4): 414–16.

Nelson, D. R. 1969. The Silent Savages. *Oceans* 1(4): 8–22.

Noe, G. E. 1987. *Carcharodon*. New York: Vantage Press.

Norman, J. R., and F. C. Fraser. 1937. *Giant Fishes, Whales and Dolphins*. New York: W. W. Norton.

Norman, J. R., and P. H. Greenwood. 1963. *A History of Fishes*. New York: Hill & Wang.

Northcutt, R. G. 1978. Brain Organization in Cartilaginous Fishes. Pp. 117–93 in E. S. Hodgson and R. F. Mathewson, eds. *Sensory Biology of Sharks, Skates, and Rays*. Arlington, Va.: U.S. Office of Naval Research.

Orr, R. T. 1959. Sharks as Enemies of Sea Otters. *Journal of Mammalogy* 40(4): 617.

Otake, T., and K. Mizue. 1981. Direct Evidence for Oophagy in Thresher Shark, *Alopias pelagicus*. *Japanese Journal of Ichthyology* 28: 171–72.

Paladino, F. V., M. P. O'Connor, and J. R. Spotila. 1990. Metabolism of Leatherback Turtles, Gigantothermy, and Thermoregulation of Dinosaurs. *Nature* 344: 858–60.

Palmer, E. W. 1980. The White Shark: Notes from Down Under. *International Marine Angler* 42(6): 6–7, 12.

———. 1981. The White Shark. *SAFIC* 5: 33–34.

———. 1984. *Fifty Years of Game Fishing*. Adelaide (privately printed).

Parker, T. J. 1983. Notes on *Carcharodon rondeletti*. *Proceedings of the Zoological Society of London* (1887): 27–40.

Parrott, A. W. 1958. *Big Game Fishes and Sharks of New Zealand*. London: Hodder & Stoughton.

Pennant, T. 1812. *British Zoology. A New Edition in Four Volumes. Vol. III: Class IV. Reptiles. IV. Fishes.* London: Wilkie & Robinson.

Phelan, J. M. 1929. Fatality from Bite of Shark. *Military Surgeon* 64: 383–84.

Piers, H. 1934. Accidental Occurrence of the Man-Eater or Great White Shark *Carcharodon carcharias* (Linn.) in Nova Scotian Waters. *Proceedings of the Nova Scotian Institute of Sciences* 28(3): 192–203.

Pike, G. C. 1962. First Record of the Great White Shark (*Carcharodon carcharias*) from British Columbia. *Journal of the Fisheries Research Board of Canada* 19: 363.

Powlik, J. J. 1989. Feeding Structures of the White Shark, *Carcharodon carcharias* (Linnaeus), with Notes on Other

Species. Unpublished master's thesis, Univ. of British Columbia.

Pratt, H. W. 1988. Elasmobranch Gonad Structure: A Description and Survey. *Copeia* 1988(3): 719–29.

Pratt, H. W., J. G. Casey, and R. B. Conklin. 1982. Observations of Large White Sharks, *Carcharodon carcharias*, off Long Island, New York. *Fisheries Bulletin. U.S.* 8: 153–56.

Primor, N., and E. Zlotkin. 1975. On the Ichthyotoxic and Haemolytic Action of the Skin Secretion of the Flatfish *Pardachirus marmoratus* (Soleidae). *Toxicon* 13: 183–87.

Putnam, F. W. 1874. Tooth of a Man-Eater that Attacked a Dory near St. Pierre Bank. *Bulletin of the Essex Institute of Salem* 6(4): 72.

Radcliffe, L. 1930. Youth Killed by Huge Shark. *Copeia* 1930(3): 89–90.

Rafinesque, C. S. 1810. *Caratteri di alcuni nuovi generi e nuove specie di animali e piante della Sicilia, con varie osservazioni sopra i medisimi*. Palermo.

Randall, J. E. 1963. Dangerous Sharks of the Western Atlantic. Pp. 339–61 in P. W. Gilbert, ed. *Sharks and Survival*. Boston: D. C. Heath.

———. 1973. Size of the Great White Shark (*Carcharodon*). *Science* 181: 169–70.

———. 1987. Refutation of Lengths of 11.3, 9.0, and 6.4 M Attributed to the White Shark, *Carcharodon carcharias*. *California Fish and Game* 73(3): 163–68.

Reiger, G. 1973. *Profiles in Saltwater Angling*. Englewood Cliffs, N.J.: Prentice-Hall.

Richardson, J. 1836. *Fauna Borelia-Americana, or the Zoology of the Northern Parts of British America. III. The Fish.* London: Richard Bentley.

Roedel, P. M., and W. E. Ripley. 1950. California Sharks and Rays. *California Division of Fish and Game, Fisheries Bulletin* 75.

Romer, A. 1966. *Vertebrate Paleontology*. Chicago: University of Chicago Press.

Rondelet, G. 1554. *Libri de Piscibus Marinis, in Quibus verae Piscium effigies expressae sunt*. London: Matthiam Bonhomme.

———. 1558. *La première (et seconde) partie de l'histoire entière des poissons*. Lyon.

Roughley, T. C. 1951. *Fish and Fisheries of Australia*. Sydney: Angus & Robertson.

Royce, W. F. 1963. First Record of White Shark (*Carcharodon carcharias*) from Southeastern Alaska. *Copeia* 1963(1): 179.

Ruhen, O. 1974. *Shark Attacks and Adventures with Rodney Fox*. Adelaide: O'Neill.

Scattergood, L. W. 1962. White Sharks, *Carcharodon carcharias*, in Maine, 1959–1960. *Copeia* 1962(2): 446–47.

Schaeffer, B. 1967. Comments on Elasmobranch Evolution. Pp. 3–35 in P. W. Gilbert, R. F. Mathewson, and D. P. Rall, eds. *Sharks, Skates and Rays*. Baltimore: Johns Hopkins Press.

Schaeffer, B., and M. Williams. 1977. Relationships of

Fossil and Living Elasmobranchs. *American Zoologist* 17(2): 293–302.

Scharp, H. 1975. *Shark Safari*. Cranbury, N.J.: A. S. Barnes.

Scholander, P. F. 1957. The Wonderful Net. *Scientific American* 196(4): 96–107.

Scholl, J. P. 1983. Skull Fragments of the California Sea Lion (*Zalophus californianus*) in the Stomach of a White Shark. *Journal of Mammalogy* 64(2): 332.

Schroeder, W. C. 1938. Records of *Carcharodon carcharias* (Linnaeus) and *Pseudopriacanthus altus* (Gill) from the Gulf of Maine, Summer of 1937. *Copeia* 1938(1): 46.

———. 1939. Additional Gulf of Maine Records of the White Shark *Carcharodon carcharias* (Linnaeus) from the Gulf of Maine in 1937. *Copeia* 1939(1): 48.

Schultz, L. P., and M. H. Malin. 1963. A List of Shark Attacks for the World. Pp. 509–67 *in* P. W. Gilbert ed. *Sharks and Survival*. Boston: D. C. Heath.

Schwartz, F. J., and G. H. Burgess. 1975. *Sharks of North Carolina and Adjacent Waters*. Morehead City, N.C.: North Carolina Department of Natural and Economic Resources.

Scott, T. D., C. J. M. Glover, and R. V. Southcott. 1980. *The Marine and Freshwater Fishes of South Australia*. Adelaide: Government Printer.

Scud, B. E. 1962. Measurements of a White Shark, *Carcharodon carcharias*, Taken in Maine Waters. *Copeia* 1962(3): 659–61.

Searls, H. 1978. *Jaws 2*. New York: Bantam.

———. 1987. *Jaws—The Revenge*. New York: Berkley.

Smith, A. 1849. Pisces. Pp. 1–77, *Illustrations of the Zoology of South Africa*. London: Smith Elder.

Smith, J. L. B. 1951. A Juvenile of the Man-Eater *Carcharodon carcharias* (Linnaeus). *Annals and Magazine of Natural History* 12(4): 873–82.

———. 1961. *The Sea Fishes of Southern Africa*. Cape Town: Central News Agency.

———. 1963. Shark Attacks in the South African Seas. Pp. 363–68 in P. W. Gilbert, ed. *Sharks and Survival*. Boston: D. C. Heath.

Soucie, G. 1976. Consider the Shark. *Audubon* 78(5): 2–35.

Southgate, M. T. 1989. "Watson and the Shark" [cover illustration]. *Journal of the American Medical Association* 262(20): 2782.

Springer, S. 1939. The Great White Shark, *Carcharodon carcharias* (Linnaeus), in Florida Waters. *Copeia* 1939(2): 114–15.

———. 1963. Field Observations on Large Sharks of the Florida-Caribbean Region. Pp. 95–113 *in* P. W. Gilbert, ed. *Sharks and Survival*. Boston: D. C. Heath.

———. 1971. It Began with a Shark. Pp. 308–319 *in* G. Scherz, ed. *Dissertations on Steno as Geologist*. Odense, Denmark: Odense University Press.

———. 1973. Lamnidae. pp. 13–15 in J. C. Hureau and Th. Monod, eds. *Check List of the Fishes of the North-Eastern Atlantic and of the Mediterranean*. *Vol. I*. Paris: Unesco.

Springer, S., and P. W. Gilbert. 1963. Anti-Shark Measures. Pp. 465–76 *in* P. W. Gilbert ed. *Sharks and Survival*. Boston: D.C. Heath.

Springer, V. G., and J. P. Gold. 1989. *Sharks in Question: The Smithsonian Answer Book*. Washington, D.C.: Smithsonian Institution Press.

Squire, J. L., Jr. 1967. Observations of Basking Sharks and Great White Sharks in Monterey Bay, 1948–1950. *Copeia* 1967(1): 247–50.

Stafford-Deitsch, J. 1987. *Shark: A Photographer's Story*. San Francisco: Sierra Club Books.

Starks, E. C. 1917. The Sharks of California. *California Fish and Game* 3(4): 145–53.

Stead, D. G. 1933. *Giants and Pygmies of the Deep*. Sydney: Shakespeare Head Press.

———. 1963. *Sharks and Rays of Australian Seas*. Sydney: Angus & Robertson.

Steno [Neils Stensen]. 1667. *Elementorum Myologiae Specimen . . . Canis Carchariae Dissectum Caput*. Florence.

Stevens, J. D., ed. 1987. *Sharks*. New York: Facts on File.

Stewart, B. S., and P. K. Yochem. 1985. Radio-Tagged Harbor Seal *Phoca vitulina richardsi*, Eaten by White Shark, *Carcharodon carcharias*, in the Southern California Bight. *California Fish and Game* 71(2): 113–15.

Storer, D. H. 1851. On a New Species of *Carcharias* (*C. atwoodi*). *Proceedings of the Boston Natural History Society* 3: 71–72.

Strasburg, D. W. 1963. The Diet and Dentition of *Isistius brasiliensis*, with Remarks on Tooth Replacement in Other Sharks. *Copeia* 1963(1): 33–40.

Strong, W. R., R. C. Murphy, B. D. Bruce, and D. R. Nelson. 1991. Movement Patterns of Bait-Attracted White Sharks, *Carcharodon carcharias*, with Notes on Feeding and Social Interactions. Abstract of presentation at *"Sharks Down Under" Symposium, February 24–March 1, 1991*. Sydney.

Swift, J. 1983. *The Complete Poems*. New Haven, Conn.: Yale University Press.

Taylor, L. R. 1985. White Sharks in Hawaii: Historical and Contemporary Records. *Memoirs of the Southern California Academy of Sciences* 9: 41–48.

Taylor, L. R., L. J. V. Compagno, and P. J. Struhsaker. 1983. Megamouth—A New Species, Genus and Family of Lamnoid Shark (*Megachasma pelagios*, Family Megachasmidae), from the Hawaiian Islands. *Proceedings of the California Academy of Sciences* 43(8): 87–110.

Taylor, R., and V. Taylor. 1981. *The Great Shark Suit Experiment*. Sydney: Ron Taylor Productions.

Taylor, V. 1978a. The Filming for *Jaws*. Pp. 29–37 *in* R. Taylor, V. Taylor, and P. Goadby, eds. *Great Shark Stories*. New York: Harper & Row.

———. 1978b. The Great White Expedition. Pp. 45–49 *in* R. Taylor, V. Taylor, and P. Goadby, eds. *Great Shark Stories*. New York: Harper & Row.

———. 1978c. Great White Death. Pp. 95–105 in R. Taylor, V. Taylor, and R. Goadby, eds. *Great Shark Stories*. New York: Harper & Row.

———. 1979. Great White Shark: Predator That Doesn't Eat People. *Oceans* 12(3): 38–42.

———. 1981. A Jawbreaker for Sharks. *National Geographic* 159(5): 664–67.

———. 1983. Filming Great White Sharks. *Oceans* 16(6): 3–7.

Templeman, W. 1963. Distribution of Sharks in the Canadian Atlantic (with Special Reference to Newfoundland Waters). *Bulletin of the Fisheries Research Board of Canada* 140: 1–77.

Tester, A. L. 1963. The Role of Olfaction in Shark Predation. *Pacific Science* 17: 145–70.

Thiele, C. 1979. *Maneater Man: Alf Dean—The World's Greatest Shark Hunter*. Adelaide: Rigby.

Thomson, K. S. 1976. On the Heterocercal Tail in Sharks. *Paleobiology* 2: 19–38.

———. 1990. The Shape of a Shark's Tail. *American Scientist* 78: 499–501.

Thompson, J. R., and S. Springer. 1965. Sharks, Skates, Rays, and Chimaeras. *U.S. Fish and Wildlife Service, Circular 28*. Washington, D.C.

Thorson, T. B., D. B. Watson and C. M. Cowan. 1966. The Status of the Freshwater Shark of Lake Nicaragua. *Copeia* (1966) 3: 385–402.

Tinker, S. W. 1973. *Sharks and Rays: A Handbook of the Sharks and Rays of Hawaii and the Central Pacific Ocean*. Rutland, Vt.: Charles E. Tuttle.

———. 1978. *Fishes of Hawaii*. Honolulu: Hawaiian Service.

Tricas, T. 1985. Feeding Ethology of the Great White Shark, *Carcharodon carcharias. Memoirs of the Southern California Academy of Sciences* 9: 81–91.

Tricas, T., and J. E. McCosker. 1984. Predatory Behavior of the White Shark (*Carcharodon carcharias*) with Notes on Its Biology. *Proceedings of the California Academy of Sciences* 43(14): 221–38.

Tschernezky, W. 1959. Age of *Carcharodon megalodon? Nature* 184(4695): 1331–32.

Tuve, R. L. 1947. Technology of the U.S. Navy "Shark Chaser." *Proceedings of the U.S. Naval Institute* 73: 522–27.

Uchida, S., F. Yasuzumi, M. Toda, and N. Okura. 1987. On the Observations of Reproduction in *Carcharodon carcharias* and *Isurus oxyrinchus*. [abstract only] The Systematics, Ecology, and Physiology of Elasmobranchs. University of Tokyo, March 17–18 [symposium].

van Dam, C. 1988. In Wind and Water. *The Sciences* January/February: 36–39.

van der Elst, R. P. 1979. A Proliferation of Small Sharks in the Shore-Based Natal Sport Fishery. *Environmental Biology of Fishes* 4(4): 349–62.

———. 1981. *A Guide to the Common Sea Fishes of Southern Africa*. Cape Town: Struik.

Vaz-Ferreira, R. 1981. South American Sea Lion—*Otaria flavescens*. Pp. 39–65 *in* S. H. Ridgway and R. J. Harrison, eds. *Handbook of Marine Mammals. Volume 1: The Walrus, Sea Lions, Fur Seals and Sea Otter*. New York: Academic Press.

Verne, J. 1870. *Vingt milles lieues sous les mers* [Twenty Thousand Leagues under the Sea]. Paris: Hetzel. (1962 Bantam Edition, New York. Translated by Anthony Bonner.)

Vladykov, V. D., and R. A. McKenzie. 1934–35. The Marine Fishes of Nova Scotia. *Proceedings of the Nova Scotian Institute for Sciences* 19(1): 1–113.

Walford, L. A. 1935. The Sharks and Rays of California. *California Department of Fish and Game, Fisheries Bulletin* 45: 1–66.

Wallett, T. 1983. *Shark Attack in Southern African Waters*. Cape Town: Struik.

Webster, D. K. 1962. *Myth and Maneater: The Story of the Shark*. London: Peter Davies.

White, E. I, W. Tucker, and N. B. Marshall. 1961. Proposal to Repeal the Ruling Given in Opinion 47 and to Use the Plenary Powers to Stabilize the Generic Names *Carcharhinus* Blainville, 1816, *Carcharodon* A. Smith, 1838, and *Odontaspis* J. L. R. Agassiz, 1838, in Their Accustomed Senses (Class Pisces). *Bulletin of Zoological Nomenclature* 18(4): 273–80.

Whitley, G. P. 1939. Taxonomic Notes on Sharks and Rays. *Australian Zoologist* 9(3): 227–62.

———. 1940. *The Fishes of Australia: Part I, The Sharks*. Sydney: Royal Zoological Society of New South Wales.

———. 1963. Shark Attacks in Australia. Pp. 329–38 *in* P. W. Gilbert, ed. *Sharks and Survival*. Boston: D. C. Heath.

Wise, H. D. 1937. *Tigers of the Sea*. New York: Derrydale Press.

Wolf, N. G., P. R. Swift, and F. G. Carey. 1988. Swimming Muscle Helps Warm the Brain of Lamnid Sharks. *Journal of Comparative Physiology* 157B: 709–15.

Wood, F. G. 1959. Man Eats Maneater. *Mariner* [notebook of Marineland of Florida], p. 4.

Wood, G. L. 1982. *The Guinness Book of Animal Facts & Feats*. Middlesex, England: Guinness Superlatives.

Woodward, A. S. 1889. *Catalogue of Fossil Fishes of the British Museum. Part I*. London: British Museum.

Younghusband, P. 1982. Sharks at Bay! *International Wildlife* 12(1): 4–10.

Zern, E. 1952. *Zane Grey's Adventures in Fishing*. New York: Harper & Brothers.

# ILLUSTRATION CREDITS

# INDEX

Entries for this Index have been drawn from both the text and the illustrations. Page numbers given in **bold-face** type refer to illustrations. People, places, or subjects discussed in the notes are identified by page numbers followed by the letter n. Because references to and illustrations of the great white shark occur throughout the book, you will find only a skeleton entry for "Great white shark"; rather, particular details, for example "Color" or "Caudal fin," have been indexed, and then under these headings.